Attention Deficit Hyperactivity Disorder

For many researchers, clinicians, teachers, patients, and family members, the discourse on ADHD has been occurring in silos. Traditional ADHD camps are organized primarily in terms of neurological and cognitive perspectives and to a lesser extent psychoanalytic/psychodynamic perspectives. Those with an interest in ADHD have not been able to obtain a comprehensive understanding of the disorder and consequently have been restricted in psychotherapy treatment options. This book argues for the integration of the three perspectives on ADHD.

Drawing on the expertise of an international range of contributors, the volume addresses questions from a psychoanalytic vantage point which have considerable meaning in clinical work with children who have ADHD. They examine the role of trauma and attachment problems as both a possible antecedent to ADHD, and as an outgrowth of ADHD which predisposes the child to limitations in emotion regulation, social adversity, and even maltreatment. Several questions pertinent to psychodynamic treatment and relevant case studies are discussed including: a) the viability of psychoanalysis/psychodynamic treatment for ADHD children, b) the impact of early traumatic experience on the child's specific weaknesses in attention, over-reactivity and dysregulation, c) contributions of problems in object relations and regressive defences to ADHD symptoms and d) the importance of other intrapsychic issues.

This book was originally published as a special issue of the *Journal of Infant, Child and Adolescent Psychotherapy.*

Francine Conway is a Professor at the Gordon F. Derner Institute of Advanced Psychological Studies at Adelphi University, USA, and has been treating children diagnosed with ADHD for the past 14 years. In addition to her clinical experience, she has taught courses on ADHD and provided clinical supervision for students working with ADHD.

Attention Deficit Hyperactivity Disorder

Integration of Cognitive, Neuropsychological, and Psychodynamic Perspectives in Psychotherapy

Edited by
Francine Conway

Routledge
Taylor & Francis Group
LONDON AND NEW YORK

First published in paperback 2024

First published 2014
by Routledge
4 Park Square, Milton Park, Abingdon, Oxon OX14 4RN

and by Routledge
605 Third Avenue, New York, NY 10158

Routledge is an imprint of the Taylor & Francis Group, an informa business

British Library Cataloguing in Publication Data
A catalogue record for this book is available from the British Library

ISBN: 978-1-138-78048-4 (hbk)
ISBN: 978-1-03-292953-8 (pbk)
ISBN: 978-1-315-77018-5 (ebk)

DOI: 10.4324/9781315770185

Typeset in Times New Roman
by Taylor & Francis Books

Contents

Citation Information vii
Notes on Contributors ix

1. Introduction: Attention Deficit Hyperactivity Disorder in Children and the Psychoanalytic Process
James McCarthy and Francine Conway 1

2. ADHD via Psychoanalysis, Neuroscience, and Cognitive Psychology: Why Haven't We Fielded a Team?
Lucy Zabarenko 5

3. The Neural and Neurocognitive Determinants of ADHD
Chaya B. Gopin and Dione M. Healey 13

4. Psychoanalytic Treatment of ADHD Children in the Frame of Two Extraclinical Studies: The Frankfurt Prevention Study and the EVA Study
Marianne Leuzinger-Bohleber, Katrin Luise Laezer, Nicole Pfenning-Meerkoetter, Tamara Fischmann, Angelika Wolff and Jonathan Green 32

5. Trauma and ADHD – Association or Diagnostic Confusion? A Clinical Perspective
Kate Szymanski, Linda Sapanski and Francine Conway 51

6. ADHD and Complex Trauma: A Descriptive Study of Hospitalized Children in an Urban Psychiatric Hospital
Francine Conway, Maria Oster and Kate Szymanski 60

7. The Reality-Sampling Deficit and ADHD: Indication for an Active Technique
Barry Jones 73

8. Psychoanalytic Conceptualizations of the Internal Object in an ADHD Child
Björn Salomonsson 87

9. Trouble Paying Attention
Daniel Gensler 103

10. Is ADHD a Real Neurological Disorder or Collection of Psychosocial Symptomatic Behaviors? Implications for Treatment in the Case of Randall E.
Burton Norman Seitler 116

11. Psychodynamic Play Therapy With a Six-Year-Old African American Boy Diagnosed With ADHD
Gabrielle F. Cione, Lila A. Coleburn, Eric A. Fertuck and Peter Fraenkel 130

Index 145

Citation Information

The chapters in this book were originally published in the *Journal of Infant, Child and Adolescent Psychotherapy*, volume 10, issue 1 (May 2011). When citing this material, please use the original page numbering for each article, as follows:

Chapter 1
Introduction: Attention Deficit Hyperactivity Disorder in Children and the Psychoanalytic Process
James McCarthy and Francine Conway
Journal of Infant, Child and Adolescent Psychotherapy, volume 10, issue 1 (May 2011) pp. 1–4

Chapter 2
ADHD via Psychoanalysis, Neuroscience, and Cognitive Psychology: Why Haven't We Fielded a Team?
Lucy Zabarenko
Journal of Infant, Child and Adolescent Psychotherapy, volume 10, issue 1 (May 2011) pp. 5–12

Chapter 3
The Neural and Neurocognitive Determinants of ADHD
Chaya B. Gopin and Dione M. Healey
Journal of Infant, Child and Adolescent Psychotherapy, volume 10, issue 1 (May 2011) pp. 13–31

Chapter 4
Psychoanalytic Treatment of ADHD Children in the Frame of Two Extraclinical Studies: The Frankfurt Prevention Study and the EVA Study
Marianne Leuzinger-Bohleber, Katrin Luise Laezer, Nicole Pfenning-Meerkoetter, Tamara Fischmann, Angelika Wolff and Jonathan Green
Journal of Infant, Child and Adolescent Psychotherapy, volume 10, issue 1 (May 2011) pp. 32–50

Chapter 5
Trauma and ADHD – Association or Diagnostic Confusion? A Clinical Perspective
Kate Szymanski, Linda Sapanski and Francine Conway
Journal of Infant, Child and Adolescent Psychotherapy, volume 10, issue 1 (May 2011) pp. 51–59

Chapter 6
ADHD and Complex Trauma: A Descriptive Study of Hospitalized Children in an Urban Psychiatric Hospital
Francine Conway, Maria Oster and Kate Szymanski
Journal of Infant, Child and Adolescent Psychotherapy, volume 10, issue 1 (May 2011) pp. 60–72

Chapter 7
The Reality-Sampling Deficit and ADHD: Indication for an Active Technique
Barry Jones
Journal of Infant, Child and Adolescent Psychotherapy, volume 10, issue 1 (May 2011) pp. 73–86

Chapter 8
Psychoanalytic Conceptualizations of the Internal Object in an ADHD Child
Björn Salomonsson
Journal of Infant, Child and Adolescent Psychotherapy, volume 10, issue 1 (May 2011) pp. 87–102

Chapter 9
Trouble Paying Attention
Daniel Gensler
Journal of Infant, Child and Adolescent Psychotherapy, volume 10, issue 1 (May 2011) pp. 103–115

Chapter 10
Is ADHD a Real Neurological Disorder or Collection of Psychosocial Symptomatic Behaviors? Implications for Treatment in the Case of Randall E.
Burton Norman Seitler
Journal of Infant, Child and Adolescent Psychotherapy, volume 10, issue 1 (May 2011) pp. 116–129

Chapter 11
Psychodynamic Play Therapy With a Six-Year-Old African American Boy Diagnosed With ADHD
Gabrielle F. Cione, Lila A. Coleburn, Eric A. Fertuck and Peter Fraenkel
Journal of Infant, Child and Adolescent Psychotherapy, volume 10, issue 1 (May 2011) pp. 130–143

Please direct any queries you may have about the citations to clsuk.permissions@cengage.com

Notes on Contributors

Gabrielle F. Cione, M.A., is a Doctoral Candidate in the Clinical Psychology Subprogram of the City University of New York (CUNY), USA. Her research and clinical interests concern racial and sexual minority youth.

Lila A. Coleburn, J.D., Ph.D., is a Clinical Psychologist with a multi-ethnic private psychotherapy practice in Manhattan, USA. She is also a Clinical Supervisor in the Clinical Psychology Subprogram of the City University of New York (CUNY), USA. Her clinical focus is on developmentally-informed psychodynamic psychotherapy with children, adolescents, and adults.

Francine Conway, Ph.D., is an Associate Professor of Psychology at the Derner Institute of Advanced Psychological Studies, Adelphi University, USA.

Eric A. Fertuck, Ph.D., is an Associate Professor in the Clinical Psychology Subprogram of the City University of New York (CUNY), USA. He is also on the faculty of the Columbia University Department of Psychiatry. His research and clinical focus is on personality disorders through the lenses of psychoanalytic and social neuroscientific perspectives.

Tamara Fischmann, Ph.D., is a Lecturer at the Department of Human Sciences, University of Kassel, Germany. She is a Researcher at the Sigmund Freud Institute and a Psychoanalyst in private practice. Her research interests include research methodology, neuroscience, and dream research.

Peter Fraenkel, Ph.D., is an Associate Professor of Clinical Psychology in the Clinical Psychology Subprogram of the City University of New York (CUNY), USA, and Director of the Ackerman Institute's Center for Work and Family, which includes empirically-supported, community-based programs for families facing the challenges of homelessness, domestic violence, and immigration. Dr. Fraenkel is the author of *Sync Your Relationship, Save Your Marriage: Four Steps to Getting Back on Track*, co-author of *The Relational Trauma of Incest: A Family-Based Approach to Treatment*, and author of numerous publications on time, technology, work and family, collaborative community-based family programs, integrative approaches to systemic therapy, and child sexual abuse.

Daniel Gensler, Ph.D., is a Clinical Psychologist and Director of the Child and Family Center at the William Alanson White Institute in New York City, USA.

Chaya B. Gopin, Ph.D., is a Postdoctoral Fellow at the Zucker Hillside Hospital, North Shore-Long Island Jewish Health System, New York, USA.

Jonathan Green, M.D., is a Professor of Child & Adolescent Psychiatry at the University of Manchester, UK, and Honorary Consultant Child & Adolescent Psychiatrist at Central Manchester and Manchester Children's Hospitals University NHS Trust and Manchester Biomedical Research Centre. He is a leading expert in the field of attachment research.

Dione M. Healey, Ph.D., is a Senior Lecturer in the Department of Psychology, University of Otago, New Zealand.

Barry Jones, MB, BSc, ChB, MRCPsych, is a Consultant Child Psychiatrist and Psychoanalyst.

Katrin Luise Laezer, Ph.D., is a Psychologist and Sociologist, working as a Researcher at the Sigmund Freud Institute in Frankfurt, Germany. Moreover, she is a Scientific Assistant at the Department of Human Sciences, University of Kassel, Germany. She is in psychoanalytical training (German Psychoanalytical Association).

Marianne Leuzinger-Bohleber, Ph.D., is Director of the Sigmund Freud Institute in Frankfurt, Germany, and Professor of Psychoanalytic Psychology at the University of Kassel, Germany. She is a member of the International Psychoanalytic Association (IPA) and Vice-President of the Research Board of the IPA. Moreover, as a Psychoanalyst, she chairs the Research Committee of the German Psychoanalytical Association.

James McCarthy, Ph.D., is Director of Psychology, Director of Research at Queens Children's Psychiatric Center, New York, USA.

Maria Oster, M.A., is a Doctoral Candidate in the Clinical Psychology Doctoral Program at Adelphi University, USA.

Nicole Pfenning-Meerkoetter is a Psychologist, working as a Scientific Assistant at the Sigmund Freud Institute and conducting her Ph.D. on the conditions of knowledge production in current psychoanalytic research. Since 2005, she has been in psychoanalytic training (German Psychoanaytical Association).

Björn Salomonsson, M.D., Ph.D., is a Psychoanalyst with the Swedish Psychoanalytic Society, Stockholm. He has a private practice; is a Consultant Psychoanalyst at the Mama Mia Child Health Centre; and a Researcher at the Karolinska Institute.

Linda Sapanski, M.A., is a Doctoral Candidate in Clinical Psychology at the Derner Institute of Advanced Psychological Studies at Adelphi University, USA. In July 2011, she began a two-year fellowship at Yale Child Study Center, USA, working primarily with children who have experienced or witnessed trauma.

Burton Norman Seitler, Ph.D., is a Psychoanalyst/Clinical Psychologist in private practice. He is also the Director of Counselling and Psychotherapy Services-R (C.A. P.S-R), in Ridgewood and Oakland, New Jersey, USA; faculty member and Director of the Child and Adolescent Psychotherapy Studies Program, New Jersey Institute for Psychoanalysis and Psychotherapy (NJI) in Teaneck, New Jersey, USA.

Kate Szymanski, Ph.D., is an Associate Professor of Psychology at Derner Institute of Advanced Psychological Studies at Adelphi University, USA. Her research and clinical interests concentrate on trauma and coping in children and adults. She is currently developing a psychodynamic group treatment for traumatized adolescents. Dr. Szymanski is affiliated with Tuesday's Children, a nonprofit organization for 9/11 families. She has a private practice in Garden City, NY, USA.

Angelika Wolff is a Child Psychoanalyst in private practice. She is the former Director of the Institute for Analytic Child and Adolescent Psychotherapy in Frankfurt, Germany. She directs and consults on numerous research projects in the field of early prevention in infancy.

Lucy Zabarenko, Ph.D., is a faculty member at the Washington Center for Psychoanalysis and the Pittsburgh Psychoanalytic Center, USA. She is the author of books and articles on medical education, psychoanalytic theory and education, and cognitive psychology.

Introduction: Attention Deficit Hyperactivity Disorder in Children and the Psychoanalytic Process

James McCarthy, Ph.D.
Francine Conway, Ph.D.

> "The child can use the analyst as a new love object, an auxiliary ego, a new object of identification, or an object of externalizing inner conflicts and the splitting of ambivalence" (Sandler, Kennedy, and Tyson, 1980, p. 107).

This statement made by Anna Freud reflects Freud's belief that the emergence of psychopathology is influenced by multiple factors, including an underlying neurobiological vulnerability, that complicate the ubiquity of unconscious conflicts throughout the stages of personality development. In calling attention to the analyst's divergent roles with a child, she also cautioned against the danger of maintaining a developmental orientation to psychopathology which is unidimensional by commenting, "I criticize above all the lack of data to support the concept of the unempathic mother as the pathogenic agent" (Anna Freud, 1983, p. 385).

Anna Freud's recommendation that the analyst can become both an active presence in children's lives and a new object in their inner world remains a cornerstone of contemporary psychodynamic treatment approaches. Her identification of the analyst as a potential, auxiliary ego for the child whose aim is to promote ego development underlies the principles of child psychotherapy. If the therapeutic process is understood as an emotional experience involving unconscious communication that fosters comprehensive ego development in the child and psychological growth in the family, then a psychoanalytic orientation is not in any way mutually exclusive with cognitive-behavioral and psychopharmacological efforts at symptom reduction.

Two essential goals of psychoanalytic psychotherapy with children and adolescents consist of establishing a therapeutic alliance that broadens and deepens the child's emotional communication and formulating interventions which address the child's particular developmental immaturities and adjustment problems. The contradictions inherent in simultaneously discerning unconscious emotional communication while using techniques designed to address specific problems and impairments in functioning requires a willingness to integrate therapeutic approaches (Lewis, 1997). Some degree of comfort with the ambiguity inherent in these contradictory goals is an essential aspect of a having a psychoanalytic orientation. Defining the purpose of the psychoanalytic process as the overall facilitation of emotional, cognitive, and adaptive functioning, sets the stage for integrative treatment with children who have Attention Deficit Hyperactivity Disorder (ADHD), especially since studies have established that children and adolescents with ADHD usually have a variety of emotional and behavioral problems.

The articles in this monograph illustrate the relevance of an integrative approach to the child with ADHD within a psychoanalytic framework. To begin, Dr. Zabarenko calls attention to the contributions of psychoanalysis, neuroscience, and cognitive approaches to understanding ADHD. Arguing for the formation of a "team approach" of these three perspectives, she encourages analysts and researchers to adopt the tools provided by each and explore ways in which the three perspectives are intercorrelated. To respond to Dr. Zabarenko's challenge, one must have some working knowledge of the contributions of neuropsychology. Drs. Gopin and Healey offers a review of a variety of theoretical models formulated to account for the heterogeneous array of cognitive and behavioral deficiencies that characterize individuals with ADHD. In their article, a review of the recent literature on the neural and neurocognitive determinants of ADHD is presented, and the importance of conceptualizing the disorder within a developmental framework is emphasized.

The authors of the articles in this issue invite the reader to maintain an attitude of openness about the multiplicity of etiological causes, the complexities of trauma, and the importance of difficulties in affect regulation commonly found in children with marked ADHD. The authors stress the value of psychoanalytic theories for illuminating the ego impairments and the obstacles to the negotiation of developmental opportunities experienced by a great many of these children and youth. Even though problems in attention and concentration are widespread in children and adolescents with many types of psychopathology, such as Early Onset Schizophrenia and acute, pediatric Bipolar illness, the papers generally refer to children who have severe, long standing deficits in concentration, sustained attention, and impulsiveness that interfere with their daily functioning and which can't be accounted for solely on the basis of a discreet trauma or a severe psychiatric disorder.

An integrative, psychoanalytic understanding of the therapeutic process is informed by developmental psychopathology research studies that delineate interacting systems impeding healthy maturation in groups of high risk children. Little is known about the mechanisms by which attentional deficits compound problems in attachment and emotion regulation resulting in part from either trauma, or from a genetic predisposition to emotional dysregulation (Cicchettii, Ackerman, and Izard, 1995; Shields and Cicchetti, 1998). Barkley (2010) believes that emotion dysregulation is a primary, fundamental component of ADHD, which contributes as much to the compromised functioning as do deficient problem solving skills and executive function deficits. Investigations of comorbidity in children with ADHD often highlight their heterogeneity and the 40–50 percent rates of co-occurrence of ADHD with disruptive behavior disorders. Implicit in these research considerations is the interplay among executive function deficits, cognitive weaknesses in social and emotional information processing, and problems with self-regulation. For example, Crawford, Kaplan, and Dewey (2006) report that a higher number of co-existing disorders in children with ADHD correlates with worse performance on tests of memory and visual-motor skills, as well as worse problems in everyday functioning. Beginning with the 1936 publication of *The Ego and the Id*, psychoanalytic writers have discussed only some of the developmental issues corresponding to these research questions under the rubric of cognitive maturation and abnormalities in the development of the ego.

From a psychoanalytic vantage point, the articles address five related questions which have considerable meaning in clinical work with children who have ADHD. First, is psychoanalysis a viable option for treatment of ADHD children? Dr. Leuzinger-Bohleber, on the basis of clinical experience results of the Frankfurt Prevention Study and the EVA Study, offers psychoanalysis as an alternative to psychostimulant only treatments. A discussion of short case studies illustrated through seven psychodynamic subgroups of children with ADHD is presented.

Second, has the role of trauma and attachment problems been fully explored as both a possible antecedent to ADHD, and as an outgrowth of ADHD which predisposes the child to limitations in emotion regulation, social adversity, an even maltreatment? Third, to what extent has the impact of early traumatic experience contributed to the child's specific weaknesses in attention and in curtailing overreactivity and dysregulation in an age-appropriate manner? Dr. Szymanski and colleagues address this question by calling attention to the strong relationship between trauma and ADHD. Dr. Conway and colleagues discuss this issue of differential diagnosis of ADHD by focusing on the prevalence of chronic stressors, even traumatic events, in the lives of ADHD children. The National Child Traumatic Network has taken up the issue of complex trauma in children. The term "complex trauma" describes the "experience of multiple, chronic and prolonged, developmentally adverse traumatic events, most often of an interpersonal nature (e.g., sexual or physical abuse, war, community violence) and early-life onset" (van der Kolk, p. 403). It is likely that many children with ADHD are emotionally dysregulated due to their experience of chronic traumatic life events resulting in what the authors term "attachment trauma." Both Drs. Szymanski and Conway call attention to the need for those providing psychotherapy treatments to also consider the impact of trauma on the child's ability to pay attention and concentrate. Dr. Jones gives a case illustration of metallization based therapy and introduces the idea of a more active technique, linking metallization base therapy and Ferenczi's lost practice.

Fourth, have underlying problems in object relations and a conflict related reliance on regressive defenses contributed to poor attention and to poor self-control? Dr. Salomonsson's discusses his model, which combines Ego Psychology and Object Relations perspectives to explore the nature of the internal object of the ADHD child, an object which the child may experience as closed and rejecting. He presents the case of a six-and-a-half year old boy and offers a psychoanalytic interpretation of selected treatment interventions.

Finally, how have the patterns of emotional and cognitive deficits and the unconscious conflicts become evident in the child's transference configurations, in addition to the family transactions? Three case presentations address this point. Dr. Gensler's discussion of a contextual, psychodynamic approach to the therapy of a seventh grade boy with attention problems addresses this issue. Neuropsychological and psychoanalytic concepts that are relevant to attention are reviewed followed by a comprehensive discussion of the treatment of that case. A summary of the case demonstrates a contextual, psychodynamic approach to the therapy of children with attention problems. Dr. Seitler presents a case regarding the treatment of an ADHD boy, which posits that ADHD is typically related to a form of agitated depression and amenable to psychodynamic treatment. The final case presented by Cione and colleagues discusses a psychodynamic approach to play therapy in working with a six-year-old boy. This article describes the effective, two-year psychodynamic treatment of an African American boy with ADHD using psychodynamic techniques related to emotion regulation.

Although ADHD is generally thought of as a chronic and persistent neurological, behavioral, and developmental disorder, the work presented in this monograph makes a strong argument for psychodynamic or psychoanalytic treatment of ADHD. It is our hope that this issue will begin to resolve the ongoing debate about the relevance of psychodynamic or psychoanalytic-oriented psychotherapy for the treatment of ADHD individuals. This issue will have accomplished its goal if there is a subtle shift in the context through which we understand ADHD. Most would agree that a central issue among individuals diagnosed with ADHD is the difficulty these individuals experience in regulating their emotions and controlling their impulses. Psychoanalytic views on the process of the development of self-regulatory abilities in the child are crucial in understanding how the child's interpersonal interactions support or impinge on emotion regulation functioning.

REFERENCES

Barkley, R. (2010), Why emotional impulsiveness should be a central feature of ADHD? *The ADHD Report*, *18*: 1–5.

Cicchetti, D., Ackerman, B. P., & Izard, C. E. (1995), Emotions and emotion regulation in developmental psychopathology. *Development and Psychopathology*, *7*: 1–10.

Cione, G., Coleburn, L. A., Fertuck, E. A., & Fraenkel, P. (2011, this issue). Psychodynamic play therapy with a six-year-old African American boy diagnosed with ADHD. *Journal of Infant, Child, and Adolescent Psychotherapy*, *10*, 129–141.

Conway, F., Oster, M., & Szymanski, K. (2011, this issue). ADHD and complex trauma: A descriptive study of hospitalized children in an urban psychiatric hospital. *Journal of Infant, Child, and Adolescent Psychotherapy*, *10*, 59–71.

Crawford, S. G., Kaplan, B. J., & Dewey, D. (2006), Effects of coexisting disorders on cognition and behavior in children with ADHD. *Journal of Attention Disorders*, *10*: 192–9.

Freud, A. (1936), *The Ego and the Mechanisms of Defense*. London: Hogarth Press.

Freud, A. (1983), Problems of pathogenesis. *Psychoanalytic Study of the Child*, *38*: 383–8.

Gensler, D. (2011, this issue). Trouble paying attention. *Journal of Infant, Child, and Adolescent Psychotherapy*, *10*, 102–114.

Gopin, C. B. & Healey, D. M. (2011, this issue). The neural and neurocognitive determinants of ADHD. *Journal of Infant, Child, and Adolescent Psychotherapy*, *10*, 13–31.

Jones, B. (2011, this issue). The reality-sampling deficit and ADHD: Indication for an active technique. *Journal of Infant, Child, and Adolescent Psychotherapy*, *10*, 72–85.

Leuzinger-Bohleber, M., Laezer, L., Pfenning, N., Fischmann, T., Wolff, A., & Conway, F. (2011, this issue). Psychoanalytic treatment of ADHD children in the frame of two extraclinical studies: The Frankfurt Prevention study and the EVA study. *Journal of Infant, Child, and Adolescent Psychotherapy*, *10*, 32–50.

Lewis, O. (1997), Integrated psychodynamic psychotherapy with children. *Child and Adolescent Clinics of North America*, *6*: 53–68.

Salomonsson, B. (2011, this issue). Psychoanalytic conceptualizations of the internal object in an ADHD child. *Journal of Infant, Child, and Adolescent Psychotherapy*, *10*, 86–101.

Sandler, J., Kennedy, H., & Tyson, R. (1980), *The Technique of Child Analysis: Discussions with Anna Freud*. Cambridge, MA: Harvard University Press.

Seitler, B. N. (2011, this issue). Is ADHD a real neurological disorder or collection of psychosocial symptomatic behaviors? Implications for treatment in the case of Randall E. *Journal of Infant, child, and Adolescent Psychotherapy*, *10*, 115–128.

Shields, A. & Cicchetti, D. (1998), Reactive aggression among maltreated children: The contributions of attention and emotion dysregulation. *Journal of Clinical Child Psychology*, *27*: 381–95.

Szymanski, K., Sapanski, L., Conway, F. (2011, this issue). Trauma and ADHD—Association or diagnostic confusion? A clinical perspective. *Journal of Infant, Child, and Adolescent Psychotherapy*, *10*, 51–58.

van der Kolk, B. A. (2005). Developmental trauma disorder: Toward a rational diagnosis for children with complex trauma histories. *Psychiatric Annals*, *35*, 401–408.

Zabarenko, L. (2011, this issue). ADHD via psychoanalysis, neuroscience, and cognitive psychology: Why haven't we fielded a team? *Journal of Infant, Child, and Adolescent Psychotherapy*, *10*, 5–12.

ADHD via Psychoanalysis, Neuroscience, and Cognitive Psychology: Why Haven't We Fielded a Team?

Lucy Zabarenko, Ph.D.

Believing that the best approach to treating and understanding ADHD is a team formed from representatives of neuroscience, psychoanalysis, and cognitive psychology, in this article I begin by investigating why such a team has not been forged. A brief review of the literature in each field illustrates what each discipline might reasonably contribute to our knowledge about the syndrome. Suggestions are then presented about processing the data from such a team emphasizing the advantages of models using iterative multivariate statistics.

INTRODUCTION

Compared to the courtly style of dealing with structural change in the healing professions, there is something appealing about the dispatch with which players are shuffled and shelved in professional sports. If a quarterback makes two fatal errors or misses an opportunity for a pass, he is benched. If a pitcher allows three hits, he may be relieved or get a chance to call for a bunt. If skaters dazzle with the precision of their school figures, they might still prevail even if their freestyle lacks pizzazz. Yet Attention Deficit Hyperactivity Disorder (ADHD), one of the most prevalent neuropsychiatric disorders and arguably one whose management causes some of the highest levels of misery to patients and their families, resists solutions and has somehow not evoked the team approach—a strategy which has a good track record.

In this essay I will assemble data about the need for a three-part approach to ADHD from psychoanalysis, the neurosciences, and cognitive psychology by (1) examining some possible explanations for the lack of such an approach, (2) citing promising recent achievements in each area which augur well for ADHD at this time, and (3) suggesting some beginning methodological strategies for use in the campaign.

WHAT'S TAKEN SO LONG?

Public interest in and attention to ADHD is vivid enough that the title elicits 26,300,000 responses in 11.6 seconds on a first e-mail pass. In the two-week period before the final drafting of this article, there was at least one feature article in *The Washington Post*, my daily newspaper (Kelly, 2011). Yet the professional literature is pocked with knowledge gaps. Even in so basic an area as prevalence, for example, there are only approximations: Gilmore (2000) states that ADHD accounts for 50 percent of referrals to child psychiatrists and psychoanalysts. Fonagy (2004) quotes two sources to confirm his statement that "for ADHD, heritability is estimated to vary from 55 percent to 82 percent (2004, p. 104)—a very large range."

Palumbo's (2011, in press) admirable summary of knowledge in the field covers historical and diagnostic issues, and ADHD is classified with Executive Function Disorders (EFD). After an exhaustive survey of the literature, the author reaches the following disheartening conclusions (Palumbo, pp. 4–5): "No data are available on prevalence rates in these disorders in children or adults. Nor are there any data on the sex ratio among males and females" (p. 10).

Psychoanalysis

The contributions on ADHD in the psychoanalytic literature are so slim as to be summarized easily. Carney's (2002a) excellent compilation was a start, and her case description of treating ADHD in an adult (2002b) is valuable if daunting. A more recent work of Salmonsson (2006) provides a spritely updated review of what coverage there is and details his clinical ventures (2004, 2006, 2007a, 2007b). He urges psychoanalytic treatment as a viable modality in ADHD but is explicit about its conceptual challenges:

"It is important to keep in mind the biological correlates of these disorders but the analyst cannot take a position . . . on aetiology as defined in natural science . . . (he) can only regard symptoms of ADHD . . . like any other symptom in the consulting room . . . They express inner conflicts and the child's way of expressing them . . . whatever the theoretical framework, the analyst must maintain an analytic frame of mind . . . and an optimal containing attitude" (2006, p. 130).

Fonagy et al. (2002, p. 312) add that "the dominant risk model in modern developmental psychopathology . . . while undoubtedly accurate . . . fails to generate effective models of intervention." We shall return to the profundity and importance of this statement below in considering the issue of models.

Palumbo (2011, in press) adds that "for the psychodynamically informed practitioner . . . " the first problem is to develop an adequate understanding of the neuropsychological deficits in patients' development" (p. 1). "Insufficient attention has been given to the psychodynamics that are at play in these patients; most foci are on the cognitive impairments and their sequelae" (pp. 2–3). Any treatment must be based:

> " . . . not only the relational dimensions of . . . (the patients') experiences and the meaning they have assigned to their exposure to the environment but also the neuropsychological strengths and weaknesses that each patient brings to the treatment." He emphasizes relevant material on the frequent co-morbidity of brain damage, dysfunctionality, and psychiatric disorders. "Symptoms of depression, substance abuse and negativity are common in those affected" (p. 3).

There are two additional factors, familiar yet powerful, which may have slowed dynamic approaches. One is the perception by analysts that the organic nature of the illness can make patients unsuited for the strenuous work of self-discovery. Also, the widespread use of effective drugs and their possible side effects are feared as possibly contaminating impediments to analytic work. The use of drugs for ADHD has itself been debated vigorously for decades, and a survey of this literature is outside the scope of this article. However, as long as medications work, that is, control and/or ameliorate symptoms, and the long-term side effects of the drugs are in doubt, it is clear that many parents will use them, and to a degree adult patients will continue to try them. As many authors have pointed out, in addition to the possibility of dangerous long-term side effects, there remains the compounded danger of misdiagnosis so that very active or rambunctious children are mistakenly medicated instead of accommodated in classrooms, families, and the culture at large.

Neuroscience

First, we need to realize that despite general enthusiasm for broadening the applied scope of knowledge about the nervous system, that stance generates fears as well. For example, that "neuroscience will pose a fundamental challenge . . . to many religions" (Farrah et al., 2009). The reply that, as with Gallilean and evolutionary discoveries, "the physicalism of neuroscience . . . (cannot) detract from the meaning of human life" comforts some but for others leaves uneasy doubts. As evidence mounts that "underlying personality, love, morality and spirituality...all have physical correlates in brain function," a Frankensteinian nervousness mounts. On another front, voices have been raised (Blass, 2007; Brenner, 2004) decrying the influence of neuroscience on psychoanalysis and dynamic psychotherapy as limiting "the significance of the unique . . . concern with the understanding of meanings" (Blass, p. 19).

Also, a glance at the expanding neuroscientific literature and the discoveries already available will persuade any researcher that simply tracking the momentum and content of new findings can seem overwhelming. However, a group of distinguished and erudite guide-translators have provided a number of enlightened, accessible summaries that explain the significance and meanings of the work (Dimasio, 2010; Doidge, 2007; Le Doux, 2002; Levin, 2009; Sachs, 2010; Sapolsky, 2005). Still, the volume, fluidity, and complexity of neuroscientific findings can discourage as well as excite.

Cognitive Psychology

Learning the language and dialect of colleagues is not always easy. An example from cognitive psychology provides a sample of accounts which bristle with acronyms embedded in sentences of indeterminate length. Less than one-third of a sentence published recently follows:

> "Recent studies have shown that potentiation of glutamergic-mediated transmission with ligands such as N-methyl-D-aspartate (NMDA) partial agonist D-cycloserine (DCS), the alpha amino-3-hydroxyl-5-methl-4-isoaxazole-proprionate(AMPA) receptor potentiator 2[2,6,-difluoro-4-({2-henylsulfony l)amino]ethyl}thio)phenoxy]acetamide(PEPA), or . . . ." (Cleva et al., 2011)

Certainly problems in verbal communication may have delayed a team approach to ADHD in all three of the disciplines we have been considering. In addition, I propose that the history of psychology may burden the field of cognition with a special kind of insularity, usually not acknowledged. In a previous brief history of learning theory, cognition, and psychoanalysis, I have emphasized that it is important to recall that these fields emerged almost simultaneously at the end of the nineteenth century (Zabarenko, 2011). Learning and its epigenetic progeny—cognitive, developmental, educational psychology—have been the province of psychology from its earliest days. Further, early investigations in these fields took place (and to a degree do still) in academic settings without any strong need to do more than suggest applications. Entranced with the thought of rigorous research so near the center of humanity, psychologists came to value purity perhaps excessively.

In addition to unfortunate baggage from the past, currently all three fields are absorbed in research to assemble new evidence and if possible weave it into existing or novel paradigms and in vital struggles to mature scientifically from within itself as well as within the larger scientific community. Psychoanalysis is wrestling with exclusivity and pluralistic theories; neuroscience toils mightily to keep up with new instrumentations and simultaneously to establish its relevance; cognitive psychology, also struggling to be relevant, still longs to adhere to the style of strict empiricism which has served it so well.

WHAT HAVE THESE THREE DISCIPLINES TO OFFER TO THE STUDY OF ADHD?

Psychoanalysis

One example of the species of clinical exploration which analytic thinking enables is to be found in case histories. Carney's (2002) extensive work with an adult patient is always worth restudying, as is Fonagy et al.'s description of behaviors in children coming to school (2004, p. 472): " . . . anxious, moody, irritable, and explosive . . . Minor upsets trigger intense affective storms—episodes of uncontrolled emotion . . . This affective lability mirrors the kaleidoscopic quality of the children's sense of self."

Salmonsson's (2006) excerpts of his clinical work not only provide whole verbatim dialogues with the children but also theoretical concepts: ADHD children suffer from "semiotic fragility (2006, p. 1039), they 'ward off' not only the import (of interpretations) but also the words themselves as concrete things thrown at them...they hated my words" (2006, p. 1030). He offers also his thoughts about medication: "Information sieves into the analysis and affects transference and countertransference...Medication does not prevent the child's propensity to flutter between different semiotic levels, but it sometimes helps him to concentrate on these issues when addressed in analysis" (p. 1038). Clinical difficulties, "... external material . . . should be handled with care . . . extra important initially in the treatment. It is a strain to remain unperturbed by pressure from parents, teachers and staff" (p. 1039). He closes this article with five technical recommendations (p. 1044) for treating children with ADHD. The suggestions are reasoned and accessible, valuable considerations for dynamically oriented clinicians of many professional backgrounds.

Neuroscience

When there are gifted scholars trained in two of the three fields we have been surveying, it may appear to be improbable luck, but whatever the affect it would be foolish not to sample their work. Fred Levin is a life-long student of neuroscience and a practicing adult, child, and adolescent psychoanalyst who has been working at connecting the findings from both fields for more than 30 years.

His understanding of ADHD, as is Barkley's (1997), is informed by the concept of the executive control network (ECN) " . . . the highest system of the brain which enables us to establish and maintain control over mental processing in an efficient manner" (Levin, 2003, p. 108). In addition to conceiving of the disorder in terms of the dysfunctionality of the ECN, Levin weaves into the discussion of the disorder concepts about what this might mean neurophysiologically. He broadens the scope of the topic: "...from the enormous complexity of the prefrontal cortex to . . . the general hierarchical mobilization and control 'of simpler units of behavior into more com plex ones ... to maintaining the pursuit of current goals over discontinuous periods of time . . . to being able to decompose sequences of events or messages into their component parts or resynthesize them into entirely new messages or behaviors' (p. 171n) and accommodates the depth and complexity in thinking about the disorder. It is possible for . . . attentive behavior to fail because of physiological disturbances in the ECN" (p. 112). Also, "traumatized patients become unable to differentiate properly between what is memory of thought, of a real event or of a wish (p. 113)."

In a recent work, Levin (2009) emphasizes material which demonstrates "...how psychoanalysis activates (the) learning of 'emotional attention'" (p. xix) and lists ADHD among the disorders in which the cerebellum (CB) is involved. More exactly, he argues that *"the cingulate cortex may . . . be an important neural interface between attention and motivation"* (p. 47, emphasis the author's) and urges "considering the role of the CB in language, executive functions and special cognition" (p. 169). He notes that several studies in boys with ADHD "confirm a role for the vermis (of the CB) in this disease . . . (as a) critical modulator of forebrain dopamine outflow . . . stimulation of the vermis seems to correct dopamine availability" (pp. 170, 172).

Cognition

Two generic phenomena will help to understand the distance which persists between clinical and empirical approaches to ADHD. One is the historical roots of the study of learning which began in academic laboratories. The legatees of the fields spanning cognition retain an understandable wish to retain in current work the careful, precise delineation of controls, variables, and research design that are its tradition. The second impediment is that, although there is dawning understanding on the part of those who deal with ADHD in the trenches of schools and clinical settings, cognition may be in fact their basic science and worth mastering, the idea can be intimidating. Often it seems as though the two fields are backing toward each other looking away from the site of contact. But there are optimistic signs.

McVay and Kane (2009), studying working memory, goal neglect, and mind wandering in an executive-control task, found that " . . . mind wandering rates varied with working memory capacity and predicted goal-neglect errors . . . indicating that . . . these differences were due, in part to variation in conscious thought" (p. 196). Also, they urge that "further assessment of subjective experience during cognitive tasks . . . should provide evidence for or against particular views of executive control" (p. 204). Note that (1) there is a hint of humor in the title of this piece and (2) the phenomena described strongly resemble ADHD.

Callaghan et al. (2011) studied the effects of early stress on learning. In this research, young animals that had experienced early-life maternal deprivation were trained to fear noise; the fear was then extinguished and their responses compared to normally reared rats. The stressed animals "were more likely to exhibit . . . stress-mediated relapse after extinction . . . and (also) exhibited a return of fear when the inhibitory neurotransmitter GABA was blocked" (p. 20). "Our results suggest that..early life adversity . . . is a potent risk factor for the development of anxiety in young people and . . . these people will be more likely to exhibit relapse after exposure-based treatment" (Callaghan et al., p. 27).

While the results will hold no surprises for clinicians, note that learning here has been used as a modality in addressing ADHD impairment, and the conclusions address and quantify anxiety. Forty years ago such an ecumenical stance was not to be found and that circumstance was demurely celebrated.

Mehta et al. (2011) also studied the effects of stress via early maternal separation and concluded that "genetic background and environmental factors are critical determinants in the development of cognitive deficits in subjects with a history of life stress" (p. 29). In this work, care was taken to investigate genetic determinants along with stress, thus enabling conclusions on heredity, stress, and their interaction. The use of maternal separation as a stress in the above two studies will no doubt capture the attention of clinicians who emphasize attachment and relational theories in their work.

Having hopefully established that all three disciplines of psychoanalysis, neurosciences, and cognitive psychology can and to an extent have provided findings of use in the study of ADHD, there remains the problem of how best to organize the data and weave it into information.

HOW BEST TO USE THE DATA?

In the consulting room we assume we can sift and sort data which is heavily encoded and involves scanning several layers of inference simultaneously. This assumption rests on a carefully circumscribed set of algorithms, with the scaffolding of coherent theories and a generally agreed upon body of technique. Vigilant for error, we hope we have set up enough detectors to enable correction. Venturing into a multidisciplinary universe wanting to understand a clinical entity, we may need to re-tool our armaments. The suggestions that follow are not offered as original but rather as essential enough to receive careful attention from the experiment.

Thrift: Pack as Much Into the Research Design as Possible

The studies summarized above both investigated early life stress as exemplified by early maternal deprivation (Callaghan et al., 2011; Mehta, 2011). Based on their knowledge that neural transmission and genetic factors can affect stress, they designed experiments to test for these additional variables. Note that this efficiency depends on an adequate intelligence about which variables are hypothesized to have what kinds of effects.

Accommodation: Think of Statistical Tools as Iterative

Especially when doing research in a multivariate universe, there is every reason to guess that results will arrive in that universe. Tests for significance need to be identified and their topography scanned for direction to guide subsequent tools. In clinical investigations, it can be assumed that there will be unexpected disappointments and serendipitous gold. Statistical tools should be planned to miss nothing.

Modelling: Use Clinical Intuition to Conceptualize Data

Fonagy's (p. 3) comment about the defects of the current risk model used in studies of ADHD provides by a contrasting example what waste (or worse, error) can occur when researchers neglect to build models that catch and suggest hypotheses. If the experiment fails to turn up at least one idea the designers did not expect, it probably needs to go back to the drawing board.

Clinical work can be thought of as the interplay of many hypotheses, ever ready to be accorded explanatory value and to be located further away from causality or discarded altogether. Models contain and permit these processes better than linearity and in their construction have the best chance of promoting valid conceptualization.

CONCLUSIONS

Wondering why three likely candidates—psychoanalysis, neuroscience, and cognition—have not forged a team for the study of ADHD, I have proposed some possible causes, verified that these disciplines have much to offer such an enterprise, and how the new mix of results might be refined. Empiricists of the world, arise. You have nothing to lose but your puzzlement.

REFERENCES

Barkley, R. (1997), *ADHD and the Nature of Control*. New York: Guilford Press.

Blass, R. B. & Carmeli, Z. (2007), The case against neuropsychoanalysis. On fallacies underlying psychoanalysis' latest scientific trend and its negative impact on psychoanalytic discourse. *Int. J. Psa.*, *88*: 19–40.

Brenner, C. (2004), Creativity and psychodynamics. *Q.*, *73*: 511–5.

Callahan, B. L. & Richardson, R. (2011), Maternal separation results in early emergence of adult-like fear and extinction learning in infant rats. *Behav. Neurosci.*, *125*: 20–8.

Carney, J., ed. (2002a), Self-regulation: Issues of attention and attachment. *Psa. Inq.*, *22*.

———— (2002b), Self- and interactive regulation: Treating a patient with ADHD. *Psa. Inq.*, *22*: 355–71.

Damasio, A. (2010), *Self Comes to Mind: Constructing the Conscious Brain*. New York: Pantheon.

Doidge, N. (2007), *The Brain That Changes Itself. Stories of Personal Triumph from the Frontiers of Brain Science*. New York: Penguin.

Farah, M. J. & Murphy, N. (2009, Feb. 27), Neuroscience and the soul. *Sci.*, *323*: 1168.

Fonagy, P. & Target, M. (2002), Early intervention and the development of self-regulation. *Psa. Inq.*, *22*: 307–35.

Fonagy, P., Gergely, G., Jurist, E., & Target, M. (2004), *Affect Regulation, Mentalization, and the Development of the Self*. New York: The Other Press.

Gilmore, K. (2000), A psychoanalytic perspective on attention-deficit/hyperactivity disorder. *J. Amer. Psychoanal. Assn.*, *48*: 1259–93.

Kelly, M. (2011, Feb. 10), How to get everyone in focus. *Washington Post*, Local Living Section, p. 10.

LeDoux, J. (2002), *The Synaptic Self. How Our Brains Become Who We Are*. New York: Penguin.
Mehta, M. & Schmauss, C. (2011), Strain-specific cognitive deficits in adult mice exposed to early life stress. *Behav. Neuro.*, *125*: 29–36.
Levin, F. M. (2003), *Psyche and Brain. The Biology of the Talking Cures*. Madison, CT: IUP.
———, ed. (2009), *Emotion and the Psychodynamics of the Cerebellum. A Neuro-psychoanalytic Analysis and Synthesis*. London: Karnac.
Levin, F. M. & Trevarthen, C. (2000). Subtle is the lord. The relationship between consciousness, the unconscious and the executive control network (ECN) of the brain. In: *The Annual of Psychoanalysis, Vol. XXVIII*, J. A. Winer (ed.). Hillsdale, NJ: The Analytic Press, pp. 105–25.
McVay, J. C. & Kane, M. J. (2009), Conducting the train of thought: Working memory capacity, goal neglect, and mind wandering in an executive control task. *J. Exp Psych.: Learning, Memory and Cognition*, *35*: 196–204.
Mehta, M. (2011), Strain-specific cognitive deficits in adult mice exposed to early life stress. *Beh. Neuro.*, *125*: 29–36.
Palumbo, J. (2011, in press). Executive disorders and self-deficits. In: *Mental Health and Social Problems: A Social Work Perspective*, A. Gitterman & N. Heller (eds.). New York: Routledge.
Sacks O. (2010), *The Mind's Eye*, New York: Knopf.
Salmononsson, B. (2004), Some psychoanalytic viewpoints on neuropsychiatric disorders in children. *The International Journal of Psychoanalysis, 85*: 117–36.
——— (2006), The impact of words on children with ADHD and DAMP. Consequences for psychoanalytic technique. *Int.*, *87*: 1029–48.
——— (2007a), 'Talk to me baby, tell me what's the matter now.' Semiotic and developmental perspectives on communication in psychoanalytic infant treatment. *Int. J. Psa.*, *88*: 127–46.
——— (2007b), Semiotic transformations in psychoanalysis with infants and adults. *Int. J. Psa.*, *88*: 1201–21.
Sapolsky, R. M. (2005), *Monkeyluv: And Other Essays on Our Lives as Animals*. New York: Schribner.
Zabarenko, L. (2011) Teaming creativity, psychoanalysis and neuroscience: The bridge to nowhere? Presented at Creativity Study Group, January, Washington, DC.

The Neural and Neurocognitive Determinants of ADHD

Chaya B. Gopin, Ph.D.
Dione M. Healey, Ph.D.

Individuals diagnosed with Attention-Deficit/Hyperactivity Disorder (ADHD) present with a wide array of cognitive and behavioral deficiencies. Over the past few decades, researchers have proposed a variety of theoretical models to account for and to better characterize this highly heterogeneous disorder. This paper reviews the recent literature on the neural and neurocognitive determinants of ADHD and emphasizes the importance of conceptualizing the disorder within a developmental framework. Implications for treatment are discussed.

INTRODUCTION

Attention-Deficit/Hyperactivity Disorder (ADHD) is a pervasive, highly impairing, neurodevelopmental disorder that is characterized by developmentally inappropriate levels of inattention and/or hyperactivity/impulsivity (*DSM-IV*-TR; American Psychological Association, 2000), which become manifest during the preschool years for most afflicted individuals (Campbell, 1995). Currently, ADHD is the most commonly diagnosed behavioral disorder of childhood (Castellanos and Tannock, 2002), conservatively estimated to affect approximately 4–6 percent of the child population in the United States (American Psychiatric Association, 2000). In addition, ADHD is the most common diagnosis received by youngsters who are referred for mental health services (Egger and Angold, 2006; Gadow, Sprafkin, and Nolan, 2001; Keenan and Wakschlag, 2000; Wilens, Biederman, Brown, Monuteaux, Prince, & Spencer, 2002). Individuals diagnosed with ADHD are reported to be at increased risk for low academic achievement and impaired social skills, with evidence of such dysfunction already present during the preschool period (Wilens et al., 2002). As such, the cost ascribable to ADHD in the United States was recently estimated to exceed $42.5 billion annually (Pelham, Foster, and Robb, 2007).

Considerable research across various disciplines has examined potential risk factors for ADHD. While the specific cause of the disorder is currently unknown, findings suggest a multifactorial etiology (Faraone, 2000; Sprich-Buckminster, Biederman, Milberger, Faraone, and Lehman, 1993) comprising complex interactions among multiple genes of small effect size and a host of environmental factors. Notably, ADHD is a highly heterogeneous disorder, and it is unlikely that all children diagnosed with ADHD have the same etiology or underlying pathophysiology (Doyle et al., 2005).

Since the emergence of ADHD as a diagnostic entity, investigators have formulated a variety of theoretical models to account for the heterogeneous array of cognitive and behavioral deficiencies that characterize individuals with ADHD. In addition, recent advances in neuroimaging and neuropsychological assessment have significantly influenced the current conceptualizations of ADHD. This article will review the recent advances in neuroimaging and neuropsychological assessment, as well as the prominent, current conceptualizations of ADHD which are based on these findings.

REVIEW OF NEUROIMAGING RESEARCH

Structural Magnetic Resonance Imaging (MRI) Findings

Investigations into potential abnormalities in the brain structures of children with ADHD have revealed reductions in the size/volume of regions within the prefrontal cortex, an area of the brain that is involved in planning and decision making (Castellanos et al., 1996; Castellanos et al., 2002; Durston et al., 2004; Filipek et al., 1997; Hynd et al., 1990; Kates et al., 2002; Mostofsky et al., 2002; Sowell et al., 2003). Similarly, studies have reported reductions in the size of the caudate nucleus, a structure that is involved in the circuitry underlying numerous cognitive functions (e.g., memory, affect, inhibition; Castellanos et al., 1996; Castellanos et al., 2002; Filipek et al., 1997; Hynd et al., 1993). Individuals diagnosed with ADHD have also been observed to have reduced volume in the globus pallidus, which regulates voluntary movement (Aylward et al., 1996; Castellanos et al., 1996), and reduced area has been documented in the corpus callosum, which transfers information from the right and left hemispheres of the brain to one another (Baumgardner et al., 1996; Giedd et al., 1994; Hynd et al., 1991; Hill et al., 2003; Lyoo et al., 1996; Semrud-Clikeman et al., 1994).

Abnormalities have also been reported in regions outside of the frontal lobes and the striatum. For instance, studies have revealed that individuals with ADHD have reduced volume in several parts of the cerebellum, an area of the brain that adjusts and coordinates motion so as to produce integrated, fluid movements (Berquin et al., 1998; Castellanos, 2001; Castellanos et al., 2002; Castellanos et al., 1996; Durston et al., 2004; Mostofsky et al., 1998; Posner and Petersen, 1990). In addition, reduced volume has reportedly been evident in the posterior cortical region responsible for visuospatial processing (Durston et al., 2004; Filipek et al., 1997; Sowell et al., 2003). Several (Berquin et al., 1998; Castellanos et al., 1996; Castellanos, 2001; Castellanos et al., 2002; Hill et al., 2003) but not all (Durston et al., 2004; Filipek et al., 1997; Hynd et al., 1990; Mostofsky et al., 2002) studies have reported reduced whole brain size in children with ADHD.

In addition, because cortical thickness is often thought of as a proxy measure of an individual's cognitive abilities, Shaw and colleagues (Shaw et al., 2006; Shaw et al., 2007a; Shaw et al., 2007b) recently compared the cortical thickness of children with and without ADHD. These researchers found that children with ADHD exhibited delays in cortical maturation by as much as two to three years relative to their typically developing peers. Of note, though, the two groups did exhibit a similar sequential pattern of cortical maturation over time.

Functional MRI findings

Functional MRI (fMRI) studies have also been conducted to characterize the anomalies associated with ADHD. When using this technique, participants generally engage in a task or behavior while investigators look for activation levels within regions that are believed to be essential components of that behavior. In line with the various structural abnormalities found in the brains of individuals with ADHD, a diverse array of aberrant neurocognitive functions have been detected through the use of fMRI. These include deficits in inhibitory control (Casey et al., 1997; Durston et al., 2003; Schulz et al., 2004; Schulz et al., 2005; Tamm et al., 2004; Vaidya et al., 1998), conflict resolution (Bush et al., 1999; Tamm et al., 2004), motor control (Rubia et al., 1999), timing (Durston et al., 2007), attention (Cao et al., 2008; Sonuga-Barke & Castellanos, 2007; Uddin et al., 2008), and working memory (Valera et al., 2005).

Diffusion Tensor Imaging Findings

Diffusion tensor imaging (DTI) is yet another imaging method that has recently been used to provide information regarding the irregularities that may underline ADHD pathology (Casey, Nigg, and Durston, 2007). DTI is an MRI technique that is used to study the organization of white matter fibers, which carry nerve impulses from one brain region to another (Ashtari et al., 2005). Results of the first DTI study conducted in children diagnosed with the disorder suggested that ADHD is a neurodevelopmental disorder that affects the organization and configuration of neural circuitry (Ashtari et al., 2005). In particular, brain regions associated with the right hemisphere motor circuitry (i.e., right supplementary motor area, right anterior limb of the internal capsule) were found to be involved in the pathophysiology of ADHD. The results suggested that the cerebellum of children with ADHD was abnormal relative to that of age-matched controls.

Subsequent DTI studies have produced variable results. Some studies have replicated and/or extended the aforementioned findings regarding the anomalies observed in the white matter tract development (Casey et al., 2007; Hamilton et al., 2008; Pavuluri et al., 2009). Another investigation demonstrated that alterations in the white matter circuitry associated with attention and executive functioning was aberrant in adults who had been diagnosed with ADHD in childhood (Makris et al., 2007). Yet other studies have reported an increase in myelination of white matter fiber bundle density in the right frontal lobe (Li et al., 2010) and in the tracts that connect prefrontal and occipito-partietal regions with the cerebellum and striatum (Silk et al., 2009). Based on these collective results, Li and colleagues (2010) suggested that some children with ADHD may exhibit deficiencies in the myelination of nerve sheaths, which impinges upon the transfer of information through the white matter bundles, whereas other individuals display excessive myelination of nerve sheaths. In the latter instance, though, the hyperplasia does not enable adequate compensation for the deficits in cognitive functioning associated with ADHD.

REVIEW OF NEUROCOGNITIVE RESEARCH

In accordance with the wealth of neuroimaging findings, data from neuropsychological assessments lend further support to the notion that ADHD symptomatology is associated with abnormalities in a wide array of brain regions. These findings are detailed, by domain, below.

General Intellectual Abilities

Several investigators have reported that children who are diagnosed with ADHD perform significantly lower on measures of overall cognitive ability (Full Scale IQ) than their age-matched peers (for review, see Frazier, Demaree, and Youngstrom, 2004; Barkley, DuPaul, and McMurray, 1990). As these authors note, such a difference may be indicative of a pattern of mild, global cognitive dysfunction, or it could reflect the culmination of multiple, specific areas of cognitive impairment (Frazier, Demaree, and Youngstrom, 2004). Given the medium effect size of the difference in intellectual abilities, some researchers (e.g., Murphy et al., 2001) have included IQ as a covariate in their investigations of specific neuropsychological deficits associated with ADHD. Murphy and colleagues (2001) contend that such covariation is essential for determining whether unique deficiencies in any particular domain are present. However, other investigators have noted that covarying for intellectual functioning is ill-conceived, as doing so may parcel out abilities that are common to both IQ and the domain in question, and in the process obfuscate/eradicate any differences that may be present (e.g., Faraone et al., 1993; Seidman et al., 1997).

Attention

Among specific neurocognitive functions, attention is one of the primary abilities reported to be compromised in ADHD. As such, it is not surprising that numerous researchers have attempted to identify the specific attentional weaknesses that characterize the disorder. As Tsal, Shalev, and Mevorach (2005) point out, attention is a complex construct composed of several different functions, including selective attention (defined by the authors as "focusing attention on relevant information while effectively ignoring distracting information"), executive attention (i.e., "inhibiting responses to irrelevant stimulus aspects"), sustained attention (i.e., "maintaining attention over a prolonged period of time in order to detect infrequent signals"), and orienting of attention (i.e., "directing attention to a designated location and reorienting to a new location"). Although prior studies demonstrated weaknesses in each of these aspects of attention (i.e., Heaton et al., 2001; Brandeis et al., 1998; Barkley, 1997; Pearson, Yaffee, Loveland, and Norton, 1995; Richards et al., 1990; Douglas and Peters, 1979; Douglas, 1972), Tsal, Shalev, and Mevorach (2005) were the first to systematically examine the particular pattern of attentional weaknesses associated with ADHD. In their elegantly designed study, these authors demonstrated that, while most individuals diagnosed with ADHD exhibited deficits in sustained attention, more than half of ADHD participants displayed difficulties with one of the other three aspects of attention. As the authors noted, these results highlighted the heterogeneity in symptom profiles that is often reported, and they emphasized the importance of considering an individual's particular pattern of performance when considering treatment options.

Processing Speed

Individuals diagnosed with ADHD have consistently been reported to exhibit slower and more variable reaction times (RT) than do their typically developing peers (van der Meere, Shalev, Borger, and Gross-Tsur, 1995; Oosterlaan and Sergeant, 1998; Borger et al., 1999; Borger and van der Meere, 2000; Leth-Steensen, Elbaz, and Douglas, 2000; Kuntsi, Oosterlaan, and Stevenson, 2001; Banaschewski et al., 2003). It has been suggested that the increased variability in reaction time may underlie other aspects of cognitive dysfunction, such as difficulty with inhibitory control (Lijffijt, Kenemans, Verbaten, and Van Engeland, 2005). However, it is also possible that such variability is itself secondary to lapses in sustained attention (Leth-Steensen et al., 2000; Hervey et al., 2006).

Executive Functioning

Frontal lesions frequently result in distractibility, impulsivity, and hyperactivity (Pennington and Ozonoff, 1996), symptoms that are also evident in ADHD. Therefore, it is not surprising that theoretical models of ADHD highlighting impairment in executive functioning, which is associated with prefrontal cortex (PFC) dysfunction, have preponderated over the past few decades. Executive functioning refers to a set of higher order cognitive skills that help one organize, initiate, monitor, and modify goal directed behavior; motivation, problem solving, and reasoning are also involved. Models of executive dysfunction have posited that deficiencies in set-shifting (Müller et al., 2007), working memory (Mariani and Barkley, 1997; Martinussen, Hayden, Hogg-Johnson, and Tannock, 2005), and planning (Barkley, 1997; Pennington, Groisser, and Welsh, 1993) not only parallel manifestations of ADHD but also are central to the pathophysiology of the disorder (see Seidman et al., 2006). Indeed, numerous investigators have found that children diagnosed with ADHD perform significantly more poorly than typically developing children on executive functioning (EF) tasks as early as the preschool period (Berlin, Hohlin, and Rydell, 2003; Hughes, Dunn, and White, 1998; Mariani and Barkley, 1997; Sonuga-Barke, Dalen, Daley, and Remington, 2002).

Motor Functioning

The notion that ADHD symptomatology is associated with motor dysfunction also has a long-standing history, already becoming popularized in the middle of the twentieth century. At that time, research into "hyperkinetic impulse disorder" and "hyperactive child syndrome," the precursors of the symptom profile we now refer to as ADHD, suggested that the disorder was a direct result of insufficient thalamic filtering, which caused the overstimulation of the cortex (for review, see Barkley, 1996). Although the syndrome is now conceptualized as one of impairment in attention and cognition rather than a primary motor disorder, difficulties with motor functioning and coordination continue to be emphasized in the literature.

Although not all individuals diagnosed with ADHD have motor impairment, estimates of those who do range from 8–52 percent (Piek, Pitcher, and Hay, 1999), which is much higher than would be expected purely by chance. Given these statistics, Blondis (1999) recommends that when making a diagnosis of ADHD, physicians should carefully assess for the presence of other developmental deficits, including developmental coordination disorders. Clinical observations during a neurological exam often reveal that children diagnosed with ADHD exhibit impairment on tasks that require the integration of sensory and motor abilities (Werry et al., 1972). These children frequently display slowing of gross motor movements (e.g., heel to toe taps) as well as motor overflow (i.e., involuntary associated movements; Denckla and Rudel, 1978). Parents and teachers frequently report that, in addition to demonstrating attentional weaknesses and/or hyperactivity, these children have poor handwriting, a finding that has been well documented (McMahon and Greenburg, 1977; Shaywitz and Shaywitz, 1984; Szatmari, Oxford, and Boyle, 1989; Barkley, 1990; Whitmont and Clark, 1996).

In summarizing the literature, Steger and colleagues (2001) have pointed out that it is the quality and speed of simple motor sequences that differentiates children with ADHD from their typically developing peers. Some investigators have further qualified these findings, reporting that it is only those children with the inattentive subtype who perform significantly worse than their same-aged peers on tasks of manual dexterity (Piek, Pitcher, and Hay, 1999). Nevertheless, there appears to be a strong association between the degree of fine motor difficulty and the severity of ADHD symptomatology (Whitmont and Clark, 1996). In addition, at least some aspects of motor impairment appear to remit when children are treated with psychostimulant medication (Sheppard et al., 2000), suggesting a different way in which this form of treatment may assist in reducing the level of functional impairment associated with ADHD.

Language Abilities

Several investigations have been conducted to assess whether there are any specific areas of language impairment evident among those with ADHD. Loge, Staton, and Beatty (1990) reported that children diagnosed with ADHD exhibited impairment in reading comprehension relative to their typically developing peers. Carte, Nigg, and Hinshaw (1996) further uncovered that children diagnosed with ADHD have difficulty on tasks of rapid naming. However, both groups of investigators theorized that the deficits were not indicative of primary language impairment. Rather, impairments in the ability to control and/or direct attention was hypothesized to underlie the aforementioned deficits in reading comprehension (Loge, Staton, and Beatty, 1990), and organization difficulties were thought to impede the children's performance on tasks of rapid naming, which requires increased selective attention (Carte, Nigg, and Hinshaw, 1996).

Although language impairment is not thought to be an underlying feature of ADHD, investigators have reported that young children diagnosed with speech/language disorders are at increased risk for the development of ADHD (Baker and Cantwell, 1987). Follow-up evaluations conducted when such children reached their preteenage years revealed that the rate of ADHD was significantly more prevalent among the children who were language impaired as youngsters than it was among those children whose speech and language abilities developed in a timely fashion (Beitchman et al., 1996). When the analyses included children who had been diagnosed with speech and/or language impairment during their early childhood years, the findings were no longer significant.

Visuospatial Abilities

In contrast to the generally intact language abilities of the left hemisphere, visuospatial functioning, which is localized to the right hemisphere, has been reported to be an area of relative weakness for individuals diagnosed with ADHD. Results of several investigations have revealed that children who are both inattentive and impulsive tend to exhibit increased difficulty on tasks that assess visuomotor precision (Raggio, 1999; Resta and Eliot, 1994). It is possible that such deficits are a reflection of poor motor control rather than primary impairment in visuospatial functioning. Nevertheless, other investigators have demonstrated that individuals who are diagnosed with ADHD, both with and without hyperactivity, do indeed demonstrate deficits on tasks that assess visuospatial functioning (Garcia-Sanchez, Estevez-Gonzalez, Suarez- Romero, and Junque, 1997). Gracia-Sanchez and colleagues (1997) reported that those who were diagnosed as being inattentive but not hyperactive/impulsive exhibited more impairment on visuospatial tasks than did their hyperactive counterparts.

Given their findings, these researchers have suggested that ADHD may be a right hemisphere disorder, since the right hemisphere of the human brain is known to play a role in mediating the processing of both visuospatial and emotional information as well as maintaining attention. This theory has been posited by several other researchers (Heilman, Voeller, and Nadeau, 1991; Stefanatos and Wasserstein, 2001); however, a consensus has yet to be reached as to whether this is indeed an accurate conceptualization of the disorder.

Learning and Memory Abilities

Aspects of verbal learning and memory have also been found to be an area of relative weakness for individuals with ADHD. Felton and colleagues (1987) demonstrated that children with attentional weaknesses who did not have a comorbid reading disability exhibited specific deficits in their ability to learn and remember a supraspan word list. In contrast, those individuals did not have difficulty recalling narratives. Unlike the well-structured nature of prose, rote verbal information lacks organization. The dissociation revealed a difficulty in processing unstructured information, which required the individual to impose an organizational strategy. As such, this deficit is likely secondary to executive dysfunction rather than a reflection of primary impairment in learning/memory abilities.

Academic Achievement

Given the above-mentioned findings, it is not surprising that individuals diagnosed with ADHD have been reported to underachieve in their school work (Barkley, Fisher, Edelbrock, and Smallish, 1990; Barry, Lyman, and Klinger, 2002; DuPaul, McGoey, Eckert, and VanBrankle, 2001; Hinshaw, 1992). Frazier, Demaree, and Youngstrom (2004) conducted a meta-analysis of the data from approximately 200 studies that employed various neuropsychological measures to ascertain the specific cognitive deficits associated with ADHD. Their findings revealed that tasks assessing spelling and arithmetic abilities were more sensitive to ADHD than was general intellectual ability (Frazier, Demaree, and Youngstrom, 2004). However, the authors noted that many of the studies included in the meta-analysis did not exclude participants who had comorbid learning disabilities. Nevertheless, it is likely that the aforementioned, specific neurocognitive impairments associated with ADHD do indeed impair a child's ability to perform on par with his or her classmates, requiring teachers to employ various strategies that will assist these children in learning the necessary classroom material and skills.

Social and Emotional Functioning

Symptoms of ADHD not only impact academic functioning but also affect the development of appropriate social skills (Pelham and Bender, 1982; Pelham and Milch, 1984; Kolko, Loar, and

Sturnick; Landau and Moore, 1991; Maedgen and Carlson, 2000; Bagwell, Molina, Pelham, and Hoza, 2001; Abikoff et al., 2004; van der Oord et al., 2005). As de Boo and Prins (2007) point out, the criticism and social rejection that children diagnosed with ADHD often experience is likely due to their tendencies to initiate conversations at inappropriate times, to interrupt others, and to exhibit off-task, unpredictable, and disruptive behaviors. In addition, children who display symptoms of both inattention and hyperactivity/impulsivity have been reported to display more aggressive behaviors and emotional dysregulation than their same-aged peers, while those diagnosed with ADHD-inattentive subtype have been reported to exhibit more social passivity (Maedgen and Carlson, 2000). Given that social impairment in early childhood predicts impairment in adolescence (Greene et al., 1999), it is possible that this deficiency causes, or at the very least exacerbates, decreased self-esteem (Dooling-Litfin and Rosen, 1997; Shaw-Zirt et al., 2005), depressive disorders (Heiligenstein and Keeling, 1995), substance use disorders (Greene et al., 1997), antisocial behavior (Grenwald-Mayes, 2002), and anxiety and eating disorders (Heiligenstein and Keeling, 1995) that many individuals diagnosed with ADHD report experiencing during adolescence and adulthood. In an effort to mitigate the effects of early social difficulties, many investigators have attempted to implement psychosocial interventions designed to improve social behaviors. However, thus far such treatments have not proven to be any more effective than medication management alone (e.g., MTA Cooperative Group, 1999; Abikoff et al., 2004).

PROPOSED THEORETICAL FRAMEWORKS

Given all of the aforementioned neuroimaging and neuropsychological findings, various hypotheses have been proposed to explain the deficits that are at the core of ADHD. These theories can be loosely categorized as models that emphasize executive dysfunction, impairment in motivation/processing reward, or an amalgamation of the two. More recently, some investigators have been re-emphasizing the importance of taking a developmental perspective when conceptualizing the underpinnings of ADHD.

Executive Dysfunction Models

One of the most prominent models of ADHD was developed by Barkley (1997). In describing the role and impact that executive functioning deficits have on the development of ADHD, Barkley suggested that behavioral inhibition (defined as the ability to inhibit responses and delay reactions to events) is an essential component of four other executive functions. The executive functions that Barkley specified include: 1) working memory, which is the ability to hold information in mind for a brief period and adapt/use it; 2) self-regulation of affect, which is the ability to inhibit behavioral responses to emotional experiences; 3) internalization of speech, which leads to increased control over one's behavior, planning, and goal direction; and 4) reconstitution, which allows events to be mentally disassembled so as to extract more information about an event before preparing a response. Together, these executive abilities enable individuals to predict and control the environment (and one's behavior within it) so as to maximize gains and minimize future consequences. More generally, the interaction of these executive functions permits far more effective adaptive functioning.

Barkley's (1997) model further stipulates that the deficits in each of these executive functions, which are evident in ADHD, have an impact on the individuals functioning. Deficits in working memory decrease an individual's ability to use forethought and/or hindsight in governing behavior. Such deficits also decrease an individual's ability to estimate time. Deficits in self-regulation lead to increased emotional expression, decreased objectivity in selecting a response to an event, an inability to delay emotional responses so as to take others into account, and decreased ability to induce drive and motivational states associated with goal directed behavior. Deficits in internalized speech lead to excessive talking, a lack of reflection before acting, difficulties with organized and rule-governed self-speech, and decreased self-control and rule-governed behavior. Finally, deficits in reconstitution result in impairments in the analysis, synthesis, and formation of responses to events. Barkley hypothesized that these four executive functions are needed to ensure that only those reactions required to accomplish a task are initiated by the individual (Barkley, 1997). As such, the model also accounts for the aforementioned difficulties with both fine and gross motor control of complex movements.

Weaknesses of the Executive Dysfunction Model

Despite the abundance of data supporting the role of executive functioning deficits in ADHD, a multitude of evidence has cast significant doubt as to whether executive dysfunction constitutes the sine qua non of ADHD. Results of a meta-analysis (Willcutt et al., 2005) have called into question whether impairments in putative executive functions are either necessary or sufficient to account for the breadth of disturbances associated with the disorder, as many children who display symptoms of ADHD do not exhibit weaknesses in domains of executive functioning. This argument is further bolstered by several studies, which have demonstrated that preschoolers with ADHD do not differ from control children on executive functioning measures after controlling for deficiencies in more rudimentary processes (Berwid, Curko Kera, Marks, Santra, Bender, and Halperin, 2005; Marks, Berwid, Santra, Kera, Cyrulnik, and Halperin, 2005). These findings in preschoolers are similar to those reported by Rommelse and colleagues (2007) in school-age children.

Adding to the rationale that executive functioning deficits cannot fully explain the scope of deficiencies associated with ADHD are the findings that children diagnosed with ADHD also display deficits in nonexecutive domains, as is readily apparent from the current literature review. In light of the fact that (i) individuals with ADHD may not present with executive dysfunction, (ii) those without ADHD (e.g., individuals with other psychiatric disorders) may exhibit impoverished executive functioning skills (Geurts et al., 2004; Pennington and Ozonoff, 1996; Bornstein, 1990; Moritz et al., 2002), and (iii) impairments in nonexecutive domains have comparable if not greater discriminative capability (Jakobson and Kikas, 2007; Bruce, Thernlund, and Nettelbladt, 2006; Dewey, Cantell, and Crawford, 2007; Dewey et al., 2002; Piek, Pitcher, and Hay, 1999; Smith and Bryson, 1994), it has become increasingly clear that executive dysfunction, although clearly associated with ADHD, may lack adequate specificity to be considered the sole, defining feature of the disorder. The models that follow represent a sampling of the more recent hypotheses, which have been formulated to account for the inadequacies of a framework that establishes executive dysfunction as the sole or the main deficit in ADHD.

Impaired Motivation/Reinforcement System Model

Another model that has received considerable attention within the literature posits that individuals diagnosed with ADHD have a dysfunction in motivational and/or reinforcement systems (Sonuga-Barke, Taylor, Sembi, and Smith, 1992; Tripp and Alsop, 2001; Castellanos and Tannock, 2002; Sonuga-Barke, 2002; Doyle et al., 2005; Johansen and Sagvolden, 2004; Sagvolden, Johansen, Aase, and Russell, 2005; Luman et al., 2007). Several theoretical models have been proposed to explain this deficiency. Some investigators have emphasized that fronto-limbic, dopaminergic abnormalities result in an inability to accurately process stimuli associated with reward (Sagvolden et al., 2005; Sonuga-Barke, 2002). Others have proposed that children with ADHD have an elevated reward threshold and therefore require additional reward in order to optimize their performance (Haenlein and Caul, 1987). A third conceptualization is that individuals with ADHD are not able to use intrinsic motivation to optimize performance (Douglas, 1989; Sergeant, Oosterlann, and Van der Meere, 1999; Luman et al., 2007). It has also been suggested that the problem is not related to reward per se; rather, it is associated with decreased sensitivity to conditions of nonreward and punishment (Quay, 1988a, 1988b, 1988c, 1997).

Dual- or Multiple-Pathway Models

Given the wide variety of and variability in cognitive difficulties that are associated with ADHD, it is most likely that a dual- or multiple-pathway model must be employed to understand the causal/associative features of the disorder. In recent years, a couple of different conceptualizations have been suggested:

Cognitive-Energetic Model

The Cognitive-Energetic Model (Sergeant, Oosterlaan, and van der Meere, 1999; Sergeant, 2000) is one theory that has been proposed to explain the complex neurocognitive dysfunction that is associated with ADHD. According to this hypothesis, ADHD is a disorder of deficient executive functioning *and* impairment in the ability to regulate arousal and to exhibit appropriate, effortful control. These systems have been conceptualized as being composed of both "bottom-up," automatically generated emotional reactions, as well as "top-down" effortful self-regulatory processes (Sergeant, 2005; Sergeant, Geurts, Huijbregts, Scheres, and Oosterlaan, 2003; Casey, 2005; Eisenberg, Fabes, Guthrie, and Reiser, 2000; Martel, Nigg, & Von Eye, 2009). In addition, the former is thought to become manifest particularly under conditions that require considerable effort or executive control (e.g., when task demands are altered).

Integrated Affective and Cognitive Model

In another effort to explain the multiple developmental pathways to ADHD, Nigg and Casey (2005) sought to integrate the literature regarding the cognitive and emotional functioning deficits associated with ADHD, both at a neuroanatomical and behavioral level. The authors posited that disruptions in one of three different neural circuits can cause ADHD-like symptoms. The first pathway described in the model involves a breakdown in fronto-striatal and fronto-cerebellar circuitry that affects prefrontally mediated cognitive control. This leads to disruptions in the development of self regulation, which is manifested primarily through inattentive and disorganized behavior (i.e., ADHD – predominantly inattentive subtype). Nigg and Casey's second pathway emphasizes the role that affective processing and temperament play in the development of impulsive behaviors. The authors argue that overreactivity in the fronto-amygdalar circuitry may cause some individuals to display an extreme temperamental approach characteristic, meaning that these people tend to approach almost anything that will be rewarding and fail to avoid things that will result in punishment. This, in turn, may result in the poor self-control and the impaired social skills that are associated with ADHD. Finally, the authors point out that hypoactivity in the amygdalar-frontal circuitry can result in fearlessness and aggression due to emotional dysregulation, a lack of empathy, and an indifference to social rules. Such a symptom profile is commonly associated with the primary diagnoses of Oppositional Defiant (ODD) and/or Conduct (CD) Disorder, disorders that frequently co-occur with ADHD. Nigg and Casey state that a breakdown in any of these neural pathways can co-occur, leading to the symptoms associated with ADHD-combined type and to the comorbidities with ODD and CD.

Developmental Model

Halperin and Schulz (2006) recently hypothesized that ADHD is the direct result of noncortical neural dysfunction that is first manifest early in the ontogenetic process. According to this theory, executive functioning deficits are not due to dysfunction of the prefrontal cortex (PFC) circuitry, which mediates those functions; rather, they are secondary to dysfunction in subcortical regulatory systems. Although these abnormalities are thought to remain static throughout a person's lifetime, the development of higher order cortical functions, which emerge during childhood, adolescence, and early adulthood, enable some individuals to compensate for the underlying deficits (for review, see Halperin and Healey, 2011). Based on this conceptualization, PFC circuitry would actually be involved in the recovery from, rather than in the pathophysiology of the disorder.

SUMMARY AND FUTURE DIRECTIONS

Over the past couple of decades, numerous frameworks have been proposed to account for the abundant findings generated from the neuroimaging and neurocognitive studies designed to understand the symptoms and deficits associated with ADHD. These theories, although quite disparate, all stem from a neurological perspective of the disorder. As Rafalovich (2001) notes, ADHD seems to have been primarily conceptualized from a neurological viewpoint since the 1990s, when stimulant medication emerged as the predominant treatment for ADHD.

Currently, psychopharmacological agents continue to be considered the most effective treatments for ADHD, along with parent training and behavior modification within the classroom setting (Halperin and Healey, 2011). However, such interventions are limited in that the effects of the interventions seldom persist after the treatment has terminated (Chronis et al., 2003, 2004), and many children do not experience full symptom amelioration even during the treatment implementation (Hoza et al., 2005; Swanson et al., 2001). Therefore, considerable energy is now being focused on generating alternative methods to approach the treatment of ADHD.

Once such promising intervention, born out of the neurocognitive and neurological literature, as well as the literature on brain plasticity and rehabilitation (Halperin and Healey, 2011), is a "brain training" program. In particular, investigators have recently begun using computerized programs designed to improve attention (Shalev, Tsal, and Mevorach, 2007; Tamm et al., 2010) and working memory (Klingberg et al., 2005), as "brain training" interventions for ADHD. Klingberg and colleagues' (2005) results are encouraging, indicating improvements in both neural and behavioral functioning, following a five-week computerized training program (Cogmed). In addition, these authors reported that the gains were maintained three months beyond the termination of treatment. Similarly, Tamm et al. (2010) found significant improvements in ADHD symptomotology and neuropsychological functioning following a 12-week attention training program (Pay Attention!), with treatment gains still apparent nine months later. These results suggest that a relatively brief intervention targeting underlying neurodevelopmental processes may yield long-lasting cognitive and behavioral improvements in children with ADHD.

This next decade is sure to see many advances in the field of ADHD research and many novel treatment options. As hypotheses continue to be generated and new interventions emerge, it is imperative that clinicians and researchers remain cognizant of the information that has been gleaned, thus far, from the copious neuroimaging and neurocognitive literature and attempt to incorporate these findings into future ADHD studies.

REFERENCES

Abikoff, H., Hechtman, L., Klein, R.G., Gallagher, R., Fleiss, J., Etcovitch, J., Cousins, L., Greenfield, B., Martin, D. & Pollack, S. (2004), Social functioning in children with ADHD treated with long-term methylphenidate and multimodal psychosocial treatment. *Journal of the American Academy of Child and Adolescent Psychiatry*, *43*: 820–9.

American Psychiatric Association. (2000), *Diagnostic and Statistical Manual of Mental Disorders*, 4th edition, text rev. Washington, DC: American Psychiatric Association.

Ashtari, M., Kumra, S., Bhaskar, S.L., Clarke, T., Thaden, E., Cervellione, K.L., et al. (2005), Attention-deficit/hyperactivity disorder: A preliminary diffusion tensor imaging study. *Biological Psychiatry*, *57*: 448–55.

Aylward, E.H., Reiss, A.L., Reader, M.J., Singer, H.S., Brown, J.E. & Denckla, M.B. (1996), Basal ganglia volumes in children with attention-deficit hyperactivity disorder. *Journal of Child Neurology*, *11*: 112–5.

Baker, L. & Cantwell, D.P. (1987), A prospective psychiatric follow-up of children with speech/language disorders. *Journal of the American Academy of Child and Adolescent Psychiatry*, *26*: 546–53.

Bagwell, C.L., Molina, B.S.G., Pelham, W.E. & Hoza, B. (2001), Attention-deficit hyperactivity disorder and problems in peer relations: Predictions from childhood to adolescence. *Journal of the American Academy of Child and Adolescent Psychiatry*, *40*: 1285–92.

Banaschewski, T., Brandeis, D., Heinrich, H., Albrecht, B., Brunner, E. & Rothernberger, A. (2003), Association of ADHD and conduct disorder- brain electrical evidence for the existence of a distinct subtype. *Journal of Child Psychology and Psychiatry*, *44*: 356–76.

Barkley, R.A. (1997), Behavioral inhibition, sustained attention, and executive function: Constructing a unified theory of ADHD. *Psychological Bulletin*, *121*: 65–94.

_____ DuPaul, G.J. & McMurray, M.B. (1990), Comprehensive evaluation of attention deficit disorder with and without hyperactivity as defined by research criteria. *Journal of Consulting and Clinical Psychology*, *58*: 775–89.

_____ Fischer, M., Edelbrock, C. & Smallish, L. (1990), The adolescent outcome of hyperactive children diagnosed by research criteria: I. An 8 year prospective follow-up study. *Journal of the American Academy of Child and Adolescent Psychiatry*, *29*(4): 456–557.

Barry, T.D., Lyman, R.D. & Klinger, L.G. (2002), Academic underachievement and attention-deficit/hyperactivity disorder: The negative impact of symptom severity on school performance. *Journal of School Psychology*, *40*: 259–83.

Baumgardner, T.L., Singer, H.S., Denckla, M.B., Rubin, M.A., Abrams, M.T., Colli, M.J., et al. (1996), Corpus callosum morphology in children with Tourette Syndrome and attention deficit hyperactivity disorder. *Neurology*, *47*: 477–82.

Beitchman, J.H., Brownlie, E.B., Inglis, A., Wild, J., Ferguson, B., Schachter, D., Lancee, W., Wilson, B. & Mathews, R. (1996), Seven-year follow-up of speech/language impaired and control children: psychiatric outcome. *Journal of Child Psychology and Psychiatry, 37*: 961–70.

Berlin, L., Bohlin, G. & Rydell, A.M. (2003), Relations between inhibition, executive functioning, and ADHD symptoms: A longitudinal study from age 5 to 8(1/2) years. *Child Neuropsychology (Neuropsychology, Development and Cognition: Section C), 9*: 255–66.

Berquin, P., Giedd, J., Jacobsen, L., Hamburger, S., Krain, A., Rapoport, J., et al. (1998), Cerebellum in attention-deficit hyperactivity disorder: a morphometric MRI study. *Neurology, 50*: 1087–93.

Berwid, O.G., Curko Kera, E.A., Marks, D.J., Santra, A., Bender, H.A. & Halperin, J.M. (2005), Sustained attention and response inhibition in young children at risk for attention deficit/hyperactivity disorder. *Journal of Child Psychology and Psychiatry, 46*: 1219–29.

Blondis, T. (1999), Motor disorders and attention-deficit/hyperactivity disorder. *Pediatric Clinics of North America, 46*: 899–913.

Borger, N., van der Meere, J., Ronner, A., Alberts, E., Geuze, R. & Bogte, H. (1999), Heart rate variability and sustained attention in ADHD children. *Journal of Abnormal Child Psychology, 27*: 25–33.

_____ & van der Meere, J. (2000), Motor control and state regulation in children with ADHD: A cardiac response study. *Biological Psychology, 51*: 247–67.

Bornstein, R. A. (1990), Neuropsychological performance in children with Tourette's syndrome. *Psychiatry Research, 33*: 73–81.

Brandeis, D., van Leeuwen, T.H., Rubia, K., Vitacco, D., Steger, J., Pascual-Marqui, R.D. & Steinhausen, H.C. (1998), Neuroelectric mapping reveals precursor of stop failures in children with attention deficits. *Behavioral Brain Research, 94*: 111–25.

Bruce, B., Thernlund, G. & Nettelbladt, U. (2006), ADHD and language impairment: A study of the parent questionnaire FTF (five to fifteen). *European Child and Adolescent Psychiatry, 15*: 52–60.

Bush, G., Frazier, J.A., Rauch, S.L., Seidman, L.J., Whalen, P.J., Jenike, M.A., et al. (1999), Anterior cingulate cortex dysfunction in attention-deficit/hyperactivity disorder revealed by fMRI and the counting stroop. *Biological Psychiatry, 45*: 1542–52.

Campbell, S.B. (1995), Behavior problems in preschool children: A review of recent research. *Journal of Child Psychology and Psychiatry, 36*: 113–49.

Cao, Q., Zang, Y., Zhu, C., Cao, X., Sun, L., Zhou, X., et al. (2008), Alerting deficits in children with attention deficit/hyperactivity disorder: event-related FMRI evidence. *Brain Research, 1219*: 159–168.

Carte, E., Nigg, J. & Hinshaw, S. (1996), Neuropsychological functioning, motor speed, and language processing in boys with and without ADHD. *Journal of Abnormal Child Psychology, 24*: 481–498.

Casey, B. J. (2005). Frontostriatal and frontocerebellar circuitry underlying cognitive control. In: *Developing Individuality in the Human Brain: A Tribute to Michael I. Posner*, U. Mayr, E. Awh & S. W. Keele (eds.). Washington, DC: American Psychological Association, pp. 141–66.

_____ Castellanos, F.X., Giedd, J.N., Marsh, W.L., Hamburger, S.D., Schubert, A.B., et al. (1997), Implication of right frontostriatal circuitry in response inhibition and attention-deficit/hyperactivity disorder. *Journal of the American Academy of Child and Adolescent Psychiatry, 36*: 374–83.

_____ Epstein, J.N., Buhle, J., Liston, C., Davidson, M.C., Tonev, S.T. et al. (2007), Frontostriatal connectivity and its role in cognitive control in parent-child dyads with ADHD. *American Journal of Psychiatry, 164*: 1729–36.

_____ Nigg, J.T. & Durston, S.D. (2007), New potential leads in the biology and treatment of attention deficit-hyperactivity disorder. *Current Opinions in Neurology, 20*: 119–24.

Castellanos, F.X. (2001), Neural substrates of attention-deficit hyperactivity disorder. *Advances in Neurology, 85*: 197–206.

_____ Giedd, J.N., Marsh, W.L., Hamburger, S.D., Vaituzis, A.C., Dickstein, D.P., et al. (1996), Quantitative brain magnetic resonance imaging in attention deficit hyperactivity disorder. *Archives of General Psychiatry, 53*: 607–16.

_____ Lee, P.P., Sharp, W., Jeffries, N.O., Greenstein, D.K., Clasen, L.S., et al. (2002), Developmental trajectories of brain volume abnormalities in children and adolescents with attention-deficit/hyperactivity disorder. *Journal of the American Medical Association, 288*: 1740–8.

_____ & Tannock, R. (2002), Neuroscience of attention-deficit/hyperactivity disorder: The search for endophenotypes. *Nature Reviews. Neuroscience, 3*: 617–28.

Chronis, A.M., Fabiano, G.A., Gnagy, E.M., Onyango, A.N., Pelham, W.E., Lopez-Williams, A., et al. (2004), An evaluation of the summer treatment program for children with attention-deficit/hyperactivity disorder using a treatment withdrawal design. *Behavior Therapy*, *35*: 561–85.

_____ Pelham Jr., W.E., Gnagy, E.M., Roberts, J.E. & Aronoff, H.R. (2003), The impact of late-afternoon stimulant dosing for children with ADHD on parent and parent-child domains. *Journal of Clinical Child and Adolescent Psychology*, *32*: 118–26.

de Boo, G.M. & Prins, P.J.M. (2007), Social incompetence in children with ADHD: Possible moderator and mediators in social-skills training. *Clinical Psychology Review*, *27*: 78–97.

Denckla, M.B. & Rudel, R.G. (1978), Anomalies of motor development in hyperactive boys. *Annals of Neurology*, *3*: 231–3.

Dewey, D., Cantell, M. & Crawford, S. G. (2007), Motor and gestural performance in children with autism spectrum disorders, developmental coordination disorder, and or attention deficit hyperactivity disorder. *Journal of the International Neuropsychological Society*, *13*: 246–56.

_____ Kaplan, B.J., Crawford, S.G. & Wilson, B.N. (2002), Developmental coordination disorder: Associated problems in attention, learning, and psychosocial adjustment. *Human Movement Science*, *21*: 905–18.

Dooling-Litfin, J. K. & Rosen, L. A. (1997), Self-esteem in college students with a childhood history of attention deficit hyperactivity disorder. *Journal of College Student Psychotherapy*, *11*: 69–82.

Douglas, V. I. (1972), Stop, look and listen: The problem of sustained attention and impulse control in hyperactive and normal children. *Canadian Journal of Behavioral Science*, *4*: 259–81.

_____ (1989). Can Skinnerian theory explain attention deficit disorder. A reply to Barkley. In: *Attention Deficit Disorder: Current Concepts and Emerging Trends in Attentional and Behavioral Disorders of Childhood*, L.M. Bloomingalde & J.A. Sergeant (eds.). Elmsford, NY: Pergamon, pp. 235–54.

_____& Peters, K.G. (1979). Toward a clearer definition of the attentional deficit of hyperactive children. In *Attention and Cognitive Development*, G.A. Hale & M. Lewis (eds.). New York: Plenum, pp. 173–247.

Doyle, A.E., Faraone, S.V., Seidman, L.J., Willcutt, E.G., Nigg, J.T., Waldman, I.D., Pennington, B.F., Peart, J. & Biederman, J. (2005), Are endophenotypes based on measures of executive functions useful for molecular genetic studies of ADHD? *Journal of Child Psychology and Psychiatry*, *46*: 774–803.

DuPaul, G.J., McGoey, K.E., Eckert, T.L. & VanBrankle, J. (2001), Preschool children with attention-deficit/hyperactivity disorder: Impairments in behavioral, social, and school functioning. *Journal of the American Academy of Child and Adolescent Psychiatry*, *40*: 508–15.

Durston, S., Davidson, M.C., Mulder, M.J., Spicer, J.A., Galvan, A., Tottenham, N., et al. (2007), Neural and behavioral correlates of expectancy violations in attention deficit hyperactivity disorder. *Journal of Child Psychology and Psychiatry*, *48*: 881–9.

_____ Hulshoff Pol, H.E., Schnack, H.G., Buitelaar, J.K., Steenhuis, M.P., Minderaa, R.B., et al.> (2004), Magnetic resonance imaging of boys with attention deficit/hyperactivity disorder and their unaffected siblings. *Journal of the American Academy of Child Adolescent Psychiatry*, *43*: 332–40.

_____ Tottenham, N.T., Thomas, K.M., Davidson, M.C., Eigsti, I.M., Yang, Y., et al.> (2003), Differential patterns of striatal activation in young children with and without ADHD. *Biological Psychiatry*, *53*: 871–8.

Egger, H.L. & Angold, A. (2006), Common emotional and behavioral disorders in preschool children: Presentation, nosology, and epidemiology. *Journal of Child Psychology and Psychiatry*, *47*: 313–37.

Eisenberg, N., Fabes, R.A., Guthrie, I.K. & Reiser, M. (2000), Dispositional emotionality and regulation: Their role in predicting quality of social functioning. *Journal of Personality and Social Psychology*, *78*: 136–57.

Faraone, S.V. (2000), Genetics of childhood disorders: XX. ADHD, Part 4: Is ADHD genetically heterogeneous? *Journal of the American Academy of Child and Adolescent Psychiatry*, *39*: 1455–7.

_____ Biederman, J., Krifcher Lehman, B., Spencer, T., Norman, D., Seidman, L., Kraus, I., Perrin, J., Chen, W. & Tsuang, M. T. (1993), Intellectual performance and school failure in children with attention deficit hyperactivity disorder and in their siblings. *Journal of Abnormal Psychology*, *102*: 616–23.

Felton, R.H., Wood, F.B., Brown, I.S., Campbell, S.K. & Harter, M.R. (1987), Separate verbal memory and naming deficits in attention deficit disorder and reading disability. *Brain and Language*, *31*: 171–84.

Filipek, P.A., Semrud-Clikeman, M., Steingard, R.J., Renshaw, P.F., Kennedy, D.N. & Biederman, J. (1997), Volumetric MRI analysis comparing subjects having attention-deficit hyperactivity disorder with normal controls. *Neurology*, *48*: 589–601.

Frazier, T.W., Demaree, H.A. & Youngstrom, E.A. (2004), Meta-analysis of intellectual and neuropsychological test performance in attention-deficit/hyperactivity disorder. *Neuropsychology*, *18*: 543–55.

Gadow, K.D., Sprafkin, J. & Nolan, E.E. (2001), DSM-IV symptoms in community and clinic preschool children. *Journal of the American Academy of Child and Adolescent Psychiatry*, *40*: 1383–92.

Garcia-Sanchez, C., Estevez-Gonzalez, A., Suarez-Romero, E. & Junque, C. (1997), Right hemisphere dysfunction in subjects with attention-deficit disorder with and without hyperactivity. *Journal of Child Neurology*, *12*: 107–15.

Geurts, H. M., Verte, S., Oosterlaan, J., Roeyers, H. & Sergean, J. A. (2004), How specific are executive functioning deficits in attention deficit hyperactivity disorder and autism? *Journal of Child Psychology and Psychiatry*, *45*: 836–54.

Giedd, J.N., Castellanos, F.X., Casey, B.J., Kozuch, P., King, A.C., Hamburger, S.D., et al. (1994), Quantitative morphology of the corpus callosum in attention deficit hyperactivity disorder. *American Journal of Psychiatry*, *151*: 665–9.

Greene, R. W., Biederman, J., Faraone, S. V., Sienna, M. & Garcia-Jetton, J. (1997), Adolescent outcome of ADHD children with social disability: Results from a four year longitudinal follow up study. *Journal of Consulting and Clinical Psychology*, *65*: 758–67.

_____ Biederman, J., Faraone, S.V., Wilens, T.E., Mick, E. & Blier, H.K. (1999), Further validation of social impairment as a predictor of substance use disorders: Findings from a sample of siblings of boys with and without ADHD. *Journal of Clinical Child and Adolescent Psychology*, *28*: 349–54.

Greenwald-Mayes, G. (2002), Relationship between current quality of life and family of origin dynamics for college students with attention-deficit/hyperactivity disorder. *Journal of Attention Disorders*, *5*: 211–22.

Haenlein, M. & Caul, W.F. (1987), Attention deficit disorder with hyperactivity: A specific hypothesis of reward dysfunction. *Journal of the American Academy of Child and Adolescent Psychiatry*, *26*: 356–62.

Halperin, J.M. & Schulz, K.P. (2006), Revisiting the role of the prefrontal cortex in the pathophysiology of attention-deficit/hyperactivity disorder. *Psychological Bulletin*, *132*: 560–81.

_____ & Healey, D.M. (2011), The influences of environmental enrichment, cognitive enhancement, and physical exercise on brain development: Can we alter the developmental trajectory of ADHD? *Neuroscience and Biobehavioural Reviews*, *35*: 621–34.

Hamilton, L.S., Levitt, J.G., O'Neill, J., Alger, J.R., Luders, E., Phillips, O.R., et al. (2008), Reduced white matter integrity in attention-deficit hyperactivity disorder. *Neuroreport*, *19*: 1705–8.

Heaton, S.C., Reader, S.K., Preston, A.S., Fennell, E.B., Puyana, O.E., Gill, N., (2001), Test of everyday attention for children (TEA-Ch): Patterns of performance in children with ADHD and clinical controls. *Child Neuropsychology*, *7*: 251–64.

Heilman, K.M., Voeller, K.K.S. & Nadeau, S.E. (1991), A possible pathophysiologic substrate of attention deficit hyperactivity disorder. *Journal of Child Neurology*, *6*: S76–S81.

Heiligenstein, E. & Keeling, R. P. (1995), Presentation of unrecognized attention deficit hyperactivity disorder in college students. *Journal of American College Health*, *43*: 226–8.

Hervey, A.S., Epstein, J.N., Curry, J.F., Tonev, S., Eugene Arnold, L.E., Keith Conners, C.K., et al. (2006), Reaction time distribution analysis of neuropsychological performance in an ADHD sample. *Child Neuropsychology*, *12*: 125–40.

Hill, D.E., Yeo, R.A., Campbell, R.A., Hart, B., Vigil, J. & Brooks, W. (2003), Magnetic resonance imaging correlates of attention-deficit/hyperactivity disorder in children. *Neuropsychology*, *17*: 496–506.

Hinshaw, S.P. (1992), Externalizing behavior problems and academic underachievement in childhood and adolescence: Causal relationships and underlying mechanisms. *Psychological Bulletin*, *111*: 127–55.

Hoza, B., Gerdes, A.C., Mrug, S., Hinshaw, S.P., Bukowski, W.M., Gold, J.A., et al.> (2005), Peer-assessed outcomes in the multimodal treatment study of children with attention deficit hyperactivity disorder. *Journal of Clinical Child and Adolescent Psychology*, *34*: 74–86.

Hughes, C., Dunn, J. & White, A. (1998), Trick or treat?: Uneven understanding of mind and emotion and executive dysfunction in "hard-to-manage" preschoolers. *Journal of Child Psychology and Psychiatry*, *39*: 981–94.

Hynd, G.W., Hern, K.L., Novey, E.S., Eliopulos, D., Marshall, R., Gonzalez, J.J., et al.> (1993), Attention deficit-hyperactivity disorder and asymmetry of the caudate nucleus. *Journal of Child Neurology*, *8*: 339–47.

_____ Semrud-Clikeman, M., Lorys, A.R., Novey, E.S. & Eliopulos, D. (1990), Brain morphology in developmental dyslexia and attention deficit disorder/hyperactivity. *Archives of Neurology*, *47*: 919–26.

_____ Semrud-Clikeman, M., Lorys, A.R., Novey, E.S., Eliopulos, D. & Lyytinen, H. (1991), Corpus callosum morphology in attention deficit-hyperactivity disorder: morphometric analysis of MRI. *Journal of Learning Disabilities*, *24*: 141–6.

Jakobson, A. & Kikas, E. (2007), Cognitive functioning in children with and without attention-deficit/hyperactivity disorder with and without comorbid learning disabilities. *Journal of Learning Disabilities*, *40*: 194–202.

Johansen, E.B. & Sagvolden, T. (2004), Response disinhibition may be explained as an extinction deficit in an animal model of attention-deficit/hyperactivity disorder (ADHD). *Behavioural Brain Research, 149*: 183–96.

Kates, W.R., Frederikse, M., Mostofsky, S.H., Folley, B.S., Cooper, K., Mazur-Hopkins, P., et al. (2002), MRI parcellation of the frontal lobe in boys with attention deficit hyperactivity disorder or Tourette syndrome. *Psychiatry Research, 116*: 63–81.

Keenan, K. & Wakschlag, L.S. (2002), Can a valid diagnosis of disruptive behavior disorder be made in preschool children? *The American Journal of Psychiatry, 159*: 351–8.

Klingberg, T., Fernell, E., Olesen, P.J., Johnson, M., Gustafsson, P., Dahlstrom, K et al. (2005), Computerized training of working memory in children with ADHD — a randomized, controlled trial. *Journal of the American Academy of Child and Adolescent Psychiatry, 44*: 177–86.

Kolko, D.J., Loar, L.L. & Sturnick, D. (1990), Inpatient social-cognitive skills training with conduct disordered and attention deficit disordered children. *Journal of Child Psychology and Psychiatry, 31*: 737–48.

Kuntsi, J., Oosterlaan, J. & Stevenson, J. (2001), Psychological mechanisms in hyperactivity: I. Response inhibition deficit, working memory impairment, delay aversion, or something else? *Journal of Child Psychology and Psychiatry, 42*: 199–210.

Landau, F. & Moore, L.A. (1991), Social skills deficits in children with ADHD. *School Psychology Review, 20*: 235–51.

Leth-Steensen, C., Elbaz, Z.K. & Douglas, V.I. (2000), Mean response times, variability, and skew in the responding of ADHD children: A response time distributional approach. *Acta Psychologica, 104*: 167–90.

Li, Q., Sun, J., Guo, L., Zang, Y., Feng, Z., Huang, X., Yang, H., Lv, Y., Huang, M. & Gong, Q. (2010), Increased fractional anisotropy in white matter of the right frontal region in children with attention-deficit/hyperactivity disorder: A diffusion tensor imaging study. *Activas Nervosa Superior Redivida, 52*: 193–9.

Lijffijt, M., Kenemans, J.L.,Verbaten, M.N. & Van Engeland, H. (2005), A meta-analytic review of stopping performance in attention-deficit/hyperactivity disorder: Deficient inhibitory motor control? *Journal of Abnormal Psychology, 114*: 216–22.

Loge, D.V., Staton, R.D. & Beatty, W.W. (1990), Performance of children with ADHD on tests sensitive to frontal lobe dysfunction. *Journal of the American Academy of Child & Adolescent Psychiatry, 29*: 540–5.

Luman, M., Oosterlaan, J., Hyde, C., van Meel, C.S. & Sergeant, J.A. (2007), Heart rate and reinforcement sensitivity in ADHD. *Journal of Child Psychology and psychiatry, 48*: 890–8.

Lyoo, I.K., Noam, G.G., Lee, C.K., Lee, H.K., Kennedy, B.P. & Renshaw, P.F. (1996), The corpus callosum and lateral ventricles in children with attention-deficit hyperactivity disorder: A brain magnetic resonance imaging study. *Biological Psychiatry, 40*: 1060–3.

Maedgen, J. W. & Carlson, C. L. (2000), Social functioning and emotional regulation in the attention deficit hyperactivity disorder subtypes. *Journal of Clinical Child Psychology, 29*: 30–42.

Makris, N., Buka, S.L., Biederman, J., Papadimitriou, G.M., Hodge, S.M., Valera, E.M., et al. (2007), Attention and executive systems abnormalities in adults with childhood ADHD: A DT-MRI study of connections. *Cerebral Cortex, 18*: 1210–20.

Mariani, M. & Barkley, R. A. (1997), Neuropsychological and academic functioning in preschool children with attention deficit hyperactivity disorder. *Developmental Neuropsychology, 13*: 111–29.

Marks, D.J., Berwid, O.G., Santra, A., Kera, E.C., Cyrulnik, S.E. & Halperin, J.M. (2005), Neuropsychological correlates of ADHD symptoms in preschoolers. *Neuropsychology, 19*: 446–55.

Martel, M.M., Nigg, J.T. & von Eye, A. (2009), How do trait dimensions map onto ADHD symptom domains? *Journal of Abnormal Child Psychology, 37*: 337–48.

Martinussen, R., Hayden, J., Hogg-Johnson, S. & Tannock, R. (2005), A meta-analysis of working memory impairments in children with attention-deficit/hyperactivity disorder. *Journal of the American Academy of Child Adolescent Psychiatry, 44*: 377–438.

McMahon, S.A. & Greenburg, L.M. (1977), Serial neurologic examination of hyperactive children. *Pediatrics, 59*: 584–7.

Moritz, S., Birkner, C., Kloss, M., Jahn, H., Hand, I., Haasen, C. & Krausz, M. (2002), Executive functioning in obsessive–compulsive disorder, unipolar depression, and schizophrenia. *Archives of Clinical Neuropsychology, 17*: 477–83.

Mostofsky, S.H., Cooper, K.L., Kates, W.R., Denckla, M.B. & Kaufmann, W.E. (2002), Smaller prefrontal and premotor volumes in boys with attention deficit/hyperactivity disorder. *Biological Psychiatry, 52*: 785–94.

Mostofsky, S.H., Reiss, A.L., Lockhart, P. & Denckla, M.B. (1998), Evaluation of cerebellar size in attention-deficit hyperactivity disorder. *Journal of Child Neurology, 13*: 434–9.

MTA Cooperative Group. (1999), A 14-month randomized clinical trial of treatment strategies for attention-deficit/hyperactivity disorder. *Archives of General Psychiatry*, *56*: 1088–96.

Müller, B. W., Gimbel, K., Keller-Pliessnig, A., Sartory, G., Gastpar, M. & Davids, E. (2007), Neuropsychological assessment of adult patients with attention-deficit/hyperactivity disorder. *European Archives of Psychiatry & Clinical Neuroscience*, *257*: 112–9.

Murphy, K.R., Barkley, R. A. & Bush, T. (2001), Executive functioning and olfactory identification in young adults with attention deficit-hyperactivity disorder. *Neuropsychology*, *15*: 211–20.

Nigg, J.T. & Casey, B.J. (2005), An integrative theory of attention-deficit/hyperactivity disorder based on the cognitive and affective neurosciences. *Development and Psychopathology*, *17*: 785–806.

Oosterlaan, J. & Sergeant, J.A. (1998), Effects of reward and response cost on response inhibition in AD/HD, disruptive, anxious, and normal children. *Journal of Abnormal Child Psychology*, *26*: 161–74.

Pavuluri, M.N., Yang, S., Kamineni, K., Passarotti, A.M., Srinivasan, G., Harral, E.M. et al (2009), Diffusion tensor imaging study of white matter fiber tracts in pediatric bipolar disorder and attention deficit/hyperactivity disorder. *Biological Psychiatry*, *65*: 586–93.

Pearson, D.A., Yaffee, L.S., Loveland, K.A. & Norton, A.M. (1995), Covert visual attention in children with attention deficit hyperactivity disorder: Evidence for developmental immaturity? *Development and Psychopathology*, *7*: 351–67.

Pelham, W.E. & Bender, M.E. (1982), Peer relationships in hyperactive children: Description and treatment. *Advances in Learning and Behavioral Disabilities*, *1*: 365–436.

_____ Foster, E.M. & Robb, J.A. (2007), The economic impact of attention-deficit/hyperactivity disorder in children and adolescents. *Ambulatory Pediatrics*, *7*: 121–31.

_____& Milich, R. (1984), Peer relationships in hyperactive children/attention deficit disorder. *Journal of Learning Disabilities*, *17*: 560–7.

Pennington, B.F., Groisser, D. & Welsh, M.C. (1993), Contrasting cognitive deficits in attention deficit hyperactivity disorder versus reading disability. *Developmental Psychology*, *29*: 511–23.

_____ & Ozonoff, S. (1996), Executive functions and developmental psychopathology. *Journal of Child Psychology and Psychiatry*, *37*: 51–87.

Piek, J. P., Pitcher, T. M. & Hay, D. A. (1999), Motor coordination and kinaesthesis in boys with attention deficit-hyperactivity disorder. *Developmental Medicine & Child Neurology*, *41*: 159–65.

Posner, M.I. & Petersen, S.E. (1990), The attention system of the human brain. *Annual Review of Neuroscience*, *13*: 25–42.

Quay, H.C. (1988a). Attention deficit disorder and the behavioral inhibition system: The relevance of the neuropsychological theory of Jeffrey A. Gray. In: *Attention Deficit Disorder: Criteria, Cognition, Intervention*, L.M. Bloomingdale & J.A. Sergeant (eds.). Oxford: Pergamon, pp. 117–25.

_____ (1988b). The behavioral reward and inhibition system in childhood behaviour disorder. In: *Attention Deficit Disorder, vol. 3*, L.M. Bloomingdalte (ed.). Oxford: Pergamon, pp. 176–85.

_____ (1988c), Reward, inhibition, and attention deficit hyperactivity disorder. *Journal of the American Academy of Child and Adolescent Psychiatry*, *27*: 262–3.

_____ (1997), Inhibition and attention deficit hyperactivity disorder. *Journal of Abnormal Child Psychology*, *25*: 7–13.

Rafalovich, A. (2001), Psychodynamic and neurological perspectives on ADHD: Exploring strategies for defining a phenomenon. *Journal for the Theory of Social Behaviour*, *31*: 397–418.

Richards, G.P., Samuels, S.J., Turnure, J.E. & Ysseldyke, J.E. (1990), Sustained and selective attention in children with learning disabilities. *Journal of Learning Disabilities*, *23*: 129–36.

Rommelse, N.N.J., Altink, M.E., de Sonneville, L.M.J., Buschgens, C.J.M., Buitelaar, J., Oosterlaan, J. & Sergeant, J.A. (2007), Are motor inhibition and cognitive flexibility dead ends in ADHD? *Journal of Abnormal Child Psychology*, *35*: 957–67.

Rubia, K., Overmeyer, S., Taylor, E., Brammer, M., Williams, S.C.R., Simmons, A., et al. (1999), Hypofrontality in attention-deficit/hyperactivity disorder during higher-order motor control: a study with functional MRI. *American Journal of Psychiatry*, *156*: 891–6.

Sagvolden, T., Johansen, E.B., Aase, H. & Russell, V.A. (2005), A dynamic developmental theory of attention-deficit/hyperactivity disorder (ADHD) predominantly hyperactive/impulsive and combined subtypes. *Behavioral and Brain Sciences*, *28*: 397–468.

Schulz, K.P., Fan, J., Tang, C.Y., Newcorn, J.H., Buchsbaum, M.S., Cheung, A.M., et al. (2004), Response inhibition in adolescents diagnosed with attention deficit hyperactivity disorder during childhood: An event-related FMRI study. *American Journal of Psychiatry*, *161*: 1650–7.

_____ Newcorn, J.H., Fan, J., Tang, C.Y. & Halperin, J.M. (2005), Brain activation gradients in ventrolateral prefrontal cortex related to persistence of ADHD in adolescence. *Journal of the American Academy of Child and Adolescent Psychiatry, 44*: 47–54.
Seidman, L.J., Biederman, J., Faraone, S.V., Weber, W. & Ouellette, C. (1997), Toward defining a neuropsychology of attention deficit-hyperactivity disorder: Performance of children and adolescents from a large clinically referred sample. *Journal of Consulting and Clinical Psychology, 65*: 150–60.
_____ Biederman, J., Valera, E.M., Monuteaux, M.C., Doyle, A.E. & Faraone, S.V. (2006), Neuropsychological functioning in girls with attention-deficit/hyperactivity disorder with and without learning disabilities. *Neuropsychology, 20*: 166–77.
Semrud-Clikeman, M., Filipek, P.A., Biederman, J., Steingard, R., Kennedy, D., Renshaw, P., et al. (1994), Attention-deficit hyperactivity disorder: Magnetic resonance imaging morphometric analysis of the corpus callosum. *Journal of the American Academy of Child and Adolescent Psychiatry, 33*: 875–81.
Sergeant, J. (2000), The cognitive-energetic model: An empirical approach to attention-deficit hyperactivity disorder. *Neuroscience and Biobehavioral Reviews, 24*: 7–12.
_____ (2005), Modeling attention-deficit/hyperactivity disorder: A critical appraisal of the cognitive-energetic model. *Biological Psychiatry, 57*: 1248–55.
_____ Geurts, H., Huijbregts, S., Scheres, A. & Oosterlaan, J. (2003), The top and the bottom of ADHD: A neuropsychological perspective. *Neuroscience and Biobehavioral Reviews, 27*: 583–92.
_____ Oosterlaan, J. & Van der Meere, J.J. (1999). Information processing and energetic factors in attention-deficit/hyperactivity disorder. In: *Handbook of Disruptive Behavior Disorders*, H.C. Quay & A. Hogan (eds.). New York: Plenum Press, pp. 75–104.
Shalev, L., Tsal., Y. & Mevorach, C. (2007), Computerized progressive attentional training (CPAT) program: Effective direction intervention for children with ADHD. *Child Neuropsychology, 13*: 382–8.
Shaw, P., Eckstrand, K., Sharp, W., Blumenthal, J., Lerch, J.P., Greenstein, D., et al. (2007a), Attention-deficit/hyperactivity disorder is characterized by a delay in cortical maturation. *Proceedings of the National Academy of Sciences, USA, 104*: 19649–54.
_____ Gornick, M., Lerch, J., Addington, A., Seal, J., Greenstein, D., et al. (2007b), Polymorphisms of the dopamine D4 receptor, clinical outcome, and cortical structure in attention-deficit/hyperactivity disorder. *Archives of General Psychiatry, 64*: 921–31.
_____ Lerch, J., Greenstein, D., Sharp, W., Clasen, L., Evans, A., et al. (2006), Longitudinal mapping of cortical thickness and clinical outcome in children and adolescents with attention-deficit/hyperactivity disorder. *Archives of General Psychiatry, 63*: 540–9.
Shaw-Zirt, B., Popali-Lehane, L., Chaplin, W. & Bergman, A. (2005), Adjustment, social skills, and self-esteem in college students with symptoms of ADHD. *Journal of Attention Disorders, 8*: 109–20.
Shaywitz, S.E. & Shaywitz, B.A. (1984), Diagnosis and management of attention deficit disorder: A pediatric perspective. *Pediatric Clinics of North America, 31*: 429–57.
Sheppard, D., Bradshaw, J., Georgiou, N., Bradshaw, J. & Lee, P. (2000), Movement sequencing in children with Tourette's syndrome and attention deficit hyperactivity disorder. *Movement Disorders, 15*: 1184–93.
Silk, T.J., Vance, A., Rinehart, N., Bradshaw, J.L. & Cunnington, R. (2009), White-matter abnormalities in attention deficit hyperactivity disorder: A diffusion tensor imaging study. *Human Brain Mapping, 30*: 2757–65.
Smith, I. M. & Bryson, S.E. (1994), Imitation and action in autism: A critical review. *Psychological Bulletin, 116*: 259–73.
Sonuga-Barke, E.J. (2002), Psychological heterogeneity in AD/HD — a dual pathway model of behaviour and cognition. *Behavioural Brain Research, 10*: 29–36.
_____ & Castellanos, F.X. (2007), Spontaneous attentional fluctuations in impaired states and pathological conditions: A neurobiological hypothesis. *Neuroscience and Biobehavioral Reviews, 31*: 977–86.
_____ Dalen, L., Daley, D. & Remington, B. (2002), Are planning, working memory, and inhibition associated with individual differences in preschool ADHD symptoms? *Developmental Neuropsychology, 21*: 255–72.
_____ Taylor, E., Sembi, S. & Smith, S. (1992), Hyperactivity and delay aversion-I. The effect of delay on choice. *Journal of Child Psychology and Psychiatry, 33*: 387–98.
Sowell, E.R., Thompson, P.M., Welcome, S.E., Henkenius, A.L., Toga, A.W. & Peterson, B.S. (2003), Cortical abnormalities in children and adolescents with attention deficit hyperactivity disorder. *Lancet, 362*: 1699–1707.
Sprich-Buckminster, S., Biederman, J., Milberger, S., Faraone, S.V. & Lehman, B.K. (1993), Are perinatal complications relevant to the manifestation of ADD? Issues of comorbidity and familiarity. *Journal of the American Academy of Child and Adolescent Psychiatry, 32*: 1032–7.

Stefanatos, G.A. & Wasserstein, J. (2001), Attention deficit/hyperactivity disorder as a right hemisphere syndrome. *Annals of the New York Academy of Sciences, 931*: 172–95.

Steger, J., Imhof, K., Coutts, E., Gundelfinger, R., Steinhausen, H. & Brandeis, D. (2001), Attentional and neuromotor deficits in ADHD. *Developmental Medicine and Child Neurology, 43*: 172–9.

Swanson, J.M., Kraemer, H.C., Hinshaw, S.P., Arnold, L.E., Conners, C.K., Abikoff, H.B., et al. (2001), Clinical relevance of the primary findings of the MTA: success rates based on severity of ADHD and ODD symptoms at the end of treatment. *Journal of the American Academy of Child and Adolescent Psychiatry, 40*: 168–79.

Szatmari, P., Oxord, D.R. & Boyle, M.H. (1989), Correlates, associated impairments and patterns of service utilization of children with ADHD: Finding from the Ontario Child Health Study. *Journal of Child Psychology and Psychiatry, 30*: 205–17.

Tamm, L., Hughes, C., Ames, L., Pickering, J., Silver, C.H., Stavinoha, P., Castillo, C.L., et al. (2010), Attention training for school-ages children with ADHD: Results of an open trial. *Journal of Attention Disorders, 14*: 86–94.

_____ Menon, V., Ringel, J. & Reiss, A.L. (2004), Event-related fMRI evidence of frontotemporal involvement in aberrant response inhibition and task switching in attention-deficit/hyperactivity disorder. *Journal of the American Academy of Child and Adolescent Psychiatry, 43*: 1430–40.

Tripp, G. & Alsop, B. (2001), Sensitivity to reward delay in children with attention deficit hyperactivity disorder (ADHD). *Journal of Child Psychology and Psychiatry, 42*: 691–8.

Tsal, Y., Shalev, L. & Mevorach, C. (2005), The diversity of attention deficits in ADHD: The prevalence of four cognitive factors in ADHD versus controls. *Journal of Learning Disabilities, 38*: 142–57.

Uddin, L.Q., Kelly, A.M., Biswal, B.B., Margulies, D.S., Shehzad, Z., Shaw, D., et al.> (2008), Network homogeneity reveals decreased integrity of default-mode network in ADHD. *Journal of Neuroscience Methods, 169*: 249–54.

Vaidya, C.J., Austin, G., Kirkorian, G., Ridlehuber, H.W., Desmond, J.E., Glover, G.H. et al. (1998), Selective effects of methylphenidate in attention deficit hyperactivity disorder: A functional magnetic resonance study. *Proceedings of the National Academy of Sciences, USA, 95*: 14494–9.

Valera, E.M., Faraone, S.V., Biederman, J., Poldrack, R.A. & Seidman, L.J., (2005), Functional neuroanatomy of working memory in adults with attention deficit/hyperactivity disorder. *Biological Psychiatry, 57*: 439–47.

van der Meere, J., Shalev, R., Borger, N. & Gross-Tsur, V. (1995), Sustained attention, activation and MPH in ADHD: A research note. *Journal of Child Psychology and Psychiatry, 36*: 697–703.

van der Oord, S., Van der Meulen, E.M., Prins, P.J.M., Oosterlaan, J., Buitelaar, J.K. & Emmelkamp, P.M.G. (2005), A psychometric evaluation of the social skills rating system in children with attention deficit hyperactivity disorder. *Behavioral Research and Therapy, 43*: 733–46.

Werry, J.S., Minde, K., Guzman, A., Weiss, G., Dogan, J. & Hoy, W. (1972), Studies on the hyperactive child-VII: Neurological status compared with neurotic and normal children. *American Journal of Orthopsychiatry, 42*: 441–51.

Whitmont, S. & Clark, C. (1996), Kinaesthetic acuity and fine motor skills in children with attention deficit hyperactivity disorder: A preliminary report. *Developmental Medicine and Child Neurology, 38*: 1091–8.

Wilens, T.E., Biederman, J., Brown, S., Monuteaux, M., Prince, J. & Spencer, T.J. (2002), Patterns of psychopathology and dysfunction in clinically referred preschoolers. *Journal of Developmental and Behavioral Pediatrics, 23*: S31–S36.

_____ Biederman, J., Brown, S., Tanguay, S., Monuteaux, M.C., Blake, C. & Spencer, T.J. (2002), Psychiatric comorbidity and functioning in clinically referred preschool children and school-age youths with ADHD. *Journal of the American Academy of Child and Adolescent Psychiatry, 41*: 262–8.

Willcutt, E.G., Doyle, A.E., Nigg, J.T., Faraone, S.V. & Pennington, B.F. (2005), Validity of the executive function theory of attention-deficit/hyperactivity disorder: A meta-analytic review. *Biological Psychiatry, 57*: 1336–46.

Psychoanalytic Treatment of ADHD Children in the Frame of Two Extraclinical Studies: The Frankfurt Prevention Study and the EVA Study

Marianne Leuzinger-Bohleber, Ph.D.
Katrin Luise Laezer, Ph.D.
Nicole Pfenning-Meerkoetter
Tamara Fischmann, Ph.D.
Angelika Wolff
Jonathan Green, M.D.

We are pleased that psychoanalytic therapy with so-called "ADHD-children" has been elected as subject of this journal. As we have discussed at length in a previous article, psychoanalysts in the last few years have been increasingly engaged in a heated discussion about ADHD (Leuzinger-Bohleber and Fischmann, 2010). As many of the contributions in this volume deal with psychoanalytic conceptualizations of the genesis, psychodynamics, and interdisciplinary approaches of ADHD, we will limit our contribution to the depiction of our attempts to provide psychoanalytic treatments — within the framework of divers prevention-programs — for "children at risk" in kindergarten. Children involved here also comprise those showing a preform of ADHD. The focus of this article is on psychoanalytic treatments of these children in the frame of two large extraclinical studies. Therefore, we will only briefly delineate our motivation to engage together with our colleagues of the Institute for Psychoanalytical Child and Adolescent Psychotherapy (IAKJP) in the endeavor of such early prevention projects. Subsequently the design, some results, and the exemplary supervision- and therapy-experiences with "ADHD children" in the Frankfurt Prevention Study and of the thereupon developed and still ongoing EVA Study will be summarized. We conclude with a short outlook.

INTRODUCTION: PSYCHOANALYTIC PREVENTION STUDIES AT THE SIGMUND-FREUND-INSTITUT IN COOPERATION WITH THE INSTITUTE FOR ANALYTIC CHILD- AND ADOLESCENT-PSYCHOTHERAPY

In 2001 the German Ministry of Health published an official statement expressing the concern that the prescription of Ritalin® for Attention Deficit Hyperactivity Disorder (ADHD) children had increased at a rate of 270 percent from 1997 to 2000 (see Amft, Gerspach and Mattner, 2004; Mattner, 2006[1]). This report led to a hot controversial discussion in the public and in the media.

As many psychoanalytic colleagues we got clairaudient in the light of this report, which seemed to allude to the imminent "medicalization of psychosocial problems." ADHD describes, according to a psychoanalytic understanding, merely a conspicuity or symptomatology whose mental relevance and background in single cases is yet to be explored.

We have therefore initially collected data in a separate follow-up study of children, who have been admitted in the years 1997–1999 to the outpatient clinic of the IAKJP with an accordant symptomatology, illustrating the broad spectrum of background and psychodynamic diagnosis concealed in this external conspicuity. Staufenberg (in press) was able to show that most of the psychoanalytic treatments of so-called "ADHD children" had been proven to show quite impressing and long-lasting, positive results.

We seized the opportunity in 2002, supported by the Zinkann Foundation, to conceptualize a large research project in order to accurately appraise, amongst other aims, whether methylphenidate was administered to hyperactive children in urban kindergartens in Frankfurt, although this was prohibited by law in Germany for children up to six years old. We conjoined this research question with our concern to avail our psychoanalytic competence for the prevention of mental and psychosocial dysfunction of integration (especially of ADHD). The study was conceptualized in an interdisciplinary manner; not only psychoanalysts but also neurobiologists and brain researchers have articulated their skepticism toward an early medicamentous influence of the developing brain (Panksepp, 1998; Hüther, 2006).

[1]Mattner (2006), Amft (2006), and Gerspach (2006) gave a short overview of the historical and societal context in which this increase of Ritalin and other psychopharmacological medication for children could be understood. Mattner (2006) elaborates that the search for neurophysiological reasons for explaining socially deviant behavior has a long tradition in European countries, particularly in Germany . . . In the 1980s, the "Minimal Cerebral Dysfunction" (MCD) was widely spread (see Mattner, 2006). It was seen in close connection with the oppositional defiant disorder. This connection could already be observed in the 1950s. At that time German authors discussed "Encephalopathische Psychopathie" (Enke, 1953), "hirnorganisch-psychisches Achsensyndrom" (Göllnitz, 1954), and "frühkindliches exogenes Psychosyndrom" (Lempp, 1970). In Switzerland one used the term "frühkindliches psycho-organisches Syndrom" (POS) (Ruf-Bächtinger, 1987); Berger (1977) talked about "Teilleistungsstörungen" or "Teilleistungsschwächen."

We conducted the *Frankfurt Prevention Study* (FP) in 2003–2006. We could demonstrate clinically as well as empirically that our psychoanalytic prevention program yielded short- and long-term effects, a result that raised great interest not only in the scientific community but also in the media.

Therefore we felt encouraged to continue in our engagement of early prevention (also of ADHD) in a series of subsequent studies:

STARTHILFE[2] (2006, Ongoing)

In this subsequent project the core components of the FP (case supervision, participating observation and counseling of training candidates of the IAKJP within the day-care facilities itself, support of parental work within the facilities) are implemented. For the past four years, 10 kindergartens could apply each year to participate in STARTHILFE. Ten child-analytic training candidates receive a scholarship in order to be present one day a week in the day-care facility to observe single children and patterns of interaction within the group. The candidates are also there to avail the teachers of their view as a participating "third" in regularly held consultations as well as to assist the educators in parent talks. Every 14 days the kindergarten-team is provided with psychoanalytic case-supervision.

STARTHILFE is a great success. Each year, twice as many facilities apply than can be accepted. The feedback of the educators and parents is positive, so that there is a possibility that the City of Frankfurt will implement this project permanently (more details, see www.sigmund-freud-institut.de).

Therapy Outcome Study on the Effects of Psychoanalytical Compared to Cognitive Behavioral Psychotherapies (in Combination With Medication) of So Called ADHD Children[3](2004, Still Ongoing)

In the FP study, we had the possibility to compare those children who got psychoanalytic child therapies with a randomized control group of untreated children. In order to enlarge the study sample (to n = 40), we included children with the diagnoses ADHD from the Institute of Psychoanalytic Child Therapy and compared them with children who were in cognitive behavioral treatments in combination with medications at the Child Psychiatric University Clinic in Frankfurt. This ongoing study lead to the first interesting results (see, e.g., Laezer, 2010; more details, www.sigmund-freud-institut.de).

[2]The responsibility of the professional execution lay in the hands of Angelika Wolff (IAKJP). We would like to thank theZikann Stiftung, the Polytechnische Gesellschaft, the Crespo Foundation, the Ursula Ströher Stiftung as well astheCity of Frankfurt for their financialsupport of STARTHILFE. We also are grateful to the 30therapists andsupervisorswhi have been engaged in this study (clinical chair: Angelika Wolff, scientific chair: Marianne Leuzinger-Bohleber (names and further information: seewww.sigmund-freud-institut.de).

[3]The main responsible scientists are Luise Laezer, Birgit Gaertner, Mjriam Weissenburger, Inka Werner, Marianne Leuzinger-Bohleber, see ww.sigmund-freud-institut.de

EVA Project: Evaluation of "EARLY STEPS" and "FAUSTLOS" in Kindergartens With Social High Risk Population (2008, Ongoing)[4]

The positive results of the FP lead to a participation at the IDeA Center of the Federal Offensive for economical and scientific excellency (Landesoffensive für wirtschaftliche und wissenschaftliche Exzellenz – LOEWE) that was granted in June 2008 (see www.idea.de). The SFI conducts within this framework the EVA Project as well as the project "EARLY STEPS" (see below).

The EVA research project investigates the differential effects of two established prevention programs — FAUSTLOS (a modification of the U.S. program Second Steps, by Cierpka and Schick, 2006) and EARLY STEPS. The study focuses on so-called "children at risk," whose development is in jeopardy due to various risk factors such as migration, poverty, and so forth. The prevention program EARLY STEPS is characterized by its individual approach as it starts from a detailed understanding of the specific needs of an individual child and its family. By offering supervision to the kindergarten team, counseling to teachers and parents, and therapy for highly distressed children, adverse developmental processes are addressed and modified. In contrast to the individual approach of EARLY STEPS, FAUSTLOS is a more standardized, highly structured curriculum for teachers, which aims at the prevention of violent behavior in children. By fostering empathy, problem-solving skills, and impulse control abilities, the children are supported in their adequate development.

FIRST STEPS ("ERSTE SCHRITTE") – An Integration Project for Infants With a Migrant Background (Start 2010)[5]

In all the prevention projects the psychoanalytic thesis was supported that ADHS often is based on an insufficient early affect regulation. Particularly depressed mothers and mothers burdened with other psychic or psychosocial risks will fail to support in a "good enough" way the development of the regulation of affects and impulses of their babies. First-generation migrant women often belong to this risk group. This is one reason why we try to support such women in our project "FIRST STEPS."

The Integration Course for migrant women of the first generation has been obligatory since December 2004. FIRST STEPS is directly attached to these integration courses. The offering of FIRST STEPS is aligned to the specific needs of mothers and fathers with infants, and contact with project team members from FIRST STEPS begins during the pregnancy. The relationship to the project team motivates the young parents not to interrupt the integration courses after the birth but to participate in special courses offered by our project. Thus, we hope to decrease the danger that these young parents will retreat to a parallel society with their infants. In the following three years, the babies and toddlers and their families will be supported, accompanied, and aided in groups tailored to the stage of development of the infant.

[4]The EVA study is conducted by a large team (Scientific Chair: M. Leuzinger-Bohleber, main responsible scientsts: Luise Laezer, Nicole Pfenning, Peter Ackermann, Verena Neubert, and others as well as around 15 child therapists and supervisors, see www.sigmund-freud-isntitut.de)

[5]Scientific Team: M.Leuzinger-Bohleber, Clinical Chair: Claudia Burkhardt-Mußmann, Project team: Munise Agca, Nasim Ghaffari,Liz Holland, Sybille Stock

As FIRST STEPS shall serve as a scientifically supported model project, the short- and long-term effects of the psychoanalytic-oriented prevention project are investigated empirically in a randomized control group design (n = 100).

A specificity of all those prevention programs is the close cooperation between the research team of the SFI and experienced psychoanalytic child- and adolescent-psychotherapists of IAKJP. Both institutions are located in the same building, which enhanced the cooperation. However, we believe it is foremost the professional and amicable bond of both institutions that enables us to seize such unique opportunities to conduct these ambitious, international, interdisciplinary, and intergenerational cross-linked research as we do at the SFI in cooperation with decade-long experienced analytic child- and adolescent-psychotherapists. It was a somewhat unfamiliar and at times strange experiment for the child-therapists to offer therapies outside of their offices and to adapt and modify the setting of their treatments. They were skeptical if under these conditions it would be altogether possible to create a sheltered space without which, as is generally known, no productive psychoanalytic work can be done. Therefore, we would like to take the opportunity here to report and critically reflect our common experiences.

Another chance is that our child-analytic colleagues themselves stem from the field of early education and are able to provide their decade-long experience herein and as therapists and supervisors in institutions in case-supervisions to the educators. It seems adequate to mention that all the teams found supervision to be extremely helpful and fought to have it extended after the FP study ended, although they had doubts at the beginning of the study whether they would be able to fit supervision into their tight working schedule.

Another great chance lay in the capability of the SFI to provide the institutional, scientific, and financial resources necessary to conduct the complex secondary research of the results obtained in the prevention projects methodologically independent from the colleagues of the IAKJP. The SFI also has an opportunity to reflect on the concepts of a psychoanalytic prevention approach, the meaning and acceptance of the research measures together with them.

FRANKFURT PREVENTION STUDY: PSYCHOANALYSIS AND NEUROBIOLOGY IN DIALOGUE[6] (2003–2006)

Short Summary

The representative, randomized, controlled, and prospective *Frankfurt Prevention Study*[7] was performed from September 2003 to August 2006. In order to be able to draw a representative sample of roughly n = 500 children in the prevention/intervention group and a control-comparison group of another n = 500 children, we performed a basic assessment in all public kindergartens in Frankfurt (114 kindergartens with around 4,500 children). The main hypothesis of the study was that a two-year psychoanalytic (non-psychopharmacological) prevention and intervention program would result in a statistically significant decrease in the number of children suffering

[6] This chapter has already been published in Tisantis and Trowell (2010, pp. 159–177).

[7] The study was financially supported mainly by the Zinnkan Foundation, but also by the Research Advisory Board (RAB) of the International Psychoanalytical Association, the Hertie Foundation and the Polytechnische Gesellschaft, Frankfurt.

from psychosocial disturbances (particularly from ADHD) in their first year in school (compared to the control group).

In order to define ADHD we used the following instruments:

- Child Behaviour Checklist (CBCL4-18)
- Questionnaire on hyperactivity (Döpfner et al., 1993)
- Conner's Teacher's Rating Form (CTRF)
- Conner's Parent's Ratings Form (CPRF)
- BADO (modified basic documentation)

From spring 2004 to summer 2006, we offered the prevention and intervention program in 14 randomly chosen kindergartens. The psychoanalytic prevention and intervention program consisted of several components based on a psychoanalytic understanding of ADHD:

- intense psychoanalytic supervision of the kindergarten teams focusing the psychodynamic and psychosocial understanding of individual children and their families
- weekly offer of a psychoanalytically oriented educational program for individual children or the children's groups by members of the research team (including a violence prevention program called FAUSTLOS, developed by Cierpka and his group (Cierpka and Schick, 2006)
- parental talks and parent counseling (in groups or individually)
- psychoanalytic individual therapies (always including the parents) offered to children with severe psychopathologies (e.g., ADHS) in the kindergartens[8]
- cooperation with medical doctors, child psychiatrists, mental health institutions, welfare institutions, and potential schools, if necessary

It took almost one year until the project was fully accepted by the teams and parents in the different institutions. The best "proof" of this acceptance was that nearly all teams expressed their wish to continue the supervisions and some other elements of our prevention program after the project officially ended in August 2006. In the meantime we have obtained statistical results supporting our main hypothesis (see Leuzinger-Bohleber et al., 2010).

Response rates were good throughout the two-year investigation (T1: 89 percent; T4: 52 percent). Results comparing children of the prevention with those of the control group showed a significant decrease of hyperactivity in both groups. This finding is not surprising considering the fact that "hyperactivity" as conceptualized in the questionnaire "Verhaltensbeurteilungsbogen für Vorshulkinder VBV 3–6 (a questionnaire assessing behavior problems and social skills in preschoolers; Döpfner, Berner, Fleischmann, & Schmidt, 1993) is mainly concerned with impulsivity of the children on the one hand (as in, e.g., question 34: "... he is constantly moving and only stays sitting on a chair very shortly") and with their capability to concentrate (as in, e.g., question 19: "can only concentrate in a game or activity shortly") on the other, both of which decrease in children from ages 3 to 6. It was interesting to observe if we would find a significant

[8]It has been an open question if we will be able to offer psychoanalytic therapies to children of low and problematic social groups, children who would never find their ways into private practices of our psychoanalytic colleagues. Until now we were able to offer such therapies to 17 children. For 10 other children we saw an indication for psychoanalytic treatments but the parents were not willing to accept treatments.- We are evaluating therapy outcome of these 17 children (with F90 diagnosis) and other children of the outclinic service of the institute for Psychoanalytic Child and Adolescence Therapy in Frankfurt in another study.

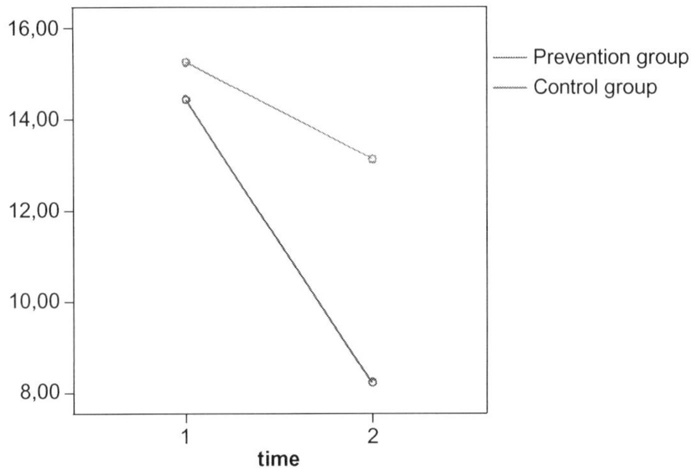

FIGURE 1 Hyperactivity of girls (comparing prevention and control group) $N_{Prevention} = 70$; $N_{Control} = 62$; Factor time: $F = 32.41$; $p = .00$.

difference between prevention- and control group-children concerning their capability to concentrate after the first year of school, a capability, which becomes highly relevant only in school not yet in kindergarten.[9]

Another interesting result is that girls seem to change more than boys in the prevention group. Taking only the ratings of the girls we find a statistically significant decrease of hyperactivity (Leuzinger-Bohleber, Staufenberg and Fischmann, 2007; see Figure 1).

What also decreases significantly is the amount of aggressive as well as anxious behavior within the prevention group children after two years (see Figures 2 and 3).

The finding of a statistically significant decrease of aggression and anxiety is a surprisingly clear indication that a psychoanalytically oriented prevention and intervention program has a positive effect on social behaviour of kindergarten children. We had not expected this result, considering that our study was a "field" study combining methods of an experimental and a naturalistic investigation.

ADHD Is Not ADHD: Some Observations Concerning Different Psychodynamic Subgroups of ADHD in the Frankfurt Prevention Study

Another aim of our study was to contribute to a differentiation of the ADHD diagnosis by looking at it from a psychoanalytic point of view. ADHD seems to have become a "fashion or rather waste basket diagnosis" for all kinds of different problems lying beyond the manifestation of hyperactive and nonattentive behaviour. We have been able to gather numerous and extensive single case observations as well as statistical data from the original sample of the 500 children of

[9] We also would like to mention that none of the 412 children in our prevention group had taken Ritalin or another Amphetamine what means that the medical doctors in Frankfurt are acting according to the German law, which does not allow these medications to be given to children younger than six years.

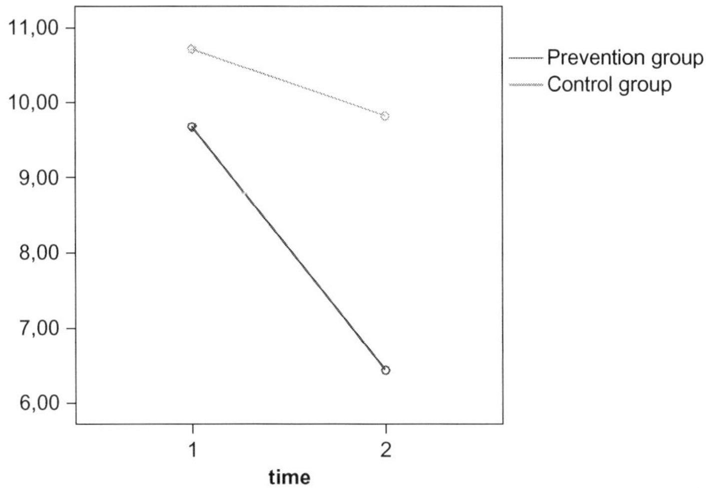

FIGURE 2 Aggressivity comparing prevention and control group $N_{Prevention} = 177$; $N_{Control} = 185$; Factor group: $F = 5.90$; $p < .02$.

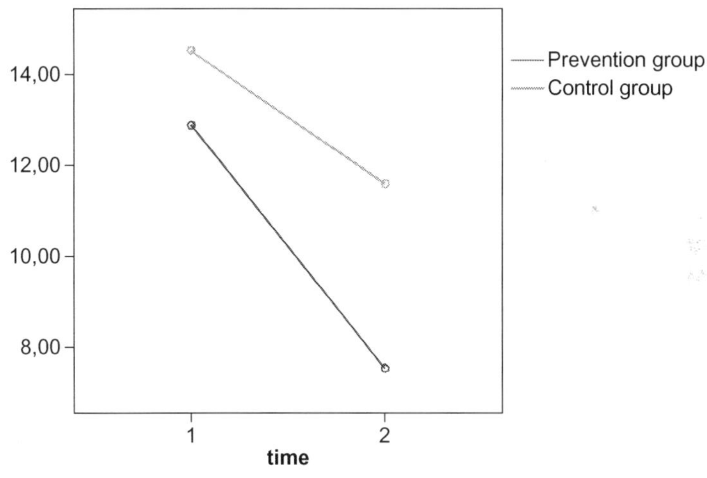

FIGURE 3 Comparison of prevention- and control group concerning anxiety $N_{Prevention} = 177$; $N_{Control} = 184$; Factor group: $F = 4.96$; $p < .03$.

our prevention/intervention group. Discussing our observations we have been able to differentiate between subgroups of children who had been diagnosed with ADHD according to the above-mentioned criteria of the Döpfner and the Conner Scales (both instruments are based on DSM-IV criteria). In other words, on a descriptive level all the following children suffered, according to DSM-IV, from ADHD which, of course, does not include comorbidities. Nevertheless it does not seem helpful for a deepened understanding of these children to stick to a "meaningful discrete diagnostic entity" (Gilmore, 2000, p. 1258). From a psychoanalytic perspective, a more dynamic, precise perception of each child´s idiosyncratic psychic and psychosocial situation offers, in our view, a better basis for an adequate treatment of the relevant child.

In the frame of this article we only want to mention these divergences subsumed under the syndrome ADHD by defining different subgroups. We have discussed them elsewhere in detail (see Leuzinger-Bohleber and Fischmann, 2010):

I. Children diagnosed with ADHD having brain organic problems
II. Children diagnosed with ADHD having an early emotional neglect
III. ADHD and trauma
IV. ADHD and culture
V. ADHD and extraordinarily talented children
VI. ADHD and mourning or depression
VII. ADHD as a compensation for growing up with a "dead mother" (André Green, Daniel Stern)

Psychoanalytic Therapies in Kindergartens: An Example

The parents of 17 children accepted help for their ADHD child because we could offer them therapy in the kindergartens. The therapists were available to treat these children twice a week in special rooms at the kindergartens. One of the most impressive child therapies was reported extensively by Christina Waldung (Waldung, Goppel and Wolff, 2006). We summarize some of her findings here. Peter (five years old) is also a child who suffered from severe early emotional neglect and who developed ADHD symptoms.

In supervision with me (L-B), a teacher reported furiously that Peter had spat in her face. "This is beyond the acceptable – I don't want to have him in my group anymore – I've tried so hard with him – and now this – I will not tolerate this – I am so disappointed . . ." I suggested in the supervision: "Of course I don't want to excuse his behavior, but perhaps Peter wanted to tell you something and has chosen you as his most beloved person in the kindergarten as the one to spit at. Let's try to understand his behavior first and then talk about how to deal with it . . ."

After this intervention, another teacher of the supervision group remembers that the female cook recalled that Peter, who had been sent away, came to the kitchen and said, "You know, sometimes I just do not want to live anymore . . ." We take his message very seriously. The head teacher of the kindergarten called Peter's father and discovered that Mr. E had just lost his job as a taxi driver because of his diabetes. The mother was severely mentally ill and had repeatedly left the family. Mr. E had tried to keep the family together, being 20 years older than his wife and more stable than her. Two older children had been taken into a children's home soon after starting school. Both had severe conduct problems and were diagnosed with ADHD. In supervision, we finally understood that Peter tried to unconsciously communicate his despair to his most beloved teacher. He probably feared that his family situation would now definitely collapse and that he would be taken away to a children's home like his two siblings. I (L-B) tried to explain in supervision: "If you have such an unbearable expectation as a child – it is well known that these children try to actively provoke something in order that they, at least, can have the fantasy that it were themselves who are responsible for the 'punishment' instead of just being the passive, helpless victim . . ." Fortunately, the father finally accepted psychoanalytic therapy for Peter. Peter has been in therapy for nearly three years and was able to be successful in normal elementary school. The therapist also worked intensively with both parents. The mother was sent to a mental hospital after Peter's birth for several months and diagnosed as psychotic. She is in constant treatment by a psychiatrist but often does not take her pills. She has left the family again and again and has had several affairs. Mr. E, whose wife had died previously, which was a traumatic experience for him, fights to keep the family together and does not want "to lose his last child." The regular contact with the therapist helped him to overcome his depression due to his unemployment and to realize how important his fatherly role is in bringing up Peter.

Peter is a highly intelligent boy. At the beginning of therapy, he was absorbed by the fantasy that, if he were a girl, he would not have the ADHD difficulties and "my mother would love me more . . ." He already showed transvestite symptoms, wanted to be a girl, and hated typical rough-and-tumble games. After these fantasies had been understood and worked through in therapy, the transvestite symptoms disappeared: he now seems to show "normal male development." Another infantile fantasy was that he had to save the marriage of his parents by lying between them in the marital bed whenever the mother returned to the father's home. Only after having understood these fantasies was he able to accept his own room and sleep alone. In therapy his overstimulated oedipal fantasies had played a central role connected with infantile grandiosity fantasies and severe guilt feelings. When these fantasies could be worked through, the aggressive-destructive behavior in the kindergarten decreased and Peter found friends in his peer group. He overcame his social isolation and developed a more stable feeling of self-confidence and a better narcissistic self-regulation.

Other relevant unconscious fantasies were connected to his infantile "explanation" of the illness of his mother. He seemed to be convinced that he had been a destructive baby who destroyed the health of his mother. Therefore, he would become "a sick person like my mother when I am growing up . . ." Often his relationships with his two siblings were topics in therapy. He was unconsciously convinced that his rivalry and aggressive impulses had been the reason why his two brothers had been sent to the children´s home. Therefore, he would also end being sent away from his beloved parents.

The regular talks of the therapist with the father seemed to help Peter to identify with him and to develop a better inner regulation structure. He developed into a creative, well-liked boy during the last years of kindergarten. His conduct problems only seldom were a problem. He also was capable of concentrating quite well. The kindergarten teachers no longer thought of him as a potential ADHD child but were convinced that he would be able to cope with school socially and academically.

However, three weeks after the beginning of school a severe crisis happened in the family. His mother became overtly psychotic again and was hospitalized. The analyst talked with the father who was convinced that his wife expected that Peter, similarly to his two brothers, would get into such severe problems in school that he would have to be taken into a children´s home as well. She forced the social worker, who had helped the family for two years, to leave. The child therapist and we expected that she also would break off the therapy of Peter.

Peter started to become aggressive in school again. Because the mother was put under medication again, she suddenly wanted to have medication (Ritalin®) for Peter, too. She said that child therapy would not help him and that he should instead take medication. We all were very concerned. Fortunately, the colleague of the University Clinic for Child and Adolescent Psychiatry to whom Peter was referred gave Ritalin to Peter in order to calm down his mother. At the same time, he advised to continue the child's therapy. Therefore, he prevented the sudden termination of the therapy.

Peter showed many side effects of Ritalin. He lost weight, developed severe sleeping problems, and changed his behavior so severely that both parents told the therapist: "He seems not be our son anymore." They themselves decided to terminate the medical therapy three months afterwards.

During these months the therapy focused on Peter's sudden aggressive outbursts again, which had been a serious problem at school. These outbursts were often triggered by feelings of impotence and helplessness, which Peter could not stand, probably because they unconsciously reminded him of his early traumatic experiences with his primary objects which had been reactivated by the hospitalization of his mother again. The above-mentioned unconscious fantasies had to be worked through again and again as well as his splittings and fragmentations in his inner object world. After some months he stabilized again and was capable of coping with the academic and social requirements of school. The therapist had regular contact with the teacher who fortunately developed a deep understanding and sympathy for Peter. Therefore, the therapist as well as the teacher became "good objects" in the outside reality and could be internalized at least partially.

Nine months after the beginning of school another crisis developed. The therapist discovered strange changes in the senso-motoric behavior of Peter. She talked to the father and asked him to consult a child neurologist. A quickly growing brain tumor was diagnosed. Peter had to be operated on at once, a dramatic event for the whole family. The mother again got sick; the father was in a desolate psychic state. The therapist took him into a crisis intervention and visited Peter at the hospital. She seemed to be an important inner and real "good object" for Peter during these days and weeks. Fortunately, the operation went well and Peter recovered soon. It was very impressing that Peter became kind of a "child therapist," caring in a touching way for the very ill children at the hospital, some of whom suffered from cancer. "These children even have a worse fate than I do . . . ," he once said in his therapeutic session which, of course, had been essential for him during these weeks because they enabled him to recognize and to cope with his archaic death anxieties and connected fantasies.

Now, in 2011, more than three years after the termination of the psychotherapy, Peter still is able to concentrate in class. He is socially integrated in a much better way and no longer as hyperactive. Peter and his parents still have a long way to go, but we are convinced that the psychoanalytic therapy helped to strengthen the boy's resilience.

All the children in Peter's family were diagnosed with ADHD. Peter's development may illustrate that even if there should be a genetic component, psychotherapy could still help to change ADHD symptoms by understanding the traumatic early relationships (for the theoretical considerations, see Leuzinger-Bohleber, Canestri and Target, 2009).

Some Considerations on Psychoanalytical Treatments of So-Called ADHD Children[10]

The story of Peter illustrates some speculations on possible reasons for the enormous worldwide increase of children diagnosed with ADHD and treated with Ritalin or other amphetamines. Peter showed many symptoms, which could lead to a diagnosis of ADHD. Indeed, our colleagues in the

[10]The following section and the conclusions of this paper are based on the summary of a former paper (Leuzinger-Bohleber and Fischmann, 2010).

department of child and adolescent psychiatry diagnosed him as suffering from ADHD. However, the traumatic experiences of his early childhood due to his psychotic mother, his depressed, organically ill and finally unemployed father, the fate of his two siblings as well as the poverty of the family may be possible biological roots of ADHD and cannot be considered as the main reasons for the psychic suffering of this boy. Therefore, some authors (e.g., Amft, Gerspach, and Mattner, 2004) talk about the danger of a "medicalization of social problems." As Peter´s crisis in his first year of school might illustrates, medication sometimes seems to be a great seduction to deal with difficult children like him and to adapt them in an efficient and socially accepted way to the requirements of the modern schools in our Western societies. Without any doubt, medication is sometimes an option to de-escalate an unbearable social situation. Thus, it seemed a necessary prevention measure not to exclude Peter during crisis situation in his first class of school in order not to exclude him from the school and to put him into a children's home like his elder siblings. Nevertheless, as the psychotherapy and the development of Peter might show, medication cannot solve the problems of these children in depth who, like Peter, often struggle with difficult internalized conflicts and/or current problems in their external realities. These determinants of their suffering from ADHD should be understood in detail to really help them to cope productively with their life and learning situations. Therefore, we plead for critical and differentiated analyses of multiple fields of problems concerning the growing up of children in postindustrial and globalized societies. When talking about ADHD, traumatic biographical, societal, and cultural factors should be taken as serious as the findings from modern neurobiology and brain research.

As already mentioned, these clinical, conceptual, and empirical findings of the Frankfurter Prevention Study motivated us to further studies. We would like to summarize one, that is, the ongoing EVA Study. The EVA Study is a modification of the design of the FP and is realized in those regions of Frankfurt which are particularly burdened with social and integration problems (e.g., high unemployment, high percentage of migrants and refugees, poverty, crime). Therefore, in contrast to the FP, we chose the experiences of child therapists to be in the kindergartens once a week.

DAS EVA-PROJEKT (EVALUATION OF THE EARLY PREVENTION PROJECTS EARLY STEPS AND FAUSTLOS IN KINDERGARTENS WITH A HIGH PERCENTAGE OF RISK CHILDREN (2008, ONGOING)[11]

Within the framework of this article we would like to present here only some first results and two clinical examples.

[11] This project is a replication study of the Frankfurt Prevention Study (FP). The study is a cluster randomized design in 14 kindergartens comparing the effectiveness of two prevention programs: EARLY STEPS and FAUSTLOS with "children at risk." In contrast to the FP experienced child psychoanalysts are working weekly in the kindergartens, offering child therapies and crises interventions for parents there and support the teachers in their daily work, supervision is provided every second week.

The excellent but time consuming attachment instrument, the MANCHESTER CHILD ATTACHMENT STORY TASK (developed by Jonathan Green and his research group) has been added as measure, to test our hypothesis that only by the psychoanalytic oriented program EARLY STEPS we will be able to achieve a change of the attachment pattern from an unsecure to a secure attachment pattern.

With our research question in EVA, we recur on findings of attachment theory (cf. Fonagy, 2010), which state that securely attached children will more often show socially adequate behavior, less aggression, and will more often come up with creative solutions for problems than insecurely and disorganized attached children. From there a change in attachment type toward more secure attachment will be one of an enduring effect. Independently from a still-to-be-assessed change of attachment style, we surmise that profound developmental disorders will be met rather by the project EARLY STEPS, yielding a more "normal" development of severely affected children.[12]

First Empirical Results

We can only present one of our preliminary findings in the frame of this article. We have just finished analyzing the data of the MCAST from the first point of measurement. Interestingly we found that, compared to other "normal" samples of children in EVA, we encountered a surprisingly low percentage of secure attachment (B: 35 percent) but a very high percentage of disorganized attachment (D: 23 percent). Also, the percentage of avoidant-insecurely attached children (A) is very high (A: 33 percent). These first results illustrate that our sample indeed included a high number of "children at risk" (see Table 1).

Some Clinical Observations Based on the Supervision and Psychoanalytic Therapies in the Kindergartens

The following are two short exemplary summaries of child therapies conducted within EVA.

I. „Mama, Mama, please don´t leave me..."—„Why do you cry: I am here...."

In one of the supervisions, a teacher gives a report on a four-year-old boy, who attracts attention because of his extremely aggressive behavior and lack of concentration. He hits children, for example, with a fork directly into the face and does not show any signs of reaction, even when extremely injuring the other children. Even though there are massive conflicts within the institution on a daily basis and the teachers often scold and punish him, he still absolutely and categorically wants to come to kindergarten. His mother, "a cold and aloof woman," often threatens him with keeping him at home as punishment. The teachers also present Ahib in supervision

[12]This study realizes a Cluster Randomized Controlled Trial-Design (CRCT), where day-care facilities are randomly allocated to one of the two intervention conditions. The choice of the day-care facilities is based on the representative baseline evaluation of the Frankfurt Prevention Study of the SFI, which was conducted in 2003 in all of its municipal day-care facilities with a sample of N = 5300 children. In this baseline evaluation the collectivity of children were evaluated regarding asocio-statistical criterion (financial support of daycare fee) as well as personality characteristics of the children (aggressivity, hyperactivity, anxiety) were screened. Based on this baseline of those daycare centers were included in the EVA Study, which had a high percentage of children of families with low socio-economic status and impressed with higher occurrence of screened personality characteristics. To safeguard the sampling further social-statistic indicators on urban district levels (percentage of citizens with migration background, percentage of unemployment, youth-unemployment as well as expert judgments) were included.

The determination of sample size of N = 14 daycare centers was performed according to a mathematical calculation of CRCT-Designs. Control of cluster effects was secured by estimation of the Intracluster-Correlation-Coefficient (ICC) on the basis of the results of the Frankfurt Prevention Study.

TABLE 1
Distribution of Attachment Pattern in Different Samples, Including the EVA Study

Sample	*Number of Children*	*Attachment Style*			
		Avoidant-Insecure (A)	*Secure (B)*	*Ambivalent-Insecure (C)*	*Disorganised Attachment (D)*
West Europe (9 samples, van lizendoorn & Kroonenberg, 1988)	510	28%	66%	6%	–
USA (21 samples, van lizendoorn et al., 1992)	1584	21%	67%	12%	–
Israel Cities (Sagi et al., 2002)	758	3%	72%	21%	3%
Project EVA	**234**	**33%**	**35%**	**9%**	**23%**

because his younger brother has now been registered to the center as well "we cannot cope with another child like this . . . "

When determining his family situation, we find out that his mother is of African origin and a single mother. "She told me, that her husband died on the day of the birth of her second child . . . the little cries so loudly every night, that the mother is afraid that she will be given notice by the landlord. He is extremely anxious to lose her and always cries "*Mama, Mama, please don't leave me . . .*" The mother is despaired. It does not help when she reassures him that she is there.

In supervision there is the assumption, that the impression of the teacher, that Mrs. X is "cold, arrogant and emotionally aloof" is possibly an expression of a dissociation caused by a severe traumatization (sudden death of the husband, thereby possibly triggered birth). We offer her a crisis-intervention with a child-therapist who is at the daycare center once a week.

Mrs. X. accepts the offer. She tells the therapist that her husband has died in an airplane crash. The family fled a war zone in Africa. It emerges that Mrs. X. indeed lives in a dissociative state and can barely find emotional access to her children. From this her little son is right in fearing that his mother is going to abandon him: she is mentally chronically absent and has in that sense "abandoned" him. This sheds a different light on the lacking affect regulation and the largely missing reliable inner structures of Ahib and makes them more comprehensible.

Regretfully, Mrs. X. is not willing to accept the extended therapeutic offer for her and her children. However, the few crisis-intervention talks seem to have helped in she now more often seeks help and support in her commune, which in parts helps to alleviate her isolation and the excessive demands put on her. At any rate the sleep disorder of the two-year-old seemed to have allayed. Even Ahib is developing well after an educator has turned to him in a special war allowing him a kind of "emotional afterripening."

„The mother should be dead..."

Mustafa attracted the attention of our team during MCAST: in a scary obvious degree he exhibited a disorganized attachment style (D). For example in the scene where the child loses the mother in the supermarket, he plays that the mother hits the child prior to losing it. Afterward he turns the tables and wants to kill the mother. He buries the mother underneath the furniture of the dollhouse and plays nonstop for 20 minutes that the mother is being hit, killed, and suffocated. "She is still not dead, still not . . ." He seems to be unable to find out of his affect storm by himself.

Even though Mustafa belongs to the FAUSTLOS group, we decide out of ethical reasons to initiate a psychoanalytic assessment. This reveals that Mustafa did not only experience aggressive affect breaches in MCAST, but also has frequently shown them in kindergarten and at home. When conflicts arise, he beats down on his opponent almost insensibly, no matter if it is a playmate, his older sister, the educator, or his mother.

Mustafa lives in an extremely irksome family situation. The violent father, an alcoholic, left the family two years ago; due to this, the youth welfare has assigned the family a family helper. The mother, a Turk who barely speaks any German, has two adult children back in Turkey and seems to be isolated in Germany. She seems depressive and latently also violent. The family lives in poverty on the bottom fringe of society.

The mother is willing to seek therapeutic help for herself and Mustafa. Luckily a Turkish speaking therapy can be offered within the facility itself. Therapy has begun and has led to a first pacification of the child's aggressive behavior in kindergarten.

These two exemplary chosen children have suffered from cumulative, early traumatization, which may be assumed to be one of the reasons they never had a chance to develop an inner affect- and impulse-control. Many of these children develop, as mentioned earlier, a so-called ADHD. We hope to abate the likelihood to develop such a syndrome via early prevention and psychoanalytic treatments and will have the opportunity to review this hope with "strong data."

Further Considerations on Psychoanalytic Treatments in Kindergartens

It is essential to allude ex-ante that implementation of psychotherapies within the frame of compulsory health insurance in Germany is only permitted in accredited practices. For our studies we obtained an exceptional permission, which is limited to the projects.

With regards to content of implementation of analytic child-psychotherapies within the facilities of kindergartens there are some manifest problems attached, beginning with the question how to establish and conserve the necessary frame. Kindergartens are usually noisy; there is little adequate sheltered and somewhat agreeable room which therapists can internally claim as "theirs" even if they bring with them their own play material. The child has to be withdrawn from his playgroup by the therapist, as the educator cannot bring the child to his therapy session. This necessarily breaches the abstinence and has some implication for the constitution of transference. The same is true for the circumstance where the therapist is perceived by the child and the parents as part of the institution; therefore, the sheltered intimate room is in question here as well.

With it is significant that we are part of the kindergarten, trying to reach children and parents there and take them into therapy (whereas this is the genuine aim) should not be underestimated, although if we were not there, those children might never have the opportunity to get an analytic child-therapy let alone by the realistic truth that their parents would not have found the strength to get the children into therapy. We also are dealing here with children whose development toward a "good enough" inner object relationship is fundamentally at stake, and the development of a beneficial therapeutic relation has an accordant uncertain prognosis. We therefore are in need of a continuing professional reflection on the emerging group processes together with the analytic child therapists of the project. A concluding evaluation of the experiences, which is relatively new in Germany, will be only possible after the completion of the project.

In any case, a long-term analytic child-therapy within the kindergarten within the framework of this project is only feasible with a few children. The fact that even several children are put into focus in such a way seems, in our view, to have an impact on the educational climate within the kindergartens. The teachers become aware again that for all the necessary activities, supportive measures, and everyday rituals, they are dealing with children who have their own history and bring along their emergent behavioral patterns that have to be met by the teacher for the sake of the children. The teachers must accept and understand these children as best they can and not become overrun by the problems and risk to forfeit their professionalism. As we tried to illustrate, these few case examples of child therapies, despite these unconventional factors and the modified setting, prove to be extremely helpful for these children at risk and their families. We will report more systematically on these findings in future publications.

SUMMARY AND CONCLUSION

In contrast to the understanding of ADHD according to a "medical model" ("defects in the brain" or maladaption in social learning), we share the view of many psychoanalytic colleagues, for example, Dieter Bürgin (2005), that attention deficit and hyperactivity are symptoms that can build a *syndromebut never an illness*, even if an underlying (common) genetic base is postulated. Furthermore, no internationally accepted cut-off point exists defining quantitatively attention deficit or hyperactivity. We summarized different psychoanalytic conceptualizations of ADHD, observations and data from the Frankfurt Preventions Study and the EVA study as well as from some psychoanalytic treatments with hyperactive children in the frame of these projects. We wanted to illustrate that a psychoanalytic perspective on ADHD focuses on the different underlying structures of the personality due to the idiosyncratic life history of the child with its early object relations, traumatizations, ego- and self–developments, its specific deficiencies, and forms of relational and emotional exchanges in the child's current family situation. Our diagnostic and clinical experiences reveal a wide range of structural and object-relational levels in such children: *there is no monocausal etiology*. Often ADHD may have a genetically based overreactivity and hypersensitivity to various stimuli as infants, which was misunderstood by the caretakers. The consequent failure to regulate drive impulses and affects result in a disruption of what Bürgin (2005) called the "narrative function," depleting the ego of secondary-process functions. We think that children of one subgroup of ADHD are sharing such early "dismatched" object relations or an overstimulation combined with a missing security in attachment helping to prevent being overfloated with stimuli and stress (see Hüther, 2006). These early experiences in their object relations also have left deficiencies concerning *attention* seen as a highly complex ego function that develops in a specific relational context, influenced by genetic factors, early emotional exchanges, temperament, and micro traumata. "Children diagnosed with ADHD often demonstrate normal attention and activity when doing something they like, but experience difficulty in doing so when the demand comes from the external world. Thus attention deficit is thought to reflect an early dysfunction of the ego brought about by the primary object's failure to contain and focus (center) attention, and to construct trust in a co-established temporality. A number of ego dysfunctions arise out of this failure in holding. One of the most serious is the failure to learn to use verbal symbolizations in order to express emotion, thus leaving imperative action as a prominent mode of avoiding being overwhelmed by unbearable feelings" (Sugarman, 2006, p. 238).

As we have tried to show in different papers (Leuzinger-Bohleber et al., 2006, 2008, 2009; Leuzinger-Bohleber, Canestri and Target, 2010; Leuzinger-Bohleber and Fischmann, 2010), other subgroups of ADHD children might have quite different biographical roots, for example, a history of early neglect, traumatization, undigested dramatic life events, current dismatch between their specific personality traits, cultural differences, and the educational system in which they live. Therefore, we formulated a plea for a differentiated diagnostic view, taking into account idiosyncratic biographical factors, current family and institutional situations, and neurobiological and genetic determinants of ADHD as contemporary, pluralistic psychoanalysis offers.

We also discussed that Embodied Cognitive Science and neurobiological research performed by Huether and his research team, Jaak Panksepp, and many other contemporary researchers, for example, Antonio Damasio, Gerald D. Edelman, and Eric Kandel, offer an understanding of ADHD, which seems in excellent concordance with psychoanalytic conceptualizations. Understanding the brain as a self-regulating system in constant interaction with the environment, with astonishing possibilities to correct maladaptations and "inadequate sensory motor coordinations" in new relational experiences may underline the possibilities to help children with ADHD to overcome their difficulties in professional new object relations (see Leuzinger-Bohleber and Pfeifer, 2002). The summary of the child therapy with Peter might serve as an illustration of these observations. To develop such new self-regulations in the realm of affects and behaviors, first in therapeutic and afterward in social situations, seems to be a unique therapeutic chance for these children. This chance is missed by offering an exclusively medical treatment, often experienced as the unconscious truth by the child that "there is something wrong in my brain. It has some kind of a 'defect.' I am not a normal kid. Without medication I am a human being, which is not bearable for my parents, siblings, peers, and teachers... I am a wild animal which cannot tame itself..."

Seen from a psychoanalytic perspective, ADHS has always been understood as a product of complex interactions of (mostly unconscious) idiosyncratic, biographical, relational, institutional, societal, neurobiological, neurophysiological, and genetical factors. This is one reason we think that psychoanalysis with its unique conceptualizations to understand psychic realities as products of such a complex intertwining of unconscious and reality factors, taking into account biological as well as societal roots of human behavior, could be regarded as the best available approaches capable of dealing theoretically and therapeutically with children suffering from ADHD. We fully agree with Gilmore (2000) when she writes: "However, I believe that the analytic process, especially in the form that is familiar to child analysts, offers the best opportunity to treat the underlying disturbance of ADHD in children and adults" (p. 1291).

It is beyond the limits of this article to describe the textbook which a group of experienced child analysts in Frankfurt has written describing the specific technique for the psychoanalytic treatment of children with ADHD (see Staufenberg et al., 2006; Staufenberg, in press). This textbook was the common ground for all 17 treatments, which were offered to children suffering from ADHD within the framework of the Frankfurt Prevention Study and the ongoing ones in the EVA Study. We have not been able to summarize our clinical experiences in detail here. Nevertheless we hope to communicate that our clinical observations as well as our empirical findings have supported our view that contemporary psychoanalysis, due to its richness of conceptualizations and clinical experiences, taking into account neurobiological as well as societal factors at the same time, should be considered as attractive field for understanding and treating children with ADHD.

REFERENCES

Achenbach, T.M. (1991a), *Manual for the Child Behavior Checklist / 4-18 and 1991 Profile*. Burlington: University of Vermont Department of Psychiatry.

_____ (1991b), *Manual for the Teacher's Report Form and 1991 Profile*. Burlington: University of Vermont Department of Psychiatry.

Amft, H. (2006). ADHS: Hirnstoffwechselstörungen und/oder Symptom einer kranken Gesellschaft? Psychopharmaka als Mittel einer gelingenden Naturbeherrschung am Menschen. In: *ADHS Frühprävention statt Medikalisierung. Theorie, Forschung, Kontroversen*, M. Leuzinger-Bohleber, Y. Brandl, and G. Hüther (eds.). Göttingen: Vandenhoeck & Ruprecht, pp. 70–90.

_____ Gerspach, M. & Mattner, D. (2004), *Kinder mit gestörter Aufmerksamkeit. ADS als Herausforderung für Pädagogik und Therapie. 2. Auflage*. Stuttgart: Kohlhammer.

Berger, E., ed. (1977), *Teilleistungsschwächen bei Kindern*. Bern.

Bürgin, D. (2005), Attention deficit hyperactivity disorder and trauma. Presented at 44th Congress of the IPA, Rio de Janeiro, Brazil, July 28.

Cierpka, M. & Schick, A. (2006). Das Fördern von emotionalen Kompetenzen mit FAUSTLOS bei Kindern. In: *ADHS - Frühprävention statt Medikalisierung. Theorie, Forschung, Kontroversen*, M. Leuzinger-Bohleber, Y. Brandl & G. Hüther (eds.). Göttingen: Vandenhoeck & Ruprecht, pp. 286–301.

Döpfner, M., Berner, W., Fleischmann, T., & Schmidt, M. (1993), *Verhaltensbeurteilungsbogen für Vorschulkinder*, VBV 3-6. Weinheim: Beltz.

Enke, W. (1953), Ätiologie und Therapie bei Schwererziehbarkeit. *Medizinische Klinik*, *48*: 231–5.

Fischer, G. & Riedesser, P. (1998), *Lehrbuch der Psychotraumatologie*. München/Basel: Reinhardt.

Fitzgerald, P.D. & Edstrom, L.V. (2006). SECOND STEP: A violence prevention curriculum. In: *The Handbook of School Violence and School Safety: From Research to Practice*, S. Jimerson & M. Furlong (eds.). Mahwah, NJ: Erlbaum, pp. 383–94.

Fonagy, P. (2010). Veränderungen der klinischen Praxis: Wissenschaftlich oder pragmatisch begründet? In: *Die Psychoanalyse im Pluralismus der Wissenschaften*, K. Münch, D. Munz & A. Springer (eds.). Gießen: Psychosozial-Verlag, pp. 33–81.

_____ Target, M., Steele, H. & Steele, M. (1998), Reflective-functioning manual, version 5, for application to adult attachment interviews. Unpublished manuscript, University College London.

Gerspach, M. (2006). Zum Verstehen von Kindern mit Aufmerksamkeitsstörungen. In: *ADHS - Frühprävention statt Medikalisierung. Theorie, Forschung, Kontroversen*, M. Leuzinger-Bohleber, Y. Brandl & G. Hüther (eds.). Göttingen: Vandenhoeck & Ruprecht, pp. 91–110.

Gilmore, K. (2000), A psychoanalytic perspective on attention-deficit/hyperactivity disorder. *Journal of the American Psychoanalytic Association*, *48*: 1258–93.

Göllnitz, G. (1954), *Die Bedeutung der frühkindlichen Hirnschädigung für die Kinderpsychiatrie*. Leipzig: Thieme.

Goodman R. (1999), The extended version of the strengths and difficulties questionnaire as a guide to child psychiatric caseness and consequent burden. *Journal of Child Psychology and Psychiatry and Allied Disciplines*, *40*: 791–9.

Green, J., Stanley, C., Smith, V. & Goldwyn, R. (2000), A new method of evaluating attachment representations in young school-age children: The Manchester Child Attachment Story Task. *Attachment and Human Development*, *2*: 48–70.

Hüther, G. (2006). Die nutzungsabhängige Herausbildung hirnorganischer Veränderungen bei Hyperaktivität und Aurmerksamkeitsstörungen. Einfluss präventiver Maßnahmen und therapeutischer Internventionen. In: *ADHS - Frühprävention statt Medikalisierung. Theorie, Forschung, Kontroversen*, M. Leuzinger-Bohleber, Y. Brandl & G. Hüther (eds.). Göttingen: Vandenhoeck & Ruprecht, pp. 222–37.

Laezer, L. (2010), Therapievergleichsstudie von hyperaktiven Kindern. Presented at the Congress of the Child and Adolescent Psychiatry, March, Hamburg.

Lempp, R. (1970), *Frühkindliche Hirnschädigung und Neurose*. Bern: Huber.

Leuzinger-Bohleber, M. (2009), *Frühe Kindheit als Schicksal? Trauma, Embodiment, soziale Desintegration. Psychoanalytische Perspektiven*. Stuttgart: Kohlhammer.

_____ & Fischman, F. (2010). Attention-deficit-hyperactivity disorder (AD/HD): A field for contemporary psychoanalysis?: Some clinical, conceptual and neurobiological considerations based on the Frankfurt prevention study. In: *Assessing Change in Psychoanalytic Psychotherapies with Children and Adolescents*, J. Tsiantis & J. Trowell (eds.). London: Karnac, pp. 139–77.

_____ & Pfeifer, R. (2002), Remembering a depressive primary object? Psychoanalysis and embodied cognitive science: A dialogue on memory. *International Journal of Psychoanalysis*, *83*: 3–33.

_____ Brandl, Y. & Hüther, G. (Eds.) (2006), *ADHS - Frühprävention statt Medikalisierung. Theorie, Forschung, Kontroversen*. Göttingen: Vandenhoeck & Ruprecht.

Leuzinger-Bohleber, M., Canestri, J. & Target, M., eds. (2009), *Frühe Entwicklung und ihre Störungen. Klinische, konzeptuelle und empirische psychoanalytische Forschung. Kontroversen zu Frühprävention, Resilienz und ADHS*. Frankfurt: Brandes & Apsel.

_____ Canestri, J. & Target, M. (2010). Controversies on different approaches in psychoanalytic research on early development and ADHD. In: *Early Development and its Disturbances: Clinical, Conceptual and Empirical Research on ADHD and Other Psychopathologies and its Epistemological Reflections*, M. Leuzinger-Bohleber, J. Canestri & M. Target (eds.). London: Karnac Books, pp. 3–50.

_____ Staufenberg, A. & Fischmann, T. (2007), ADHS-Indikation für psychoanalytische Behandlungen? *Praxis der Kinderpsychologie und Kinderpsychiatrie*, *56*: 356–85.

_____ Fischmann, T., Göppel, G., Läzer, K.L. & Waldung, Ch. (2008), Störungen der frühen Affektregulation: klinische und empirische Annäherungen an ADHS. *Psyche - Z Psychoanal*, *6*: 621–53.

Mattner, D. (2006). ADS – die Biologisierung abweichenden Verhaltens. In: *ADHS - Frühprävention statt Medikalisierung. Theorie, Forschung, Kontroversen*, M. Leuzinger-Bohleber, Y. Brandl & G. Hüther (eds.). Göttingen: Vandenhoeck & Ruprecht, pp. 51–69.

Mayr, T. & Ulich, M. (2006), *Perik. Positive Entwicklung und Resilienz im Kindergartenalltag (Beobachtungsbogen und Begleitheft)*. Freiburg i. Br.: Herder.

Panksepp, J. (1998), Attention deficit disorders, psychostimulants, and intolerance of childhood playfulness: A tragedy in the making? *Current Directions in Psychological Science*, *7*: 91–8.

Ricken, G., Fritz, A., Schuck, K.D. & Preuss, U. (2007), *Hannover-Wechsler Intelligenztest für das Vorschulalter (WPPSI-III)*. Bern: Huber.

Ruf-Bächtiger, L. (1987), *Das frühkindliche psychoorganische Syndrom*. Stuttgart: Thieme.

Staufenberg, A. M. (2011), *Zur Psychoanalyse der ADHS*. Frankfurt: Brandes & Apsel.

_____ Bürgin, D., von Freyberg-Döpp, D., Hédervári-Heller, É., Wolff, A., Leuzinger-Bohleber, M. (2006), Manual zur psychoanalytisch-psychotherapeutischen Behandlung psychosozialer Integrationsproblemen bei Kinder. Die Frankfurter Präventionsstudie. Unpublished manuscript.

Sugarman, A., reporter. (2006), Attention deficit hyperactivity disorder and trauma. *International Journal of Psychoanalysis*, *87*: 237–41.

Tsiantis, J. & Trowell, J., eds. (2010), *Assessing Change in Psychoanalytic Psychotherapies with Children and Adolescents*. London: Karnac.

Waldung, C., Göppel, G. & Wolff, L. (2006). Ein Fallbeispiel (Die Frankfurter Präventionsstudie). In: *ADHS - Frühprävention statt Medikalisierung. Theorie, Forschung, Kontroversen*, M. Leuzinger-Bohleber, Y. Brandl & G. Hüther (eds.). Göttingen, Germany: Vandenhoeck & Ruprecht, pp. 256–62.

Trauma and ADHD – Association or Diagnostic Confusion? A Clinical Perspective

Kate Szymanski, Ph.D.
Linda Sapanski, M.A.
Francine Conway, Ph.D.

In recent years, a growing body of research has developed to examine the relationship between exposure to traumatic events in childhood and Attention Deficit Hyperactivity Disorder (ADHD; Daud and Rydelius, 2009; Famularo et al., 1996; Ford et al., 2000; Lipschitz, Morgan and Southwick, 2002; McLeer et al., 1998; Cuffe, McCullough and Pumariega, 1994; Husain, Allwood and Bell, 2008). It is not surprising that these two areas are being evaluated, as cognitive and emotional disruptions that occur in response to trauma, such as difficulty concentrating, dysregulated affect, irritability, and hyperarousal, either overlap with ADHD symptomatology or exasperate it (Barkley, Grodzinsky and DuPaul, 1992; Daud and Rydelius, 2009; De Bellis, 2001; Ford et al., 2000; Jennings et al., 1997). From an epidemiological perspective, trauma exposure and ADHD are pervasive in childhood. Up to half of children in community samples, as well as two-thirds of children in psychiatric samples, have witnessed or experienced trauma (Boney-McCoy and Finkelhor, 1995). The overall rate for ADHD diagnoses varies from seven to twenty-nine percent among school-age children (see review by Barkley, 2006). Because both phenomena are prevalent, it is not surprising that they often overlap (Wozniak et al., 1999). There is an existing body of research that attempts to assess the trauma-ADHD link and to isolate possible mechanisms behind it. We will present a comprehensive review of the literature covering the trauma-ADHD relationship, and we will illustrate it using descriptive data from a hospitalized sample of children and adolescents. This article will address the following questions pertaining to trauma-ADHD association: First, is exposure to trauma a risk factor for the development of ADHD? Second, is the diagnosis of ADHD a misrepresentation of symptoms related to traumatic exposure? The clinical implications of both questions in context of identifying and treating children and adolescents who present with ADHD will be discussed.

TRAUMA AND ADHD

The *Diagnostic and Statistical Manual for Mental Disorders* (DSM-IV-TR; American Psychiatric Association, 2000) outlines two criteria for an experience to be considered traumatic. First, an individual is confronted with actual or threatened death or serious injury, or with serious threat to his/her physical integrity. Trauma may also occur if an individual witnesses such events happening to others. Second, the individual must respond to the event with intense fear, helplessness, or horror, which, in children, may manifest as disorganized, agitated behavior. Common examples of childhood trauma include physical and sexual abuse, maltreatment, life-threatening accidents, death of a caregiver or family member, man-made disasters, life-threatening illness, exposure to community violence, and exposure to domestic violence (Herman, 1997). Our discussion of trauma also extends to events that may not always meet both DSM-IV criteria; however, children experience them as extremely distressing and often develop Post Traumatic Stress Disorder (PTSD) in their aftermath. These events include homelessness, foster care placement, and incarceration of a parent or caregiver (Applebaum and Burns, 1991; North, Smith and Spitznagel, 1994; Pecora et al., 2006; Stoppelbein and Greening, 2000).

Exposure to traumatic events, especially prolonged or repetitive exposure, leads to widespread psychological and biological consequences (van der Kolk, 2005). Current findings suggest that exposure to aversive environmental stressors lead to reduced coping abilities, impaired affect regulation, and decreased self-regulation of behavior (Cicchetti and Toth, 2005). Disruption of these affect modulating capacities place the developing child at risk for severe emotional and behavioral problems such as anxiety, depression, dissociation, impulsivity, aggression, cognitive distortions, attachment disorders, substance abuse, emotional instability, developmental delays, and disruptive disorders (Bergen et al., 2003; Haugaard, 2004; Kaufman, 2008; Kearney, 2010; Putnam, 2003; van der Kolk, 2005). Traumatized children might also develop symptoms of PTSD, such as intrusive recollections, avoidance, and hyperarousal.

According to the DSM-IV-TR, central criteria for diagnosing Attention Deficit/Hyperactivity Disorder (ADHD) are the presence of symptoms of inattention, impulsivity, and hyperactivity that are present to a degree that is atypical on the basis of age. These symptoms have to interfere with or disrupt at least two major areas of functioning, such as school, home, or social situations (American Psychiatric Association, 2000). Children with ADHD have deficits in impulse control, attentional focusing, and stress management, which put them at high risk for functional impairment (Hinshaw, 2002; Barkley, 2006). They are more likely to be perceived as defiant, noncompliant, aggressive, and less able to engage in work (Monastra, 2008). Seventy-five percent of children diagnosed with ADHD have evidence of severe impairment in most aspects of their life: familial, educational, social, and even legal domains are affected (Angold and Costello, 1996). ADHD is often comorbid with Oppositional Defiance Disorder (ODD) and Conduct Disorder (CD; Barkley et al., 1990; Costello et al., 1996; Lahey et al., 1994). Children diagnosed with these disruptive behavior disorders often experience worse psychosocial impairment than children with depression, anxiety, or other psychiatric disorders (Costello et al., 1996; Ford, 2002). Their functional difficulties may be due to the externalizing nature of the symptoms involved in this behavior. Physical impulsivity and associated acting-out behaviors are more noticeable and disruptive than more internalized symptoms, such as those present in depression and anxiety.

IS TRAUMA A RISK FACTOR FOR ADHD?

There is an ongoing debate in the literature regarding the possible relationship between trauma and ADHD (Ford et al., 2000). Researchers have asked whether or not traumatic events contribute to or exacerbate ADHD symptomatology. It is well documented that exposure to environmental stressors could be substantially disorganizing for children and adolescents, resulting in motor restlessness, difficulty concentrating, explosive aggressive outbursts, and emotional constriction (Rydelius, 1981; van der Kolk, 1987). Many of these problems correspond to those present in ADHD, thereby increasing children's vulnerability to this disorder. The presence of PTSD, with its symptoms of hyperarousal and intrusion, may exacerbate ADHD's lack of attention, poor impulse control, and hyperactivity (Daud, Skoglund and Rydelius, 2005; Weinstein, Staffelbach and Biaggio, 2000). In a follow-up study of severely deprived Romanian orphans adopted before they were 43 months old, Stevens et al. (2008) found that ADHD-like symptoms of inattention and overactivity were associated with disinhibited attachment and conduct problems due to the institutional hardship. Posttraumatic reactions of increased arousal and hypervigilance may contribute to problems with stress regulation and anger control typical for disruptive behaviors disorders. ADHD, CD, and ODD all involve difficulties modulating affect (Wakschlag et al., 2005). Traumatized children's feelings of emotional numbing, avoidance, and disengagement from others may facilitate ADHD's functional impairment at home and school and in social relationships such as intrafamilial conflict, school suspension, and rejection by peers (Biederman, 1991; Mannuzza et al., 1988).

Research findings pertaining to the role of trauma in the development or exacerbation of ADHD are somewhat conflicted. In the study by Famularo et al. (1996), nearly one-third of severely maltreated children met criteria for an ADHD diagnosis. Ford et al. (2000) also demonstrated the relationship between chronic trauma (maltreatment) and disruptive behavior disorders. In this research, children diagnosed with ADHD and ODD were at higher risk for past exposure to traumatization. The impact of parental trauma on children's ADHD was shown by Daud and Rydelius (2009). In their study children of traumatized parents were found to be at higher risk for PTSD and ADHD. On the other hand, several investigations have failed to find a relationship between trauma and ADHD (Ford et al., 2000; Wozniak et al., 1999). These studies demonstrate no differences in rates of trauma between children with and without ADHD diagnosis. One possible explanation for this result could be a limited operationalization of the trauma construct in this research (Wozniak et al., 1999).

The conceptual assumption behind identifying trauma as a risk factor for ADHD is the idea that traumatic exposure substantially impacts a child's ability to regulate his/her affect. Children who experienced trauma are prone to be easily overwhelmed, overreact to minor stresses, have difficulties with self-soothing, react excessively in response to neutral stimuli, and have trouble modulating their anger (Luxenberg, Spinazzola and van der Kolk, 2001). Their relationships with others are altered; therefore, regulatory function of the environment is impaired. Developmentally, childhood trauma affects cognitive and linguistic growth because it alters the "social interactional process by which children acquire and use language to talk about their own and others emotions" (Cole et al., 1994, p. 66). Impairment in the child's ability to symbolize his/her emotions via use of language results in acting out and externalizing behaviors, affecting capacity for self-control (Hinshaw, 2002). Traumatized children's compromised ability to regulate affect creates a particular vulnerability for disruptive behaviors typical of an ADHD diagnosis. Inattention, hyperactivity, and detachment serve as cognitive and behavioral pathways readily available for an emotionally dysregulated child.

IS ADHD SYNDROME MASKING SYMPTOMS OF TRAUMA?

Comparing the diagnostic categories of ADHD and PTSD brings the question of their overlap. Children exposed to traumatic events, particularly multiple chronic traumas, are at high risk for PTSD (van der Kolk, 2005). Avoidance symptoms of PTSD are understood as a defensive response to the cognitively and emotionally overwhelming experience of traumatic event. They include purposeful efforts not to think about trauma as well as more general experiences of not attending to stimuli, high distractibility, and forgetfulness (APA, 2000). These symptoms mirror those of the Inattentive cluster of ADHD, which include inattention, distractibility, and avoidance of activities (Ford et al., 2000). PTSD's Hyperarousal cluster is conceptualized as an innate protective mechanism within the body to defend itself from future traumas. Hyperarousal symptoms are characterized by a pattern of increased arousal such as hypervigilance, irritability, and an exaggerated startle response (APA, 2000). Again, many of these symptoms are similar to those of the Hyperactivity cluster of ADHD such as fidgeting, excessive moving around, and restlessness (Ford et al., 2000; Cuffe et al., 1994; Wozniak et al., 1999). Similarly, PTSD's symptoms of intrusive recollection and the re-experiencing of traumatic memories can present as ADHD's symptoms of difficulty in organization and incapacity to listen. In children, re-experiencing may also lead to disorganized, agitated behavior, as the sudden remembering of frightening or painful memories may overwhelm children's developing coping mechanisms. Feelings of anxiety that characterize PTSD can mirror the Impulsivity cluster of ADHD (Cuffe et al., 1994; Wozniak et al., 1999). Taking into account that the prevalence of ADHD is quite high in psychiatric populations (Costello et al., 1996), many of the children may have been exposed to trauma and may experience undetected PTSD symptoms. Ford et al. (2000) claimed the opposite, arguing that PTSD is often misdiagnosed when ADHD is truly present. In either case, the symptom similarity between these two disorders could lead to the wrong conceptualization of the diagnosis.

A number of studies have shown PTSD to be comorbid with ADHD (Cuffe et al., 1994; Merry and Andrews, 1994; Weinstein et al., 2000) possibly due to the temperamental component for both (Comings, 1997). However, many researchers have also explored the notion of symptom overlap between these two syndromes, concluding that "many of the . . . . . thousands of children with disruptive behavior disorders may have been exposed to traumatic maltreatment and may experience undetected PTSD symptoms" (Ford et al., 2000, p. 214).

Children may respond to trauma with a wider range of symptoms than those captured by PTSD. As aforementioned, trauma in children has been found to lead to problems with affect regulation, behavior regulation, stress tolerance, mood lability, aggression, depression, and anxiety, among others. These symptoms might manifest themselves as distractibility, disorganized affect, and disruptive behaviors, all of which occur in ADHD and ODD (Rydelius, 1981; van der Kolk, 1987). Therefore, it is possible that a clinician may mistake these symptoms for those of ADHD without even acknowledging a possibility of a trauma history.

RELATIONSHIP BETWEEN TRAUMA AND ADHD IN A PSYCHIATRIC INPATIENT SETTING

When examining a dataset of hospitalized children and adolescents from a psychiatric setting, the notion of the trauma-ADHD association has particular significance in terms of diagnosis and treatment. In our clinical sample (63 inpatients) drawn from the metropolitan New York area, the majority of children experienced multiple traumas, as the average number of traumas was 2.9. Thirty-three percent of this highly traumatized population was diagnosed with ADHD. There are two possible explanations for these findings, both presenting important practical implications for clinicians.

The first explanation pertains to trauma as a risk factor for ADHD. In our sample, children diagnosed with ADHD were significantly younger than children without ADHD ($t=4.1$, $p < .0001$; ADHD $X = 11.2$, non-ADHD $\overline{X} = 13.0$). Multiple traumas occurring during early stages of psychosocial development are particularly detrimental to a child's capacity to regulate emotion. Specifically, experiencing multiple early traumas is associated with cognitive impairment, particularly in the verbal domain of functioning (Cicchetti, 2002). These children are more likely to express affect through physical actions, have difficulty with self-soothing, and experience a heightened degree of affective intensity that might take a violent form. These tendencies put such children at higher risk for PTSD or PTSD-like symptoms (van der Kolk, 2005). Intrusive memories of trauma(s), hyperarousal, and numbing can contribute to or exasperate inattention, hyperactivity, and detachment that characterize functioning of ADHD children. Difficulty with anger regulation, also an outcome of early childhood trauma, can contribute to deficits in social-problem solving, which are typical in ADHD (Harty et al., 2009). Traumatized children's deficiencies with affect modulation impact regulatory processes of intensity, tolerance, expression, differentiation of affect, anger modulation, and ability for self-care. Thus trauma's impact on emotion dysregulation in children renders them particularly vulnerable to ADHD symptomatology. Particularly, a history of prolonged childhood trauma poses such risk due to its profound negative impact on children's capacity for affect regulation (Cicchetti et al., 1991; Kaplan, 2004). In support of this notion, 76 percent of children in our hospitalized population had histories of foster placement, and 50 percent had histories of physical abuse, demonstrating that the majority of ADHD group was exposed to a chronic trauma.

Sander's (2002) intersubjective approach to affect regulation points to the importance of the environment in the regulatory process. He specifically claims the existence of an interactive loop between the environment and an individual's capacity for regulating emotions. The environment supports the development of affect regulation, and the experience of positive affect in turn facilitates the motivation to seek connection with that environment. Events that generate positive emotions are motivating factors to maintain an environmental connection. Because the majority of children experienced traumas related to the family environment (e.g., foster care, abuse), the regulatory support of the external world is severely impaired. Therefore, children are not seeking connections with others when disruption in affect regulation occurs, particularly since the others are a source of overwhelming negative affect. This may also contribute to social functioning deficit observed in ADHD. Children in our sample do not appear to have a consistent familial support that would provide them with the buffer against traumatic exposure. Overall, this population is composed of highly traumatized children whose early experiences with chronic trauma place them at a high risk for difficulties with affect regulation, which either increased their vulnerability for ADHD or exasperated its symptomatology.

As we have discussed previously the symptom similarities between these two disorders are greater than their differences, therefore the risk of misdiagnoses is rather high. In this highly traumatized population the ratio of ADHD to PTSD diagnoses was 4:1, with only eight percent of the sample diagnosed with PTSD. Consistent with the established prevalence rates of ADHD, significantly more boys than girls were diagnosed with ADHD (χ^2=3.962, $p < .05$), putting them at higher risk for undetected PTSD. Our sample is characterized by early, chronic, and multiple traumas where possible PTSD symptoms of hyperarousal/hypervigilance and avoidance/numbing may be inappropriately attributed to ADHD's clusters of hyperactivity and inattention. Disorganized or agitated behavior that children often exhibit in response to trauma, combined with commonly experienced posttraumatic anxiety, can both be factors underlying restlessness or impulsivity present in the ADHD children in this sample. According to DSM-IV-TR, a diagnosis of ADHD should not be given to "children from inadequate, disorganized, or chaotic environments" if the children "have difficulties in goal-directed behavior," which is a common struggle in traumatized children (DSM-IV-TR; Daud and Rydelius, 2009). Therefore, extra caution needs to be taken when children with the history of trauma are evaluated for ADHD, as the overlap with the symptoms of PTSD and other trauma-related psychopathology can easily lead to misdiagnosis. It is likely that PTSD diagnosis is underrepresented in this clinical sample because trauma symptoms have been mislabeled as ADHD symptoms, which are more external and easier to detect.

CLINICAL IMPLICATIONS

Our descriptive data demonstrate a high prevalence of ADHD in a clinical sample of severely traumatized children and adolescents. Difficulty with affect modulation resulting from trauma exposure may either create vulnerability for ADHD or may exasperate the disorder's symptomatology. Low prevalence of PTSD diagnosis in the sample also may suggest that the presence of trauma pathology is underrepresented due to the overlap of PTSD and ADHD diagnostic criteria (Cuffe et al., 1994; Ford et al., 2000; Wozniak et al., 1999). Based on the presented review and obtained findings, we recommend that children diagnosed with ADHD be carefully screened for trauma history in order to determine the appropriate course and type of their treatment. Furthermore, the accurate assessment of trauma symptoms, particularly the presence of PTSD, is crucial for a precise differential diagnosis of ADHD. A better understanding of the trauma-ADHD relationship will enhance clinicians' abilities to identify and properly treat children and adolescents that are at risk.

REFERENCES

Adler, L. A., Kunz, M., Chua, H. C., Rotrosen, J., & Resnick, S. G. (2004), Attention-deficit/hyperactivity disorder in adult patients with posttraumatic stress disorder (PTSD): Is ADHD a vulnerability factor? *Journal of Attention Disorders*, *8*: 11–6.

American Psychiatric Association. (2000), *Diagnostic and Statistical Manual of Mental Disorders: DSM-IV-TR*. Washington, DC: APA.

Angold, A. & Costello, E. J. (1996), Toward establishing an empirical basis for the diagnosis of oppositional defiant disorder. *Journal of the American Academy of Child & Adolescent Psychiatry 35*: 1205–12.

Applebaum, D. R. & Burns, G. L. (1991), Unexpected childhood death: Posttraumatic stress disorder in surviving siblings and parents. *Journal of Clinical Child Psychology*, *20*: 114–20.

Barkley, R. A. (2006), *Attention-deficit Hyperactivity Disorder, a Handbook for Diagnosis and Treatment*, 3rd edition. New York: Guilford Press.

———— Fischer, M., Edelbrock, C. S. & Smallish, L. (1990), The adolescent outcome of hyperactive children diagnosed by research criteria: I. An 8-year prospective follow-up study. *Journal of American Academic Adolescent and Child Psychiatry*, *29*: 546–57.

———— Grodzinsky, G. & DuPaul, G. J. (1992), Frontal lobe functions in attention deficit disorder with and without hyperactivity: A review and research report. *Journal of Abnormal Child Psychology*, *20*: 163–88.

Bergen, H. A., Martin, G., Richardson, A. S., Allison, S. & Roeger, L. (2003), Sexual abuse and suicidal behavior: A model constructed from a large community sample of adolescents. *Journal of the American Academy of Child & Adolescent Psychiatry*, *42*: 1301–09.

Biederman, J. (1991), Attention deficit hyperactivity disorder (ADHD). *Annual Journal of Clinical Psychiatry*, *3*: 9–22.

Boney-McCoy, S. & Finkelhor, D. (1995), Psychosocial sequel of violent victimization in a national youth sample. *Journal of Consulting and Clinical Psychology*, *63*: 726–36.

Cicchetti, D., Ganiban, J. & Barnett, D. (1991). Contributions from the study of high risk populations to understanding the development of emotion regulation. In: *The Development of Emotion Regulation and Dysregulation*, J. Garber & K. Dodge (eds.). New York: Cambridge University Press, pp. 15–49.

———— (2002), The impact of social experience on neurobiological systems: Illustration from a constructivist view of child maltreatment. *Cognitive Development*, *17*: 1407–28.

———— & Toth, S. L. (2005), Child maltreatment. *Annual Review of Clinical Psychology*, *1*: 409–38.

Cole, P. M., Michel, M. & Teti, L. (1994). The development of emotion regulation and dysregulation: A clinical perspective. In: *The Development of Emotion Regulation*, N.A. Fox (ed.). Monographs of the Society for Research in Child Development; Serial. No. 240, Vol. 59, Nos. 2–3, pp. 53–72.

Comings, D. E. (1997), Genetic aspects of childhood behavioral disorders. *Child Psychiatry & Human Development*, *27*: 139–50.

Costello, J. E., Angold, A., Burns, B. J., Sangl, D. K., Tweed, D. L., Erkanli, A. & Worthman, C. M. (1996), The Great Smoky Mountains study of youth: Goals, design, methods, and the prevalence of DSM-III-R disorders. *Archives of General Psychiatry*, *53*: 1129–36.

Cuffe, S.P., McCullough, E.L. & Pumariega, A.J. (1994), Comorbidity of attention deficit hyperactivity disorder and post-traumatic stress disorder. *Journal of Child and Family Studies*, *3*: 327–36.

Daud, A. & Rydelius, P.-A. (2009), Comorbidity/overlapping between ADHD and PTSD in relation to IQ among children of traumatized/non-traumatized parents. *Journal of Attention Disorders*, *13*: 188–98.

———— Skoglund, E. & Rydelius, P.A. (2005), Children in families of torture victims: Transgenerational transmission of parents' traumatic experiences to their children. *International Journal of Social Welfare*, *14*: 23–32.

Daviss, W.B., Reiser, A.F. & Thomas, J. (2000), Child maltreatment, other trauma exposure, and posttraumatic symptomatology among children with oppositional defiant and attention Deficit hyperactivity disorders. *Child Maltreatment*, *5*: 205–17.

De Bellis, M. D. (2001), Developmental traumatology: The psychobiological development of maltreated children and its implications for research, treatment, and policy. *Development and Psychopathology*, *13*: 539–64.

Famularo, R., Fenton, T., Kinscherff, R. & Augustyn, M. (1996), Psychiatric comorbidity in childhood post traumatic stress disorder. *Child Abuse & Neglect*, *20*: 953–61.

Ford, J. D. (2002), Traumatic victimization in childhood and persistent problems with oppositional-defiance. *Journal of Aggression, Maltreatment, and Trauma*, *6*: 25–58.

———— Rascusin, C. G. E., Daviss, J. R., Fleisher, A. & Thomas, J. (2000), Child maltreatment, other trauma exposure, and posttraumatic symptomatology among children with oppositional defiant and attention deficit hyperactivity disorders. *Child Maltreatment*, *5*: 205–17.

Harty, S., Miller, C. J., Newcorn, J. H. & Halperin, J. M. (2009), Adolescents with childhood ADHD and comorbid disruptive behavior disorders: Aggression, anger, and hostility. *Child Psychiatry and Human Development*, *40*: 85–97.

Haugaard, J. (2004), Recognizing and treating uncommon behavioral and emotional disorders in children and adolescents who have been severely maltreated: Introduction. *Child Maltreatment*, *9*: 123–30.

Herman, J. L. (1997), *Trauma and Recovery: The Aftermath of Violence from Domestic Abuse to Political Terror*. New York: Basic Books.

Hinshaw, S. P. (2002), Process, mechanism, and explanation related to externalizing behavior in developmental psychopathology. *Journal of Abnormal Child Psychology: An Official Publication of the International Society for Research in Child and Adolescent Psychopathology*, *30*: 431–46.

Husain, S. A., Allwood, M. A. & Bell, D. J. (2008), The relationship between PTSD symptoms and attention problems in children exposed to the Bosnian War. *Journal of Emotional and Behavioral Disorders*, *16*: 52–62.

Jennings, J. R., van der Molen, M., Pelham, W., Debski, K. & Hoza, B. (1997), Inhibition in boys with Attention Deficit Hyperactivity Disorder as indexed by heart rate change. *Developmental Psychology*, *33*: 308–18.

Kaplan, A. (2004), The role of affect regulation as a mediating mechanism between childhood trauma and adolescent and adult substance abuse. Doctoral Dissertation, Adelphi University.

Kaufman, J. (2008). Genetic and environmental modifiers of risk and resiliency in maltreated children. In: *Developmental Psychopathology and Wellness: Genetic and Environmental Influences*, J. J. Hudziak (ed.). Arlington, VA: American Psychiatric Publishing, Inc., pp. 141–60.

Kearney, J.A. (2010), Women and children exposed to domestic violence: Themes in maternal interviews about their children's psychiatric diagnoses. *Issues in Mental Health Nursing*, *31*: 74–81.

Lahey, B. B., Applegate, B. A., Barkley, R. A., Garfinkle, B., McBurnett, K., Kerdyk, L., Greenhill, L., Hynd, G. W., Frick, P. J., Newcorn, J., Biederman, J., Ollendick, T., Hart, F. L., Perez, D., Waldman, I. & Shaffer, D. (1994), DSM-IV field trials for oppositional defiant disorder and conduct disorder. *American Journal of Psychiatry*, *151*: 1163–71.

Lipschitz, D.S., Morgan, C.A. III & Southwick, S.M. (2002), Neurobiological disturbances in youth with childhood trauma and in youth with conduct disorder. *Journal of Aggression, Maltreatment & Trauma*, *6*: 149–74.

Luxenberg, T., Spinazzola, J. & van der Kolk, B.A. (2001), Complex trauma and disorders of extreme stress (DESNOS) diagnosis, Part I: Assessment. *Directions in Psychiatry*, *21*: 373–93.

Mannuzza, S., Klein, R.G., Bonagura, N., Konig, P.H. & Shenker, R. (1988), Hyperactive boys almost grown up, II: Status of subjects without a mental disorder. *Archives of General Psychiatry*, *45*: 13–8.

McLeer, S. V., Dixon, J. F., Henry, D., Ruggiero, K., Escovitz, K., Niedda, T. & Scholle, R. (1998), Psychopathology in non-clinically referred sexually abused children. *Journal of the American Academy of Child & Adolescent Psychiatry*, *37*: 1326–33.

Merry, S. & Andrews, L. (1994), Psychiatric status of sexually abused children 12 months after disclosure of abuse. *Journal of American Academy of Child and Adolescent Psychiatry*, *33*: 939–44.

Monastra, V.J. (2008), *Unlocking the Potential of Patients with ADHD: A Model for Clinical Practice*. Washington DC: American Psychological Association.

North, C. S., Smith, E. M. & Spitznagel, E. L. (1994), Violence and the homeless: An epidemiologic study of victimization and aggression. *Journal of Traumatic Stress*, *7*: 95–109.

Pecora, P.J., Kessler, R.C., O'Brien, K., White, C.R., Williams, J., Hiripi, E., English, D., White, J. & Herrick, M.A. (2006), Educational and employment outcomes of adults formerly placed in foster care: Results from the Northwest Foster Care Alumni Study. *Children and Youth Services Review*, *28*: 1459–81.

Putnam, F.W. (2003), Ten-year research update review: Child sexual abuse. *Journal of the American Academy of Child & Adolescent Psychiatry*, *42*: 269–78.

Rydelius, P.A. (1981), Children of alcoholic fathers, their social adjustment and their health status over 20 years. *Acta Paediatrica Scandinavica Supplement*, *286*: 1–89.

Sander, L. (2002), Thinking differently: Principles of process in living systems and the specificity of being known. *Psychoanalytic Dialogues*, *12*(1): 11–42.

Stevens, S.E., Sonuga-Barke, E.J., Kreppner, J.M., Beckett, C., Castle, J., Colvert, E., Groothues, C., Hawkins, A. & Rutter, M. (2008), Inattention/overactivity following early severe institutional deprivation: Presentation and associations in early adolescence. *Journal of Abnormal Child Psychology: An Official Publication of the International Society for Research in Child and Adolescent Psychopathology*, *36*: 385–98.

Stoppelbein, L. & Greening, L. (2000), Posttraumatic stress symptoms in parentally bereaved children and adolescents. *Journal of the American Academy of Child & Adolescent Psychiatry*, *39*: 1112–9.

van der Kolk, B.A. (1987), The drug treatment of post traumatic stress disorder. *Journal of Affective Disorders*, *13*: 203–13.

van der Kolk, B.A. (2005), Developmental trauma disorder. *Psychiatric Annals*, *35*, 401–8.

Wakschlag, L.S., Leventhal, B.L., Briggs-Gowan, M.J., Danis, B., Keenan, K., Hill, C., Egger, H.L., Cicchetti, D. & Carter, A.S. (2005), Defining the "disruptive" in preschool behavior: What diagnostic observation can teach us. *Clinical Child and Family Psychology Review*, *8*: 183–201.

Weinstein, D., Staffelbach, D. & Biaggio, M. (2000), Attention-deficit hyperactivity disorder and posttraumatic stress disorder: Differential diagnosis in childhood sexual abuse. *Clinical Psychology Review*, *20*: 359–78.

Wozniak, J., Crawford, M. H., Biederman, J., Faraone, S. V., Spencer, T. J., Taylor, A., & Blier, H. K. (1999), Antecedents and complications of trauma in boys with ADHD: Findings from a longitudinal study. *Journal of the American Academy of Child & Adolescent Psychiatry*, *38*: 48–55

ADHD and Complex Trauma: A Descriptive Study of Hospitalized Children in an Urban Psychiatric Hospital

Francine Conway, Ph.D.
Maria Oster, M.A.
Kate Szymanski, Ph.D

This paper embarks on a descriptive exploration of the relations between ADHD and Complex Trauma among children in an urban psychiatric hospital. To date, these two diagnostic categories have not been examined in concert. This study was based upon chart reviews of 79 children and adolescents who were receiving treatment at an urban children's psychiatric hospital. The Hospitalized Child and Adolescent Trauma and Psychopathology Questionnaire was completed for each participant and information regarding demographics, diagnosis, and complex trauma. Results showed ADHD children experience higher incidences of chronic stress, termed here as environmental trauma, and disruptions in attachment relationships referred to here as attachment trauma. We propose that experiences of chronic adverse situations during childhood, also referred to as complex trauma, cannot be extricated from ADHD symptomatology and is strongly correlated with behavior that is common among children who have deficits in psychological processes known as mentalization. Implications for development of a capacity to mentalize with ADHD children are discussed.

Attention Deficit Hyperactivity Disorder (ADHD) is one of the most frequently diagnosed mental disorders in children and adolescents in the United States (Kessler et al., 2005) with prevalence rates ranging from three percent to as high as eleven percent (Barkley and Biederman, 1997; Mash and Barkley, 2003). More specifically, based on its prevalence, ADHD appears to have become the most commonly diagnosed neurobehavioral condition of childhood (Furman, 2005). Although ADHD is now generally accepted as a mental disorder and has been since it was first entered into commonly used diagnostic manuals such as the *Diagnostic and Statistical Manual-Second Edition* (DSM-II) in 1968; and updated with DSM IV in 1994 (DSM IV, APA 1994), controversies surrounding the origins, diagnosis, and treatment persists.

The controversy exists for a number of reasons. For example, Knowledge about mental illness is constantly changing as standards for what is "knowable" and the process for knowing are continually being evaluated and re-evaluated, and the tension between empirical knowledge about ADHD versus knowledge gained from clinical experience remains (Eresund, 2007). Moreover, the influence of cultural judgments on diagnosis is inescapable and results in a lack of consensus among clinicians and those who evaluate the field (Goffman, 1961). Nonetheless, it is in this context of diagnostic ambivalence that the ADHD diagnosis is understood. For some, the cultural biases inherent in diagnosis prohibit any definitive use of one diagnostic manual or approach to the ADHD diagnosis relative to other approaches.

Despite the lack of clarity about ADHD, the dominance of neuropsychology in the discussion about diagnosis and treatment of ADHD tends to drum out other voices such as those influenced by the psychodynamic perspective (Gwynedd and Norris, 1999). For example, the view that the cause of ADHD lies in structural abnormalities in the brain leads some clinicians to endorse medication as a treatment of choice (Barkley, 1997; Castellanos et al., 1996; Fisher and Rose, 1996; Fuster, 1997). Although other perspectives endorsing a more environmental and psychological (i.e., less neurobiological) view arose in the mid-twentieth century (1940–1950s), these ideas continue to struggle to gain prominence in the ADHD discourse (Bender, 1942; Greenacre, 1941). More recently, Behavioral Therapy (BT) or behavioral management at home and at school has gained some traction, and several studies have been conducted establishing the use of this modality as an effective treatment for ADHD children in conjunction with medication (Pfiffner, Rosen and O'Leary, 1985; DuPaul and Stoner, 2003; Jensen, 2002; Barkley, 2006). Currently, the field seems to have reached an impasse where a combination of both Neurological and Behavioral approaches are being touted as offering the best treatment results for this population (DuPaul and Eckert, 1997; Barkley, 2006). Even the BT approach is offered from the perspective that the child's need for behavior modification stems from executive functioning deficits that may be neurological in nature (Barkley, 1997, 2006).

Epistemological inadequacies inherent in a nomenclature that relegates ADHD to one of three subtypes (i.e., hyperactive/impulsive), inattention, or combination of the two, fail to address differences in the types of ADHD that materialized in clinical practice of psychologists. Rafalovich's (2005) study, which explored clinicians' uncertainty regarding the diagnosis and treatment of ADHD, asserts that most clinicians are uncertain as to the origin of ADHD. A more pertinent question seems to be whether the ADHD symptomatology stems from neurological or environmental/social insults thereby determining treatment approaches (Rafalovich, 2005). Of these two positions (the first being neuropsychology, which concerns the need for pharmacological interventions, and the second being environmental deficits, which concerns the need to address issues pertaining to the child's psychological experiences of interactions with the environment) this article focuses on the latter. More importantly, this article contends that environmental insults occurring early in life pose a significant risk to the child's ability to focus and pay attention. We proposes that experiences of chronic adverse situations during childhood, also referred to as complex trauma (van der Kolk, 2005), cannot be extricated from ADHD symptomatology and is strongly correlated with behavior that is common among children who have deficits in psychological processes known as mentalization (Fonagy and Target, 1998).

Complex trauma refers to the occurrence of chronic and prolonged adverse events in a child's life that has an early onset and is generally interpersonal. These adverse events include but are not limited to sexual or physical abuse, community violence, neglect, and maltreatment (see Spinazzola et al., in van der Kolk, 2005). More alarming is the prevalence of these adversities during childhood. According to the Adverse Childhood Experiences (ACE) study, a range of adverse events occurred among approximately 11–23 percent of adults during their childhood and is significantly related to depression, suicide, violence, sexual acting out behavior, and other self-destructive behaviors (Felitti et al., 1998). More specifically, chronic adverse traumatic events impede an individual's ability to integrate sensory, emotional, and cognitive information resulting in an "unfocused response to stress" (van der Kolk, 2005, p. 402). Van der Kolk (2005) argues that neural pathways and social interactions are inextricable in early development, and among children who experience these complex traumas, not only are neurological insults present but also psychological impairments in the child's ability to develop internal models for affective and cognitive interpersonal experiences. Children who live in chronically stressful environments are greatly disadvantaged in their capacities to rely on their environment (usually the source of the stress) to soothe them. Consequently, they are caught between two purposes: one to minimize the threat posed by their environment, which at times includes the parent or caregiver, and the other to regulate their emotions (Pynos et al., 1987). Children who experience complex trauma tend to experience overwhelming anxiety, anger, aggression, hyperarousal or dissociative states, and much more. Van der Kolk (2005) asserts complex trauma experiences result in Developmental Trauma Disorder which is characterized by "exposure. . . triggered patters of repeated dysregulation in response to trauma cues. . . persistently altered attributions and expectancies [and]. . . functional impairments" (van der Kolk, p. 404).

It is our belief that complex trauma and ADHD share some common symptoms. In ADHD, as in complex trauma, the target symptoms such as poor emotion regulation and impulsivity are also found in other affective disorders that lend themselves to a wider range of treatment options. In actuality, according to Furman (2005), ". . . rates of comorbid psychiatric and learning problems, including depression and anxiety, range from 12 percent to 60 percent, with significant symptom overlap with ADHD" (p. 994). Deficits in emotion regulation may also stem from experiences of parenting the ADHD child as stressful or interruptions in the parent/child relationships during early childhood. A review of the literature gives way to the finding that parents of children with ADHD experience more stress and more dysfunctional interaction styles than do parents of children without ADHD (Anastopoulos et al., 1993; Anderson, Hinshaw and Simmel, 1994; Fischer, 1990; Johnston and Mash, 2001). Parents of children with ADHD report increased feelings of self-blame, incompetence, depression, and isolation (e.g., Nigg and Hinshaw, 1998). Not surprisingly, mothers of hyperactive children are separated or divorced more frequently than mothers of children without ADHD (Fischer, 1990).

Attention deficit hyperactivity disorder is frequently comorbid with a range of psychiatric disorders and is frequently diagnosed in hospitalized children (Conway, Oster & McCarthy, 2010). Clinicians working with ADHD children in private practice often note emotional and behavioral problems beyond the core symptoms of inattention and impulsivity/hyperactivity (Furman, 2005; Rafalovich, 2005). They share many features with other clinical disorders of childhood, including aggression and externalizing behavior, depression, and cognitive difficulties (Ethier, Lemelin and Lachorite, 2004; Mannuzza and Klein, 1999). The overlapping symptoms between children with ADHD and those with, for example, a history of child abuse (Ford et al., 2000; Wozniak et al., 1999) highlights the lack of clarity regarding differential diagnosis pertaining to trauma and ADHD.

It is widely accepted that abuse is most likely damaging to a child's self and other perceptions, resulting in learned helplessness, anxiety, and depression (Kazdin, 1985), even to the point of increased self-destructive and suicidal behavior (Widom, 1997). Abused children often experience externalizing and internalizing difficulties, compromised peer relations, and academic/cognitive impairments closely resembling ADHD. Treatment of trauma survivors often incorporates psychodynamic techniques, such an acceptance of unconscious processes; this is not the case with ADHD treatment. Therefore, it can be argued that the assumption that ADHD in children is a largely neurocognitive disorder has often neglected the underlying emotional, personality, and interpersonal issues from which many ADHD afflicted children suffer.

This article asserts that children experiencing a series of adverse life events early in life, also referred to as Complex Trauma, share a constellation of symptomatology found in children diagnosed with ADHD. As previously stated, externalizing and internalizing behavior problems, peer rejection, and cognitive difficulties are not uncommon. In addition, there tends to be shared adversities including child abuse, that is, inappropriate reactions on the part of adults (often parents) against children. Also, families of children with ADHD are marked by dysfunctional interpersonal interactional patterns. These similarities raise the question of a possible link between the etiology of these two phenomena (Complex Trauma and ADHD); namely, the idea that disrupted or insecure attachment may be leading to greater more deeply engrained emotional consequences that are ignored by less psychodynamic oriented assessment and diagnosis of and treatment for ADHD.

This article embarks on a descriptive exploration of the relations between ADHD and Complex Trauma among children in an urban psychiatric hospital. To date, these two diagnostic categories have not been examined in concert. We expect to replicate previous findings that children diagnosed with ADHD will have comorbid diagnosis with anxiety, mood disorders, and learning problems. We also expect that ADHD children will have a history of chronic stressors in their lives, including disruptions in early caregiver relationships stemming from abuse, neglect, maltreatment, death of a parent, and exposure to chronic stresses, including witness of violence and other adversities. We also expect a positive relationship between ADHD and Complex Trauma.

METHOD

Participants

This study was based upon chart reviews of 79 children and adolescents receiving treatment at an urban children's psychiatric hospital. Participants, ages 8–18, were primarily of Hispanic and African-American ethnic backgrounds. Primary diagnoses included, but were not limited to, conduct disorder, oppositional defiant disorder, attention deficit disorder, major depression, bipolar disorder, schizophrenia and schizoaffective disorder, as well as mood, depressive, and psychotic disorders not otherwise specified. Some participants were diagnosed with learning disorders and mental retardation and most had comorbid diagnoses.

Most participants in the study had experienced adverse life events including, but not limited to, physical or sexual abuse, neglect or maltreatment, abandonment by a biological parent or caretaker, and exposure to domestic or community violence.

Procedures

This study entailed a review of closed patient charts that were randomly selected by the hospital's chief psychologist using medical record numbers. Institutional Review Board (IRB) approval was obtained, and doctoral and Master's level psychology students reviewed closed charts. Careful measures were taken to ensure that participants' identities remained concealed. Each participant's data were assigned an identification number that was used to enter individual data on a collection sheet. The data collection sheet was kept in a locked file cabinet, and the only list linking participants' names to identification numbers was kept with patient files in the hospital's medical records room at all times.

Doctoral level graduate students went to the hospital to complete questionnaires regarding demographic information, psychiatric, and trauma history. Coding was based on information contained in the intake section of participants' charts. All coders were trained to complete the data sheet by two faculty members who were licensed clinical psychologists. The training included an extensive description of each questionnaire item, as well as practice coding of intake documents that were not being used in the present study.

Measures

The Hospitalized Child and Adolescent Trauma and Psychopathology (HCATP) Questionnaire was developed by the research team, which included two faculty psychologists and six doctoral students in clinical psychology. Faculty psychologists drafted the questionnaire with input from the team regarding what information would be most relevant to the study's goals. The questionnaire was piloted using ten patient charts coded by three clinical psychology doctoral students. Percent agreement was calculated for each questionnaire item. Any item with a low percent agreement was discussed and clarified by the research team, after which the item was re-written in a checklist format to promote higher construct validity and interrater reliability.

Demographic Information

Participants' demographic information such as age, sex, and ethnicity were collected as well as all Axis I and II diagnoses.

Complex Trauma History

History of adverse life events was assessed using the HCATP Questionnaire developed for a larger study. This questionnaire asks about the presence of a broad range of traumatic experiences in a child's history, including adoption/foster placement, homelessness, witnessing violence, witnessing domestic violence, being a victim of violence, sexual or physical abuse, maltreatment/neglect, death of a parent/caregiver, death of other significant family member, parent/caregiver incarceration, and parent/caregiver substance use.

For purposes of this study, complex trauma is defined as "the experience of multiple, chronic and prolonged adverse traumatic events, most often of an interpersonal nature (e.g., sexual or physical abuse, community violence) and early life onset. These exposures can occur within the child's caregiving system and include physical, emotional, and educational neglect and child maltreatment beginning in early childhood" (van der Kolk, 2005).

The current study looked at early (before age ten) and late (after age ten) onset of complex trauma including the following: *Abuse Complex Trauma,* which includes a history of chronic stressors in their lives stemming from abuse (sexual and physical); *Attachment Complex Trauma,* which includes disruptions in early caregiver relationships stemming from neglect, maltreatment, death of a parent, history of adoption, foster care placement, caregiver death, or caregiver incarceration; and *Environmental Complex Trauma,* which include exposure to chronic stresses including witness of violence and other adversities.

Results

The charts of 87 hospitalized children were reviewed. Children diagnosed with ADHD were significantly older than those with no ADHD diagnosis (ADHD *M* 12.93, *SD* 2.51 and non-ADHD *M*=11.05, *SD*=2.47). A diverse group of participants included African Americans (ADHD=71.9 percent; Non-ADHD=56.4 percent), Hispanic (ADHD=12.5 percent; Non-ADHD=29.1 percent), Caucasian (ADHD=6.3 percent; Non-ADHD=9.1 percent), and other (ADHD=9.4 percent; Non-ADHD=5.4 percent). A greater percent of ADHD children were males (75 percent) compared to 58.2 percent non-ADHD children (see Table 1).

Compared to non-ADHD children (75 percent), children diagnosed with ADHD (97 percent) experienced higher incidences of attachment and environmental complex trauma events. More specifically, ADHD children experienced one to four separate incidences that disrupted their caregiving relationships, including adoption, foster care placement, maltreatment, ACS involvement, and deaths of their mothers, fathers or caregivers. Sixty-two percent of ADHD children lived in chronically stressful environments where they witnessed violence in their homes or parental substance abuse when compared to 58 percent of their non-ADHD counterparts (see Figure 1).

Most of the incidences contributing to Complex Trauma occurred before age ten. Particularly among the ADHD group, most of the Attachment and Environmental Trauma occurred only early in life (see Table 2).

Children diagnosed with ADHD experienced significantly higher occurrences of Complex Trauma, attachment type. When both attachment and environmental complex trauma indicators

TABLE 1
Demographics

Demographics	*ADHD*	*NO ADHD*	*F*
	Mean (SD)	Mean (SD)	
Age	13.93(2.51)	11.05(2.47)	26.95***
	%	%	χ^2
Ethnicity			5.15
African American	71.9	56.4	
Caucasian	6.3	9.1	
Hispanic	12.5	29.1	
Other	9.4	5.4	
Gender	75	58.2	2.49

*** $p<.001$

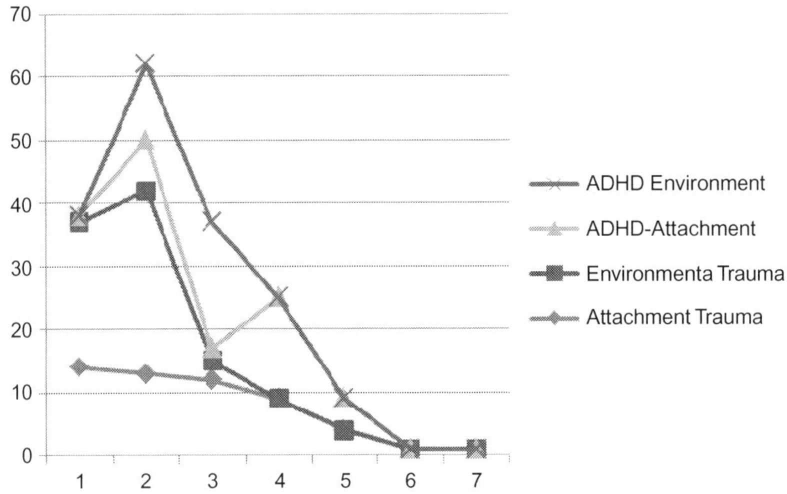

FIGURE 1 Frequencies of Complex Trauma occurring in ADHD and Non-ADHD Hospitalized Children (color figure available online).

TABLE 2
Early and Late Onset of Complex Trauma in ADHD and non-ADHD Hospitalized Children

	ADHD		*No-ADHD*	
Complex Trauma Onset	*Early Onset (%)*	*Late Onset (%)*	*Early Onset (%)*	*Late Onset (%)*
Attachment Trauma				
Foster care placement	62.5	0	30.9	5.5
Sexual abuse	31.3	3.1	25.5	5.5
Physical abuse	40.6	0	40	0
Maltreatment	59.4	0	41.8	0
Mother's death	6.3	0	7.3	3.6
Father's death	3.1	0	12.7	5.5
Caregiver's death	3.1	0	3.6	1.8
Environmental Trauma				
Parent's substance abuse	59.4	0	45.5	5.5
Domestic violence	12.5	0	16.4	0

are considered together, their occurrence is significantly higher among children diagnosed with ADHD (see Table 3).

DISCUSSION

The findings of this study shows ADHD children experience higher incidences of chronic stress, termed here as *environmental trauma*, and disruptions in attachment relationships, referred to

TABLE 3
Complex Trauma in ADHD and Non-ADHD Hospitalized Children

	ADHD		
Complex Trauma	*No Mean (SD)*	*Yes Mean (SD)*	*F*
Attachment Trauma	1.68 (1.46)	2.5 (1.13)	7.29**
Complex Trauma Environment	0.63 (0.58)	0.62 (0.49)	.008
Presence of Complex Trauma (Attachment & Environment)	2.29 (1.81)	3.12 (1.28)	5.22*
	%	%	X^2
Sexual Abuse	20	12	0.01
Physical Abuse	27	14	0.23

**p<.01, *p<.05

here as *Attachment Trauma*. Moreover, among ADHD children, the number of stressful events experienced by a child ranges from one to four with some children experiencing as many as six separate stressful life events. Most of these complex trauma events occurred before age ten. This study offers evidence that environmental stressors and disturbances in attachment relations are more likely to be found among ADHD children compared to their non-ADHD counterparts.

Complex Trauma—Attachment Type

The findings show ADHD children experience greater disruptions in early attachment relations. Developmental theories state that these early relationships are crucial to the development of the individual, and the way a child functions in the world is formed through the relationship with the primary caregiver, often the mother. Common treatment of ADHD ignores the presence of unconscious factors and filters out any focus on intrapsychic processes (Salomonsoon, 2004). This relationship has been conceptualized in many different areas of psychodynamic theory, but this discussion will focus on Fonagy's theory of mentalization and its importance in conceptualizing and treating ADHD (Fonagy et al., 2002).

The capacity to understand and regulate one's self as a separate yet interrelated entity within the environment has been thought of as an unconscious developmental process by which the child internalizes the earliest representations of self and other through interaction with the primary caregiver(s). Kernberg's (1980) developmental model indicates that beginning in childhood, relationships are internalized as mental representations of self–object interactions complete with emotional and cognitive information about the self and the objects. Personality develops as a child learns to differentiate between self and object representations and as well as how to integrate both the good and bad parts of both. Intense aggressive impulses as a result of poor early interactions can compromise the development of the internal representations, resulting in psychopathology and personality disturbances.

Over the past decade, mentalization, an expansion of previous developmental theories such as Kernberg's, has become pivotal for understanding personality development. Fonagy and colleagues (2002) adopted the term *mentalizationto* describe an individual's implicit and explicit interpretation of his or her own and others' actions as meaningful. The theory of mentalization is focused on the understanding of an individual's affective and interpersonal functioning based on his or her reflecting ability; the primary purpose is to assist individuals in successfully navigating their environment to meet their needs, wants, and wishes.

Much of the theorizing about mentalization is akin to Piaget's concept of "decentration," a developmental task where a child achieves the capacity to distinguish between "being" and "having" an experience (Piaget, 1954). This developmental task is adversely compromised by trauma. As a result of trauma, children's ability to adopt a perspective of themselves as having an experience distinct from the experiencing is impaired. Children experience a "crisis of loyalty" and respond by constricting their knowledge and experience of the trauma balanced with a compliant or defiant self-protective stance vis-a-vis the event (Summit, 1983, in van der Kolk, 2005).

Mentalization is considered to be a developmental achievement that relies on the interactions and emotional relationship between the infant and caregivers. The caregiver's contingent mirroring of and response to the child's internal states facilitates the child's development of the capacity to mentalize. Deviations from this normal developmental path are hypothesized to result in severe forms of adult psychopathology (Fonagy et al., 2002). Fonagy and colleagues theorize that an undeveloped capacity for mentalization is characterized by unstable or inaccurate perceptions or "immature modes of thinking." For example, some may function in the "equivalence mode" when appearance and reality are seen as equivalent, or in the "pretend mode" when mental states are dissociated from external reality. Also noted is a reemergence of a teleological mode of thought. Childhood maltreatment is hypothesized to cause a defensive inhibition of mentalization as a way of the individual to avoid considering the malicious intents of an abusive or neglecting figure (see Fonagy et al., 1996, in Fonagy, 1999). Alternatively, disorganized attachment can lead to a hypersensitivity to mental states, urging the individual to guess immediately what those around them feel and think in order to preempt further traumatization. In this so-called "hyperactive mentalization," mentalizing is distorted by creating pseudo knowledge, avoiding meanings or connections (Fonagy and Target, 2000).

In a study by Schneider-Rosen and Cicchetti (1991), it was found that abused toddlers showed less positive affect when looking at themselves in the mirror than controls. Beeghly and Cicchetti (1994) later showed that these toddlers had a specific deficit in their use of internal state words and that such language tended to be context-bound. Furthermore, Fonagy et al.'s (1996) Menninger Clinic study of maltreated five to eight year olds found specific deficits in tasks requiring mentalization, particularly those children referred for sexual or physical abuse. In his 1999 paper to the Developmental and Psychoanalytic Discussion Group of the American Psychology Association, Fonagy summarizes the above findings and advises that maltreatment seems to result in children's withdrawal from their internal world.

The current authors hope to incorporate the above findings to expand the current understanding of ADHD. As predicted, there is a high cormobidity of attachment trauma and ADHD. As a result, it can be inferred that early traumatic experiences in ADHD children impede the development of mentalization and instead perpetuate nonmentalizing modes of representing internal reality (i.e., equivalence or pretend modes). The ability to mentalize means to be able to "read other's minds" in order to predict their behavior in meaningful ways (Fonagy and Target, 1998). As children learn to understand other people's behavior, they learn to adapt to different situations and be flexible in their responding. This ability to explore their experiences, asserts Fonagy and Target (1998), underlies "affect regulation, impulse control, self-monitoring, and the experience of self-agency"

(p. 92). All the above named skills have been found to be deficient in children diagnosed with ADHD, yet these skills are not addressed in behavior or pharmacological therapy. Based on this theory, it can be deduced that children with ADHD have not developed the ability to manipulate or understand themselves or others within their environment, resulting in poor emotion regulation and impulsivity. ADHD children are often seen by others as being out of touch with reality or living "in their own world." Children with poor mentalization or reflective abilities are really unable to stop themselves and think rationally about the next logical move but rather go about their lives using deficient tools such as fixed attributions and fixed stereotypes to make meaning (p. 93).

A caregiver's reflection of the child's feeling states allows the child to recognize that they are feeling as well as what it is that they are feeling. Therefore, the quality of the attachment as well as the mirroring function affects a child's representations of self and other feeling states for life (Fonagy et al., 2002). There needs to be a healthy ability to contain all types of mental states on the part of the mother in order to make the child's experiences more manageable. As Winnicott (1967) described, the mother's ability to contain and model extreme feeling states allows the child to start to own his or her self-states without overwhelming anxiety or guilt. Normal emotion regulation is accomplished when the child feels secure in knowing that when he or she is in distress, the mother will be nearby to re-establish some sort of equilibrium (Fonagy and Target, 1998). The deficiency results from a disruption in mother-infant mirroring.

When a parent fails to provide the reflective experience for a child, the child often internalizes a distorted and/or empty self-representation. It will be hard for the child to differentiate thoughts and feelings of self and other as there is a failure on the part of the parent to reflect the child's individuality as part of the process. In other words, a neglected or insecurely attached child does not learn to accept his own self, and as a result is completely out of touch with his own and others experiences. Fonagy and Target (1998) states that this can lead to failures of object permanence leading to intense separation anxiety or merger with a proximal object throughout life. These dependencies are often seen in the behaviors, thoughts, and feelings of Borderline Personality Disorders patients who show impulsivity, fears of abandonment, erratic moods, and so forth. It can also be likened to children who are diagnosed with ADHD, as they have extreme difficulty relating to others, shifting environments, erratic moods, and other similar symptoms.

As previously noted, another important link between these findings and what is currently known about ADHD is the fact that such traumatic disruptions in attachment and mirroring can not only lead to emotional impairments but also neurological. It is becoming increasingly recognized that attachment or interaction with others is necessary for the development of biological regulatory functions and neural pathways (p. 412). Schore (2001) found that traumatic attachment, characterized by abuse or neglect, causes impairment in right brain functions (orbitofrontal) and leads to serious impairments in regulation of affect and bodily states. Several other studies have found that the right emotional brain and the nature of procedural memory (storage of nonverbal interpersonal interaction) are impacted by early attachment trauma. Romanian orphans, institutionalized shortly after birth and suffering severe neglect and maltreatment during most of the first year of their lives, show significant loss of cortical function in the fronto-temporal areas (Perry, 1997). In sum, early traumatic experiences in relations between children and caregivers can impair the development of procedural memory, the capacity to develop emotional thinking, memory, a sense of self and understanding others leading to affective dysregulation, impulsivity, poor regulation of anxiety, and aggression (Schore, 2001). Fonagy and Target (2002) also note the connection between early environment and biology in the development of mentalization. ADHD children exhibit all of the above mentioned characteristics and should therefore be considered for dynamic treatment approaches emphasizing the restoration of the mentalizing function.

Fonagy reported (1998) that a record review of 750 records at the Anna Freud Centre confirmed that intensive psychodynamic treatment four to five times a week was effective for children with severe, long-standing emotional disorders, such as conduct disorder, which has often been linked with ADHD. This is evidence that if psychodynamic treatment is consistent and the analysts are able to keep children in treatment, those with severe pathology such as conduct disordered children will show just as positive an outcome as children with more neurotic level disorders. More importantly, the extensive review of these hundreds of cases also narrowed down a vital similarity between the heterogeneous sample of children being examined; that is, all of them seem to lack mentalization to some degree. The severity of the disorder dictates what end of the spectrum their mentalizing functions lie. All of these children lacked a capacity to be aware of their own as well as other people's thoughts and feelings, leading to difficulties with peer relationships, affect regulation, frustration tolerance, and self-image (p. 90).

Working psychoanalytically with ADHD children can help them to find meaning in their own and other behavior by recognizing mental states. Fonagy & Target (1997) suggests that through psychoanalysis, which helps to remember past experiences in the context of a stable and empathic analytic relationship, a child can build the capacity for mentalization and overt symptoms of behavioral dysregulation will subside.

REFERENCES

Anastopoulos, A. D., Shelton, T., DuPaul, G. J. & Guevremont, D. C. (1993), Parent training for attention deficit hyperactivity disorder: Its impact on parent functioning. *Journal of Abnormal Child Psychology, 21*: 581–96.

Anderson, C. A., Hinshaw, S. P. & Simmel, C. (1994), Mother-child interactions in ADHD and comparison boys: Relationships with overt and covert externalizing behavior. *Journal of Abnormal Child Psychology, 22*: 247–65.

Barkley, R. A. (1997a), *ADHD and the Nature of Self-control*. New York: Guildford Press.

———; (1997b), *Defiant Children: A Clinician's Manual for Parent Training*. New York: Guildford Press.

———; (2006), *Attention-deficit Hyperactivity Disorder: A Handbook for Diagnosis and Treatment,*3rd edition. New York: Guilford Press.

——— & Biederman, J. (1997), Toward a broader definition of the age-of-onset criterion for attention-deficit hyperactivity disorder. *Journal of the American Academy of Child and Adolescent Psychiatry, 36*: 1204–10.

Beeghly, M. & Cicchetti, D. (1994), Child maltreatment, attachment, and the self system: Emergence of an internal state lexicon in toddlers at high social risk. *Development and Psychopathology, 6*: 5–30.

Bender, L. (1942). Postencephalitic behavior disorders in children. In: *Encephalitis: A Clinical Study*, J.B. Neal (ed.). New York: Grune & Stratton.

Castellanos, F. X., Giedd, J. N., Marsh, W. L., Hamburger, S. D., Vaituzis, A. C., Dickstein, D. P., et al. (1996), Quantitative brain magnetic resonance imaging in attention-deficit hyperactivity disorder. *Archives of General Psychiatry, 53*: 607–16.

Conway, F., Oster, M. & McCarthy, J. (2010), Exploring object relations in hospitalized children with caregiver loss. *Journal of Infant, Child, and Adolescent Psychotherapy, 9*:108–17.

DuPaul, G. J. & Stoner, G. D. (2003), *ADHD in the Schools: Assessment and Intervention Strategies*. New York: Guilford.

——— & Eckert, T. L. (1997), The effects of school based interventions for attention-deficit hyperactivity disorder: A meta-analysis. *School Psychology Review, 26*: 5–27.

Eresund, P. (2007), Psychodynamic psychotherapy for children with disruptive disorders. *Journal of Child Psychotherapy, 33*: 161–80.

Ethier, L. S., Lemelin, J. P. & Lachorite, C. (2004), A longitudinal study of the effects of chronic maltreatment on children's behavioral and emotional problems. *Child Abuse & Neglect, 28*:1265–78.

Felitti, V. J., Anda, R. F., Nordenberg, D., (1998), The relationship of adult health status to childhood abuse & household dysfunction. *American Journal of Preventive Medicine, 14*:245–58.

Fischer, K.W. & Rose, S. P. (1996). Dynamic growth cycles of brain and cognitive development. In: *Developmental Neuroimaging: Mapping the Development of Brain and Behavior*, R. W. Thatcher, G. R. Lyon, J. Rumsey & N. Krasnegor (eds.). San Diego, CA: Academic Press, pp. 263–79.

———— (1990), Parenting stress and the child with attention deficit hyperactivity disorder. *Journal of Clinical Child Psychology, 19*: 337–46.

Fonagy, P. (1999), Pathological attachments and therapeutic action. Presented at meeting of the Developmental and Psychoanalytic Discussion Group, American Psychoanalytic Association Meeting, May 13, Washington, DC.

———— Leigh, T., Steele, M., Steele, H., Kennedy, R., Mattoon, G., Target, M., & Gerber, A. (1996), The relation of attachment status, psychiatric classification, and response to psychotherapy. *Journal of Consulting and Clinical Psychology, 64*:22–31.

———— & Target, M. (1995), Towards understanding violence: The use of the body and the role of the father. *International Journal of Psychoanalysis, 76*: 487–502.

———— & Target, M. (1996), Playing with reality: I. Theory of mind and the normal development of psychic reality. *International Journal of Psycho-Analysis, 77*: 217–33.

———— & Target, M. (1997), Attachment and reflective function: Their role in self-organization. *Development and Psychopathology, 9*: 670–700.

———— & Target, M. (1998), Mentalization and the changing aims of child psychoanalysis. *Psychoanalytic Dialogues, 8*: 87–114.

———— & Target, M. (2000), Playing with reality III: The persistence of dual psychic reality in borderline patients. *International Journal of Psychoanalysis, 81*, 853–873.

————, Gergely, G., Jurist, E. & Target, M. (2002), *Affect Regulation and Mentalization*.New York: Other Press.

Ford, J. D., Racusin, R., Ellis, C. G., Daviss, W. B., Reiser, J., Fleischer, A., et al. (2000), Child maltreatment, other trauma exposure, and posttraumatic symptomatology among children with oppositional defiant and attention deficit hyperactivity disorders. *Child Maltreatment, 5*:205–17.

Furman, L. (2005), What is attention-deficit hyperactivity disorder (ADHD)?*Journal of Child Neurology, 12*: 994–1002.

Fuster, J. M. (1997), *The Prefrontal Cortex: Anatomy, Physiology, and Neuropsychology of the Frontal Lobe*. New York: Raven.

Goffman, E. (1961), *Asylums: Notes on the Social Situation of Mental Patients and Other Inmates*. New York: Anchor.

Greenacre, P. (1941), The predisposition to anxiety. *Psychoanalytic Quarterly, 10*: 66–94.

Gwynedd, L. & Norris, C. (1999), Including ADHD? *Disability and Society, 14*: 505–17.

Jensen, P. S. (2002). ADHD comorbidity findings for the MTA study: New diagnostic subtypes and their optional treatments. In: *Defining Psychopathology in the 21st Century: DSM-V and Beyond*,J. E. Helzer (ed.). Washington, DC: American Psychiatric Press, pp. 169–92.

Johnston, C. & Mash, E. J. (2001), Families of children with attention-deficit/hyperactivity disorder: Review and recommendations for future research. *Clinical Child and Family Psychology Review, 4*: 183–207.

Kazdin, A. E. (1985), *Treatment of Antisocial Behavior in Children and Adolescents*. Homewood, IL: Dorsey Press.

Kernberg, O. F. (1980), *Internal World and External Reality*. New York: Jason Aronson.

Kessler, R. C., Berglund, P., Demler, O., Jin, R., Merikangas, K. R. & Walters, E. E. (2005), Lifetime prevalence and age-of-onset distributions of DSM-IV disorders in the National Comorbidity Survey Replication. *Archives of General Psychiatry, 62*: 593–602.

Mannuzza, S. & Klein, R. G. (1999). Adolescent and adult outcomes in attention-deficit/hyperactivity disorder. In: *Handbook of Disruptive Behavior Disorders*,H. L. Quay (ed.). New York: Kluwer Academic/Plenum Press, pp. 279–94.

Mash, E. J. & Johnston, C. (1990), Determinants of parenting stress: Illustrations from families of hyperactive children and families of physically abused children. *Journal of Clinical Child Psychology, 19*: 313–28.

———— & Barkley, R. A. (2003), *Child Psychopathology*. New York: Guilford Press.

Nigg, J. T. & Hinshaw, S. P. (1998), Parent personality traits and psychopathology associated with antisocial behaviors in childhood attention-deficit hyperactivity disorder. *Journal of Child Psychology and Psychiatry, 39*: 145–9.

Perry, B. (1997). Incubated in terror: Neurodevelopmental factors in the "cycle of violence." In: *Children in a Violent Society*, J. Osofsky (ed.). New York: Guilford Press, pp. 124–49.

Pfiffner, L. J., Rosen, L. A. & O'Leary, S. G. (1985), The efficacy of an all-positive approach to classroom management. *Journal of Applied Behavior Analysis, 18*: 257–61.

Piaget, J. (1954), *The Construction of Reality in the Child*. New York: Basic Books.

Pynos, R. S., Frederick, C. J., Nader, K., (1987), Life threat and posttraumatic stress in school-age children. *Archives of General Psychiatry, 44*: 1057–63.

Rafalovich, A. (2005), Exploring clinician uncertainty in the diagnosis and treatment of attention deficit hyperactivity disorder. *Sociology of Health & Illness, 27*: 305–23.

Schneider-Rosen, K. & Cicchetti, D. (1991), Early self-knowledge and emotional development: Visual self-recognition and affective reactions to mirror self-image in maltreated and non-maltreated toddlers. *Developmental Psychology, 27*: 481–8.

Schore, A. (2001), The effects of a secure attachment relationship on right brain development, affect regulation, and infant mental health. *Infant Journal of Mental Health, 22*: 7–66.

Summit, R. C. (1983), The child sexual abuse accommodation syndrome. *Child Abuse Neglect, 7*: 177–93.

Target, M. & Fonagy, P. (1996), Playing with reality II: The development of psychic reality from a theoretical perspective. *International Journal of Psycho-Analysis, 77*, 459–79.

van der Kolk, B. A. (2005), Developmental trauma disorder: toward a rational diagnosis for children with complex trauma histories. *Psychiatric Annals, 35*: 401–8.

Widom, C. S. (1997). Child abuse, neglect, and witnessing violence. In: *Handbook of Antisocial Behavior*,D. M. Stoff, J. Breiling & J. D. Maser (eds.). New York: Wiley, pp. 159–170.

Winnicott, D. W. (1967). Mirror-role of the mother and family in child development. In: *The Predicament of the Family: A Psycho-Analytical Symposium*, P. Lomas (ed.). London: Hogarth Press, pp. 26–33.

Wozniak, J., Harding-Crawford, M., Biederman, J., Faracone, S. V., Spencer, T. J., Taylor, A.(1999). Antecedents and complications of trauma in boys with ADHD: Findings from a longitudinal study. *Journal of the American Academy of Child and Adolescent Psychiatry, 38*:48–55.

The Reality-Sampling Deficit and ADHD: Indication for an Active Technique

Barry Jones, MB, BSc, ChB, MRCPsych

Attention-deficit hyperactivity disorder (ADHD) is a common condition and one that the current evidence base highlights as not being best served by the prescription of medication alone (Jensen et al., 2007). The demand facing clinicians is twofold. For the psychiatrist, there is a need to be open to and accommodating of an analytic perspective of ADHD, as one extending understanding of the condition beyond the neurological. For the analyst, I suggest there is a requirement to be open to altering the analytic frame. It is this latter demand that I shall aim to help answer in this article, by highlighting the existence of a reality-sampling deficit in patients with ADHD. Using clinical examples, I shall examine how the concept of a reality-sampling deficit may aid our understanding of the ADHD child's internal experience and their relationship to external reality. In turn, this will lead us toward some adaptations of analytic technique, with an emphasis more upon process than content and links to mentalization-based therapy. I will discuss some relevant aspects of psychoanalytic theory as well as the current evidence base (biological, psychological, and psychodynamic) to form a platform from which we might better help the child with ADHD.

INTRODUCTION TO A THEORY OF A REALITY-SAMPLING DEFICIT

The core symptoms of age-inappropriate hyperactivity, inattentiveness and impulsivity combine to make attention-deficit hyperactivity disorder (ADHD) both a common condition and a miserable one for the child and his family (Kaplan, Sadock and Grebb, 1994; Buitelaar, 2002). In the home, a mixture of frustration and despondency frequently infiltrates the relationship between parent and child. The child moves outward from that fractured environment into the playground, where difficulty in turn-taking makes further social isolation likely. In the classroom, the child may be greeted by a teacher, exasperated by her own failed attempts to educate the inattentive child.

It is a shame, then, that the schools of psychiatry and psychoanalysis have yet to find common ground to tread in an attempt to jointly treat the suffering child, despite being called upon to. From the field of psychiatry, the UK NICE guidelines call for parent training and education programmes as first-line interventions to help those preschool-aged children and those with mild symptoms with medication reserved for those of school age with more severe symptomatology

(NICE, 2008). In the United States, the place of medication has also been called into question, with the finding of a large multicentre trial being that medication benefits were not maintained at three years of follow up in comparison to behavioural treatments (Jensen et al., 2007). In combination, these publications present us with the need to look for an addition to "psychiatric" medication to help better cater to the child's struggle. What response can analytic understanding mount? I shall attempt to provide one such analytic addition.

In his early discussions within the "Project for a Scientific Psychology," Freud the neurologist argued that mounting quantities of energy (denoted as 'Q') derived from sensory perceptions from the exterior and these were reduced by motor discharge. That is, the external world had an influence upon motor activity. An early analytic perspective began to take shape in his mind, enough to recognise that an endogenous and pervasive source of Q related to basic needs, later to be termed instincts. If Q were to mount from either source, internal or external, increased motor activity (hyperactivity) would result. His initial economic views here offer us a pointer to the later structural model and to the idea of a lack of ego strength in relation to constitutional (id) and environmental influences. That is, the child may be overwhelmed from internal and external sources.

Freud adds that if the child does suffer the misfortune of experiencing a stimulus from external reality of sufficient intensity to overwhelm the ego, the child may nonetheless escape being overwhelmed again by a mechanism "which draws the ego's attention to the imminent fresh cathexis of the hostile mnemic image [and] the ego can succeed in inhibiting the passage . . . of unpleasure" (Freud, 1895). Elsewhere I have argued that without this helpful mechanism, inattention to reality may result and excessive stimulation by an object may then once again occur and promote motor discharge (Jones and Allison, 2010).

I will now add an additional layer of complexity and pose the questions: What if the child's capacity to sample the world is askew? What then would his or her experience of the world consist of and what sequelae might we expect to encounter? Freud again paves the way by noting that the psychical apparatus "receives perceptions (which are accompanied by consciousness) and passes the excitation on to the unconscious mnemic systems: but as soon as the cathexis is withdrawn, consciousness is extinguished and the functioning of the system comes to a standstill . . . the periodic non-excitability of the perceptual system . . . at the bottom of the origin of the concept of time" (Freud, 1925). If the capacity to receive perceptions were reduced, an awareness of time would not be coherently constructed through the reality sampling process.

We are here speaking of a disturbance at the interface of internal and external reality and in the transition between primary and secondary processes. Contact with external objects would be perceived internally as temporally truncated. The excessive stimulation from an external object may straightforwardly be in the direction of excess (as in the seduction theory). Such an experience is also in keeping with the high degree of psychosocial adversity seen so often in children with ADHD. (Biederman, Faraone and Monuteaux, 2002). Importantly, though, I am adding to this the notion the idea that excessive stimulation may also be in the direction of asceticism as a result of a reality-sampling deficit.

So we should see evidence of a disturbed sense of time and of primary process activity where secondary processes might be expected to predominate. Neuropsychological testing experiments lead us precisely in this direction. Through such experiments, we are informed about problems with timing behaviour, with the consequence of temporal myopia, present-boundedness, and aversion to delay of rewards (Rubia, 2002; Sagvolden et al., 2005; Sonuga-Barke, 2002).

For the child with ADHD and an incumbent reality-sampling deficit, the world would be populated by objects that insufficiently gratify his instinct derivatives, which would flood forward with greater force under the guiding dominance of the pleasure principle. Motor discharge then allows for a reduction in anxiety and offers the possibility of representation of instinct derivatives as felt (i.e., physical) experiences, all the more important if words cannot be supplied to cathect to the instinct derivatives due to the reality sampling deficit and foreshortened contact with external objects. Hyperactivity is therefore important. Because a sense of time has not been coherently constructed, the child would have an inadequate understanding of temporal frames and appear impulsive. Inattention is entirely understandable if the child has little expectation to be gratified, such that a move from one incomplete contact to the next, in an attempt to draw together a composite of several less than satisfying experiences, presents itself as the alternative. However, this also affords little space within which to be gratified and adds to the child's difficulties.

In recognition of the importance of muscular activity, Bick describes a second skin formation as a consequence to early failures of a parental "primary skin" container function. She says that "faulty development of this primal skin function can be seen to result either from defects in the adequacy of the actual object or from fantasy attacks on it, which impair introjection" (Bick, 1968, p. 483). She points here, then, to the notion of a preobject relating state. She notes that such a development manifests itself "in states of unintegration as distinct from regression involving the most basic types of partial or total, unintegration of body, posture, motility, and corresponding functions of mind, particularly communication. The second skin phenomenon, which replaces first skin integration, manifests itself as either partial or total type of muscular shell or a corresponding verbal muscularity" (Bick, 1968).

I am suggesting the alternative idea that a deficit in the sampling of reality, irrespective of the fantasy of attack or actual environmental failures that could produce the same displacement towards reliance upon the musculature for containment. It is not necessarily a failure of containment per se but also a failure of the capacity to sample the container; that is, a deficit in this *process* that may also give rise to ADHD in some cases. Taken together, we have a link between innate, biological, and environmental influences, with the possibility of both a failure in the container externally and in the reality sampling of container from the internal world of the child.

In his discussion of repression, Freud reminds us that "the patient does not remember anything of what he has forgotten and repressed, but acts it out. He produces it not as a memory, but in action" (Freud, 1914). It is similarly possible, through the presence of a deficit in the sampling of reality, for a series of unintegrated states to exist in parallel, throughout development, and for there to be a similar impact upon memory. In these unintegrated states, disavowal by projective mechanisms is limited due to the limited contact made with reality. Instead, an incumbent reliance upon musculature (activity) follows as a means to achieve some representation of internal states and then to achieve a sense of integration. Thus, both repression and a lack of integration of a series of self-states may promote a tendency toward action.

Analytic attention should then be given to this process by which the child attempts to form a second skin. It is from this very experience that the mobility of cathexes and reliance on muscular activity spring up as a solution, but one that leaves the child or adolescent perpetually trapped in a never-ending quest for representation of instinct derivatives and subsequent gratification as he moves from one object to the next in a hyper-active state. This situation requires an adaptation by the analyst toward the process in which the child involves himself. The analyst must now adopt a position between primary and secondary process, presenting and representing himself to the patient so that the experience of a need-gratifying object can be gradually and safely achieved, thus overcoming the deficit in sampling reality.

A modification to the analytic setting, depending upon the patient presenting, is not a novel idea. When encountering patients, Ferenczi, for instance, notes the requirement for adapting a technique that had not been fully available for analysis by sticking to the fundamental principle of free association. He points out that activity is "not so much an active interference on behalf of the doctor as upon the patient, upon whom are imposed certain tasks . . . " (Ferenczi, 1927). The two phases he describes consist of a demand upon the patient to carry out certain activities previously avoided and a renouncing of these newly found pleasurable activities.

Our activity here, however, with the patient suffering from ADHD, is slightly different. The analytic work may be described within three overlapping but sequential phases, with the trend of the analytic work keeping with but not being exclusive to each phase.

PHASE ONE: FUSION

Here the focus is upon presenting and re-presenting to the patient contact with a need-gratifying object to be made use of and cathected to. With silences kept to a minimum, the presence of the child's reality sampling deficit requires frequent, explicit representation of the analyst in external reality by words and gestures. Mirroring the child's internal affective state is continuously promoted, as in the sense of an analyst involved in an active process similar to the child's. The analyst's activity is of an intensity near to a state of fusion with the patient. As the patient gains the sense of the analyst capable of sustaining interest in the patient's internal experiences, the patient gradually gain the sense of being represented in the analyst's mind. It is only then the second phase of separation can begin.

Case Example

Monica was born deaf to a single mother before being diagnosed as hearing impaired at two years of age. From that point, she had received hearing aids and intensive speech and language input and entered into a mainstream school. With this provision, she was able to hear relatively well and her speech was good. Indeed, she was rather articulate. She described her relationship with her mother as a cold one, perceiving her mother as rather intolerant and austere. Within the school environment, however, she had initially achieved well academically, but her performance then declined as she neared the move into secondary school. The teachers began to note her being easily distracted and, as her school performance deteriorated, frustrations were voiced that she did not seem to take in what the teachers had taught. She had no peer group and was rather isolated at school. After a psychiatric consultation, she received a diagnosis of ADHD whilst her mother received parent training. When her difficulties continued unabated, she was offered medication and declined.

Instead, Monica entered into analysis in her adolescence, and her presentation from the outset was chaotic. She came late to sessions, clutching her mobile phone and continuing those conversations well into the session whilst I sat patiently. She did not use the couch. She would typically move seamlessly from a telephone conversation to speaking to me, talking in a pressured manner as if objects were interchangeable to her. The content of her speech was uttered too fast to be a free association, with contradictory statements juxtaposed and with no awareness of them as mutually exclusive. It seemed to me as if she was speaking directly from the realm of the primary process, presenting parallel but unintegrated and often contradictory aspects of her mind to me. She once, for example, stated that analysis was an utter waste of time and she was better off not coming. In the same breath, she declared that her time with me was invaluable and she could not contemplate doing without it.

Monica would fidget pervasively, biting her nails and shaking her legs. When I did speak, she would raise her voice and talk over me so that I was set to silence. At the end of sessions I would announce the time to finish and she would continue to speak, moving me to stand and then to eventually open the door to indicate the ending. Such was the early period of her analysis.

After some months of this presentation, I began to bear the frustrations so familiar to her teachers, of her not taking in any of what I had to offer. She left me repeatedly with no space from which to talk, and it was only infrequently that I was ever able to complete even the briefest of interpretations. In a sporadic and piecemeal manner, I had managed to wonder aloud about her not using the couch, about her early experience of a parent whom she struggled to hear then moving out of sight as perhaps being terrifyingly recreated if she were to consider such a move to the couch. This produced no response. I wondered about a fear of having to submit to me, with the worry of all the sexual fantasies of her adolescence perhaps being in danger of becoming a reality. Still she remained in the chair, presenting in the same manner.

One day Monica began to speak of having had a restless night. She hadn't slept and had begun to itch, she told me, to the point that she had begun to wonder if she had bedbugs in her mattress. As she spoke, I scratched my arm. It was quite unconscious on my part. Suddenly, she stopped speaking and gave me a broad smile. 'Well, perhaps it is time I started to use the couch," she said, and with that she stood and moved to take her position on the couch.

What had precipitated this move to the couch, where all my analytic efforts had previously failed? I had not, I began to realise, been open to considering that Monica might be requiring an adaptation of the analytic frame and that I might have to do some work to clarify what this change might consist of, that is, to "listen" differently. I began to consider Monica's treatment of me from the outset as an irrelevance as perhaps being indicative of her having little expectation that I might gratify her needs. Like her mother, might I also be intolerant and austere? This picture might be made all the more stark by her difficulty in hearing me — not just in my spoken words but also in all the grunts and groans that would otherwise convey that I was alive to her. When I had scratched my arm, I had been able to convey that I was alive to her and to what she was saying *in action*. Her smile of satisfaction was perhaps, then, at having successfully recruited me into her muscular armor as a way of representing her feelings, that is, of recruiting me *into the process* that she had developed to cope with her deficit in sampling reality. I too had to develop a modified way of listening to her, with my whole being, including with my bodily and verbal musculature.

Parsons, in his writings, describes a flexible way of listening that rests not just upon the external analytic frame but also upon an internal one. He notes that "a secure internal setting allows flexibility in the external setting without sacrifice of its analytic quality. The internal setting can help analysts listen inwardly to themselves in a way that is free-floating with regard to their internal processes. This points beyond usual ideas of countertransference" (Parsons, 2007).

His notion rests upon the premise of the analytic framework as being an internal and external one and consequently the "strength of the concept in making possible considerable flexibility in the external setting without any sacrifice of its analytic quality" (Parsons, 2007). This flexibility affords the analyst a means of listening to his patient differently.

If we consider Monica as being "deaf to the world" in her sampling of reality, we must also recognize that the world must seem deaf to her in that people are from her perspective not involving themselves in making meaningful and sustained contact with her. I began to be more open in this way to Monica, feeling free to grunt, move, and speak to Monica. In doing so, I was far more active than usual with patients. Indeed one might, with this "usual" reference point in mind, say that I was being "hyper-active." Whilst being more in touch with what moved me inwardly and commenting upon it, I was equally consciously aware at times of openly and freely conveying "not knowing" when no insight or interpretation came to me. I spoke far more often from *within this process*, between primary and secondary levels, presenting and representing myself to Monica as someone who could tolerate a less than perfect fit between what was being said to me and what I was capable in that moment of understanding, that is, of tolerating and giving expression to a less than perfect coupled system between my internal reality and the reality that Monica presented to me.

By inhabiting this dual position, being both active in my listening and conveying both knowing and not knowing, a language was gradually developed with Monica. I had presented myself as an echo chamber to her own internal states so that she was able to feel me as being within the process with her.

Why is this so important? If we consider that an inner state of being, of bodily self-monitoring, must be brought in line with external reality if it is to achieve survival and progress toward ego integration, then the existence of a reality-sampling deficit places a greater stress upon the analyst to help in the process of coupling these two states. Modern neurobiology describes this dynamic of fluctuating coupling of inner and external world states as "core coupling," being a necessity in the establishment of a coherent sense of an "autobiographical self" (Damasio, 1999).

In line with my emphasis on the process of core coupling, Monica was gradually able to develop verbal representations of her own internal experiences. "Words are often so empty and meaningless," she said once, adding with a tentative curiosity, "except I understand more now what you're saying." She was expressing an awareness of moving toward a different, new representational system that involved words and a recognition of a world within which both she and I could exist alongside one another.

PHASE TWO: SEPARATION

Later in her analysis, Monica spoke of having been invited into a text exchange with a man, wherein prose was being created and swapped. She found that she was rather adept at this pursuit, feeling it to be enjoyable. She contrasted this with a previous experience of "lurching from crisis to crisis." This more recent experience, she said, felt more as if it had creatively emerged from her. The fact that this man had a name similar to my own led me easily into making a "you mean me" transference interpretation about her experience of using words with me. Monica began writhing around on the couch, restating her narrative of the event in protest, as if I needed to hear it again. Indeed I did. She became increasingly provocative, clipping my utterances every time I began to speak, leaving me frustrated and setting me once more to silence.

Listening inwardly to our exchange again led me to acknowledge that my interpretation had been doubly damaging to Monica. First, I had called upon her to give up the person she consciously thought she was talking about and consider me instead. This involved an act of separation and reconnecting in her mind, difficult because her reality-sampling deficit had made contact with others fragile already, so that any such contact was being anxiously guarded and prized by her (just like her primary school was prized and the separation involved in moving to secondary school was anxiety provoking). Provoking me was an attempt to ensure that contact with someone remains. Second, the "you mean me" interpretation had also held within it the notion that my understanding of reality was better than her own and she should accept this foreign thing in place of her own fragile understanding, rather than be helped to augment the latter.

For both these reasons, I began in my listening to only ever interpret *from within* the transference and with a respectful handling of projective mechanisms. After all, such functioning is indicative of an attempt to make contact with reality. Therefore, it is to be initially promoted rather than dismissed. Parsons describes a particular way of listening that is of help here, denoting "abstracting meaning from a patient's words as distinct from hearing meaning in what the patient says. In doing the former, the analyst risks distancing himself from the patient. In doing the latter, one offers himself up as 'an echo-chamber' for the patient's words" (Parsons, 2007).

Monica frequently cited this event within her analysis as evidence of her capacity to creatively engage with the world. Increasingly she voiced the desire for (and pursued) further creative experiences with a boyfriend, within a college course and in a peer group. She began to contrast this way of being as distinct from her chaotic entry into analysis, charting her development to the current point and often wondering about my evolving experience of her. Referencing herself in this way, by which I mean the act of establishing oneself and others within a context specific narrative (Jones and Miller, 2011), allowed Monica to consider herself in the here and now and imagine a potential future. Further, the growing capacity to consider herself in relation to me and consider my state of mind pointed to an increasing ability to "mentalize" (Bateman and Fonagy, 2004).

In turn, a qualitative distinction between her internal reality and external reality began to emerge, placing her in a more tenable and integrated position in her relating to the world. She moved to begin and end sessions on time, and the activity she displayed on the couch lessened. Brief silences emerged between us, within which she appeared to be able to "wait and see" what might emerge.

PHASE 3: THE FLEXIBLE ADAPTATION TO REALITY

Monica displayed increasingly an active and incisive mind wholly capable of verbally representing her own experience of the process of her analysis. Her sampling of reality appeared more continuous. For example, upon noticing herself again interrupting me and moving on to another thought instead, she paused and remarked, "It's as if I don't want to take in what you say and digest it, because I worry then you'll end and leave me alone. So I come up with the next thing and then the next to speak about, but wouldn't taking something in actually be more satisfying?" She was able to wonder then if her previous way of impulsivity and inattentiveness, of moving interchangeably and hyperactively between people, had perpetuated her plight of never being sated.

Moving was under dominance of the pleasure principle in a hyperactive search for a need gratifying object, Monica had not delayed long enough to achieve satisfaction by taking something meaningful inside of her. Her frustration then was no longer just because of her deafness (i.e., of her initial reality sampling deficit), but rather because wishes continued to be denied an existence in her mind consciously long enough to be gratified.

As she gained insight into this facet of her presentation, her hyperactivity reduced further and her capacity to mentalize increased. Her relation to external reality bore fruit as she moved to undertake a college course in business studies, where she subsequently achieved a first class degree. Whilst there she became an active and accomplished sportswoman at college; her activity was now imbued with a sense of enjoyment and direction. She has to date never revisited the psychiatrist for medication.

The Wider Evidence Base and the Reality-Sampling Deficit

Monica exhibits a clear reality-sampling deficit by way of her hearing impairment. Obviously, not all children with ADHD will display such impairment, so does this concept have use beyond Monica's isolated case? From Monica, her initial reality-sampling deficit was rectified physically by the provision of hearing aids. However, the reality-sampling deficit continued as a psychic way of being. We may then hope to find that a sampling of reality could be "psychically" disrupted in a variety of other further subtle ways, with a relative de-coupling between internal and external reality similarly occurring and again giving rise to the symptoms of ADHD. Thankfully, we do find such subtle disruptions when examining current thinking and research around the diagnosis of ADHD.

The Executive Dysfunction Hypothesis

If the ego has a diminished capacity to sample reality, as we have discussed, and therefore exhibits a reduced ability to offer up a "substrate" for gratification of id instinct derivatives, then we might expect the id under dominance of the pleasure principle to become excessively demanding. The ego is then "merely obeying the warning of the pleasure principle" and acquiescing to the demands of the id (Freud, 1923). The reality-sampling deficit here lies obviously with the ego, offering consequentially a paucity of pleasure to the id. Similarly, the fronto-striatal/executive dysfunction hypothesis (Pennington and Ozonoff, 1996) postulates a disrupted communication between the seat of executive function (the prefrontal cortex/the ego) and the brainstem (id). (For a fuller discussion of the anatomical correlates of psychoanalytic concepts, refer to Jones and Allison, 2010.)

Excessive Internal Stimulation

Adding to the excessively demanding nature of the id, in not being offered a satiating sample of reality, is the possibility that the mechanism by which pleasure is sensed is intrinsically and physiologically damaged. Such a picture is in evidence in addictive and immediately gratifying behaviours (Volkow, 2001), where dopamine receptors are fewer in number. Methylphenidate, the first line drug used in treating ADHD, increases dopamine availability, which in turn is centrally implicated in the sensation of "pleasure." Again, the id surges forward to present its demands to the ego, in keeping with the pleasure principle.

Taking the above two points together, we arrive at a picture of a reality sampling deficit that may combine with an innate propensity to seek immediate gratification, borne of a reduced capacity to generate pleasure. This parallels the psychiatric concept of a dual pathway hypothesis for ADHD (Sonuga-Barke, 2002).

I am thus far not suggesting that the reality sampling deficit is the only "route into" ADHD; rather, it is one useful concept to add to the variegated aetiologies co-existing in combination. Again, such graded, variegated aetiology is in keeping with a modern view (Castellanos et al., 2006). In light of this, we might wonder what bearing external reality has upon the impact of the reality-sampling deficit with regards ADHD.

Panksepp has described the inherent, biological importance of play in mammals. He suggests that the rising numbers of ADHD diagnoses might be a rebound phenomenon, with mounting excitation arising through enforced abstinence from play (Panksepp, 1998). Abstinence in play may overwhelm the ego and heighten the need for a play activity, urgently performed in order to reduce internal excitation once more. Similarly, the high degree of concurrent psychosocial adversity (or "external excitation") seen so often in the presentation of children with ADHD (Biederman et al., 2002) may provide further stimulation of the ego and a propensity toward action.

What does this variegated picture of the aetiology of ADHD mean with regards to clinical management of the child? Does the three-stage model discussed retain validity in relation to this complex picture?

Case Example

Gareth, a burly boy of eight years, had struggled to find a home in the care system. His early life had been marred by parental abuse and neglect, with him being frequently beaten and starved by his single mother. The visiting social worker had noted the home to be a cold environment, with no toys or children's playthings in evidence.

He had entered into a succession of foster care placements, which had broken down due to his "unruly and wild" behaviour. Ignoring instruction or boundaries and being often violent at home and school, he soon came to the attention of child psychiatry where he had attained the diagnoses of ADHD and conduct disorder. He was commenced on methylphenidate at the age of seven. His foster carer attended a "parent training" programme with him, where the initial focus was on attending to Gareth's current mental state and offering a running narrative.

In combination, this approach served Gareth reasonably well initially. His foster care noted that Gareth began to pause enough to listen to instruction at home, as did the teachers at school, but he then would continue to disobey. The "parent training" continued and began then to include elements of reward and punishment, to "shape" Gareth's behaviour to the foster carer's expectations and in line with the reinforcement theory behavioural model upon which it is largely based (McMahon and Forehand, 2003). At this point, Gareth presentation deteriorated. He became increasingly provocative, with unremitting temper tantrums continuing across settings and culminating in suspension from school.

When he entered analysis at eight years old, he was continuing to receive his methylphenidate at a therapeutic dose. However, his foster care placement was again under threat of breaking down and he was socially isolated at school, having been placed in a class for those with learning difficulties.

Phase One: Fusion

Whilst not pervasively and overtly hyperactive in early sessions, Gareth would instead sit huddled on the floor by my legs, as if grafting himself to me to keep contact. His inability to play was striking, moving from one toy to the next, as if never resting long enough to wonder within his play. Similarly, I was required to be active within sessions, often speaking as he moved from one incomplete thing to the next. Silences were minimal and a contingent marked mirroring to the fore. By this, I mean merely empathically reflecting the Gareth's feelings in such a way that he can grasp that I am showing him a safe representation of his feelings in words (Fonagy, 2008).

Both of us seldom paused for thought. Instead, as the echo chamber, I was involved in presenting my words alongside his action. From this position of fusion, however, it seemed that nothing could be fully gratifying for either of us. It was this that I began to focus on *with* Gareth, again speaking from within the transference relationship and with the supposition that contact with me was prized and separation traumatic.

Here again, the emphasis is upon the importance of core coupling. "When I was a child, like you, I would for example remark, 'I liked to play with trains, but now that I'm a grown up I can't quite remember how to. Can you help me remember?'" This technical adaptation, of concretely referencing myself, afforded a better negotiation of the 'reality sampling deficit' such that Gareth was able to confidently retain contact with me in his wondering and a curiosity about his own imagined future (in me presenting myself both as a 'doing' child and my future as a 'thinking' adult) emerged. This process promoted slowly the emergence of a space between us to play, in which he could both think and do.

Phase Two: Separation

Brief periods began to emerge of a more sustained play, whilst still keeping contact with my leg. If I spoke and deviated from the play to interpret, which was in itself chaotic and difficult for me to make sense of, I would be scolded. He was to control the separation. My interpretations again here had to be quite concrete and explicit and include references to me as child. Again, my own referencing in this way promoted the possibility of Gareth establishing himself within a temporal frame. That is, Gareth had to know that I had developed and waited within the process in which he found himself. I was an echo chamber, extending into the future and inviting him involve himself in his imagined future with me.

Gradually he moved into the centre of the room, away from me, and his play began to involve the idea of a child needing cared for, then being shut away only to wait and see if he cold be rediscovered. He became increasingly thoughtful and began to involve a wondering about me, too, about how similar we might be, about where I was from, where I might live, and with whom. This capacity, to wonder about himself in relation to me and about me marked a developing ability to mentalize.

Further, this analytic "process" approach had allowed him to emerge into the experience of and "arrive at being" (Jones and Miller, 2011) with, but separate from, an object rather than being subjected suddenly to his separateness, as he had feared. His curiosity developed within him, involving himself in an internal a space within which he was now free not to know.

Phase 3: Flexible Adaptation to Reality

Gareth continued in analysis for another year, with my own activity diminishing as play became consolidated. One afternoon he was playing cricket with me in the garden when he hit the ball into a rose bush. He began to attempt to retrieve the ball, scratching his arms as he struggled to gain access through the bush. Worried about injury, I asked him to stop. He turned and smiled. "Well, we know the ball's safe," he said. "We just can't see it." He paused and added, "I wasn't safe at home." "And I wasn't there to see it," I noted, referencing myself. Gareth nodded and we walked quietly back to the consulting room, together and separate.

When subsequently reviewed by the child psychiatrist, Gareth's was found no longer to meet the threshold criteria for ADHD, and he settled well into a long-term foster care placement and school.

Gareth's case is a composite of aetiologicals factors. Methyphenidate seemed to help in addressing the innate damaged pleasure mechanism. The parenting programme, through the focus of attending to Gareth's internal world and "contingently mirror," of that experience, began to offer a remedy to the environmental failure and lack of play. This psychological approach is borne from the ethos that "a child's willing cooperation with a parent will be enhanced by the parent having previously demonstrated a willingness to cooperate with the child" (Parpall and Maccoby, 1985) and offers overlap with the notion of developmental help (Hurry, 1998).

However, in Gareth's case the move to a cooperation and compliance with reality brought a disruption to this process. This attempt had proven problematic when boundaries were set precisely because compliance with reality brought up immediately the anxiety in Gareth of the cessation of contact with a need-gratifying object.

Winnicott (1971) describes two distinct modes of living and engaging with the world. One based on a compliance with reality involves "the world and its details being recognized, but only as something to be fitted in with or demanding adaptation." Here the feeling of separateness is stark. The other mode involves the task of perception and setting this perception in relation to one's past experience. He states that it is this method of "creative apperception" that "makes the individual feel that life is worth living, while living by compliance produces in the end a sense of futility."

The focus, within his analysis, upon a reality-sampling deficit underlined his requirement for me to be a need-gratifying object capable of creative apperception, along with demonstrating a "willing cooperation" to involve myself in his world, as above. I was of developmental help to him. Mutative interpretations were supplanted by active listening. This afforded an external representation paralleling the primary process activity that predominates and allowing a side step into word cathexis. I interjected between his psyche and burly musculature, being open to hypertrophy and ready to use my own verbal musculature to achieve word cathexis. Being open to this means being open to a flood of primary process activity and approach a running commentary *within* a process. Presenting myself to Gareth as a child and adult (the act of "referencing") afforded the sense of an object that could continue within a temporal frame and so offered the reassurance of ongoing contact. He was able then in his mind to develop a space to think and create from *within*, alongside action. He had moved from a world dominated by compliance and protests against this to a being creatively engaged with the world and capable of play.

THE ACTIVE TECHNIQUE AND THE BORDERLINE COUSIN

The clinical approach I offer above bears some similarities to one used in treating borderline patients in that the stage of fusion involves a high degree of contingent mirroring and there is a move gradually to reflective functioning and mentalizing. However, the activity displayed by the analyst in relation to ADHD, in my experience, is of a more pervasive nature. One might wonder why. It may be that when the origin of disturbance lies initially external to the child and largely within the child's environment, that the capacity to cathect to reality remains intact and so the need to actively and impulsively engage with the world is only ever episodic, when reality fails. The analyst needs perhaps to be most active with the borderline patient in these moments and less so at other times, recognizing that the sampling of reality can at times progress normally. Contrast this with the pervasive nature of ADHD, which points perhaps to the disturbance lying more internal to the child. Here, the instincts exert a continuous pressure from the ego from which it can never escape. There is a call upon the analyst then to present and represent himself for contact and cathexes in a more pervasive manner.

CONCLUSION

The concept of a reality-sampling deficit provides us with one important aetiological factor when considering ADHD, where an analytic adaptation and understanding may helpfully serve the child. Rather than competing with a medical management, it may be complimentary to clinical care.

For analytic work to prove fruitful, the analyst needs to consistently embody a shift of emphasis, replacing process over content as principally important to his work. This entails the analyst actively attending to the process by which internal states are represented through muscular activity in the child. This shift in thinking requires a particular way of listening that is more fluid than the traditional analytic frame allows for, with the analyst positioning himself between primary and secondary process activity as the echo chamber to the child's internal world and feeling free to respond from that position in an active manner.

Projective mechanisms used by the child indicate contact with reality and thus are to be respected and galvanized. The analyst works to contingent mirror the child's experience. He works alongside the child, interpreting within the transference and by using referencing to aid the child in establishing himself within a temporal frame. In doing so, he fosters the beginnings of mentalizing and the further development of higher order representation of instinct derivatives in the child. The child develops the capacity to differentiate internal and external world states. This clinical work is phase driven, with the analyst working more to approach a point of fusion initially before a trend toward the handling of separation dominates the scene. Finally, a flexible adaptation to reality is reached.

In this way, the child is helped toward a more integrated way of functioning, can learn to trust in a gratifying contact with the world, and develop a creative engagement with reality. Hyperactivity diminishes as the search for a need-gratifying object comes to an end. Inattention and impulsivity decline as the child learns to give up the notion of cumulative gratification through establishing partial contact with successive objects. Instead, gratification is derived from sustained and meaningful contact with his objects as secondary process functioning establishes itself within the child's mind. Sampling of reality gradually increased and the pre-existent reality-sampling deficit is overcome.

REFERENCES

Bateman, A. & Fonagy, P. (2004), Psychotherapy for borderline personality disorder: Mentalization-based treatment. England: Oxford University Press.

Bick, E. (1968), The experience of the skin in early object-relations. *International Journal of Psycho-Analysis*, *49*: 484–5.

Biederman, J., Faraone, S. & Monuteaux, M. (2002), Differential effect of environmental adversity by gender: Rutter's index of adversity in a group of boys and girls with and without ADHD. *American Journal of Psychiatry*, *159*: 1556–62.

Buitelaar, J. K. (2002), Epidemiology: What have we learned over the last decade? In Seija Sandberg (Ed.), Hyperactivity and Attention-Deficit Disorders, 2nd edition. Cambridge, UK: Cambridge University Press.

Castellanos, F., Sonuga-Barke, E., Milham, M. & Tannock, R. (2006), Characterizing cognition in ADHD: Beyond executive dysfunction. *Trends in Cognitive Sciences*, *10*(3): 117–23.

Damasio, A. (1999), *The Feeling of What Happens: Body and Emotion in the Making of Consciousness*. New York: Harcourt, Brace.

Ferenczi, S. (1927), The Further Development of an Active Therapy in Psychoanalysis. In S. Ferenczi (Ed.), Further Contributions to the Theory and Technique of Psychoanalysis. New York: Boni & Liveright Publishers.

Fonagy, P. (2008). The mentalization-focused approach to social development. In: Mentalization: Theoretical Considerations, *Research Findings, and Clinical Implications (Psychoanalytic Inquiry Book Series: Volume 29)*, F. N. Busch (ed.). New York: Analytic Press, pp. 3–56.

Freud, S. (1895), *Project for a Scientific Psychology. The Standard Edition of the Complete Psychological Works of Sigmund Freud, Volume 1: Pre-Psycho-analytic.* Publications and unpublished drafts, p. 324.

_____ (1914). Remembering, repeating, and working-through. Further recommendations on the technique of psycho-analysis II. In: *The Standard Edition of the Complete Psychological Works of Sigmund Freud Volume X11*, p. 150.

_____ (1923). The Ego and the id. In: *The Standard Edition of the Complete Psychological Works of Sigmund Freud, Volume 19: The Ego and the Id and Other Works*, p. 22.

_____ (1925). A note upon the mystic writing pad. In: *The Standard Edition of the Complete Psychological Works of Sigmund Freud, Volume XIX*, p. 230.

Hurry, A. (1998). Psychoanalysis and developmental therapy. In: *Psychoanalysis and Developmental Theory*, A. Hurry (ed.). London: Karnac, pp. 32–73.

Jensen, P., Arnold, L., Swanson J., Vitiello, B., Abikoff, H., Greenhill, L., Hechtman, L., Hinshaw, S., Pelham, W., Wells, K., Conners, C., Elliott, G., Epstein, J., Hoza, B., March, J., Molina, B., Newcorn, J., Severe, J., Wigal, T., Gibbons,

R. & Hur, K. (2007), 3-year follow up of the NIMH MTA study. *Journal of the American Academy of Child & Adolescent Psychiatry*, *46*(8): 989–1002.

Jones, B. & Allison, E. (2010), An integrated theory for ADHD. *Psychoanalytic Psychotherapy*, *24*(3): 279–95.

_____ & Miller, S. (submitted), Emerging as a personality disorder service. *Psychoanalytic Psychotherapy*.

Kaplan, H., Sadock, B. & Grebb, J. (1994), *Attention-deficit Disorders. Kaplan and Sadock's Synopsis of Psychiatry*, 7th edition. Baltimore, MD: Williams & Wilkins, pp. 1063–8.

McMahon, R. & Forehand, R. (2003), *Helping the Noncompliant Child*. New York: Guilford Press.

National Institute for Health and Clinical Excellence (NICE). (2008), *Attention Deficit Hyperactivity Disorder: Diagnosis and Management of ADHD in Children, Young People and Adults. NICE Clinical Guideline 72*. National Collaborating Centre for Mental Health. London: Author.

Panksepp, J. (1998), *Affective Neuroscience: The Foundations of Human and Animal Emotions*. New York: Oxford University Press.

Parpal, M. & Maccoby, E. (1985), Maternal responsiveness and subsequent child compliance. *Child Development*, *56*(5): 1327.

Parsons, M. (2007), Raiding the inarticulate: The internal analytic setting and listening beyond countertransference. *International Journal of Psychoanalysis*, *88*: 1441, 1445, 1447.

Pennington, B. & Ozonoff, S. (1996), Executive functions and developmental psychopathology. *Journal of Child Psychology and Psychiatry*, *37*: 51–87.

Rubia, K. (2002), The dynamic approach to neurodevelopmental psychiatric disorders: Use of fMRI combined with neuropsychology to elucidate the dynamics of psychiatric disorders, exemplified in ADHD and schizophrenia. *Behavioural Brain Research*, *130*: 47–56.

Sagvolden, T., Johansen, E. B., Aase, H., & Russell, V.A. (2005), A dynamic developmental theory of attention-deficit/hyperactivity disorder (ADHD) predominantly hyperactive/impulsive and combined subtypes. *Behavioural & Brain Science*, *28*: 397–419.

Sonuga-Barke, E. (2002), Psychological heterogeneity in AD/HD – a dual pathway model of behaviour and cognition. *Behavioural Brain Research*, *130*: 29–36.

Winnicott, D. W. (1971), *Playing and Reality*. London: Tavistock, p. 65.

Psychoanalytic Conceptualizations of the Internal Object in an ADHD Child

Björn Salomonsson, M.D., Ph.D.

Several factors contribute to the dearth of psychoanalytic treatments and conceptualizations of attention-deficit hyperactivity disorder (ADHD). The author argues that psychoanalysis can contribute to standard treatments of such children. The prerequisites are the child's interest in change and the analyst's insight as to the legitimate aims of such treatments: to help the child discover his inner world and the connections between emotions, thought processes, and symptoms. The patient's reception of interventions varies. Sometimes, he is open to the verbal content of words. Other times, he reacts mainly to nonverbal aspects of the analyst's communication such as tone of voice, dress, or demeanor. The motor behind these vacillations is the present state of the child's internal object. When it is harsh, unyielding, and ridiculing, interventions are taken as assaults that must be defended at. Only in moments when it is welcoming and benevolent can the child use the intervention for building up his ego. The child's so-called semiotic capacity is related to the shifting state of the internal object. This has repercussions on both transference and countertransference. The discussion is illustrated by a six-and-a-half-year-old boy in child psychoanalysis while being in remedial and pharmacological treatment.

The worldwide prevalence of attention-deficit hyperactivity disorder (ADHD) exceeds five percent (Polanczyk et al., 2007). Though the figures vary between studies and countries, they seem equal in Europe and North America. ADHD thus constitutes an enormous challenge for child psychiatry and, as is increasingly recognized, for adult psychiatry. In previous papers (Salomonsson, 2004, 2006), I have pointed out that psychoanalysts have largely refrained from analyzing ADHD children and from conceptualizing the disorder in terms of psychoanalytic theory. Their reluctance seems based on a misinterpretation of the diagnosis, namely, that it would be based on a distinct and consistent neurophysiological cause. In fact, ADHD is not diagnosed via neuroimaging or any other neurophysiological investigation. Rather, it is established when interviews with the parents and the child demonstrate a sufficient number of symptoms within the domains of hyperactivity, impulsivity, and difficulties in attention.

However, since the term "neuropsychiatric disorders" is now used for ADHD and some other disorders, it may have led therapists to believe that every such child has a demonstrable cerebral dysfunction that should not be "touched" by psychotherapy. I consider this a mistake from a scientific theoretical perspective. Every mental phenomenon, whether normal or disordered, is paralleled by neuro-chemical processes. All psychotherapists, however, whether analytic or behavioral, deal with mental suffering without knowing the patient's biochemistry or neurophysiology. The crucial issue is whether they claim that therapy will rectify the biological dysfunction or, alternately, that it might diminish the patient's suffering via the therapeutic relationship. The first claim is unjustified, whereas the second is legitimate.

Another reason for refraining from psychotherapy with ADHD children might be that stimulant medication is the treatment which most consistently has been shown to be effective. If therapy is added, it is claimed that it should be a behavioral treatment (Barkley, 2006). One reason for disregarding psychodynamic therapy is that, to my knowledge, there exists only one completed randomized controlled trial, the New York Montreal (NYM) study (Klein et al., 2004), comparing a multimodal treatment including psychotherapy with metylphenidate medication (Abikoff et al., 2004a). These studies (Abikoff et al., 2004a, b; Hechtman et al., 2004a, b) showed no advantages to psychotherapy on the children's social functioning, symptoms, or academic achievements and very small effects on parental practice.

However, one should not draw hasty conclusions. The NYM study did not clearly define the therapies' content and theoretical base. This implies that "high-grade treatment with MPH [metylphenidate] was compared with psychosocial treatments of unknown quality" (Barkley, 2006, p. 685). The therapies aimed to address "negative emotional states [experiencing criticism and rejection, demoralization and poor self-esteem] and to provide children with an ally to assist them in developing better problem-solving tactics, self-effectiveness, and greater self-control" (Klein et al., 2004, p. 797). Therapies were delivered once weekly for a year, then once monthly for another year. If one views psychotherapy as functioning by the establishment of a transference field in which symptoms and character traits are approached, the frequency and length in the NYM therapies seem vastly insufficient. In contrast, if therapies were of a supportive kind, frequency and length might be adequate. Then, however, the results did not apply to psychodynamic therapy.

Another factor is that the NYM cohort excluded children with conduct disorder. It is known from the large MTA study (The MTA Cooperative Group, 1999) that the best results were obtained from combining medication with behavioral treatment. As Barkley (2006) has emphasized, such combined treatments were especially effective on non-ADHD symptoms, such as oppositional/aggressive and internalizing symptoms, social skills, parent-child relations, and so forth. One might ask if medication is especially effective on the typical ADHD symptoms, whereas psychotherapy is more efficacious for the emotional and relational non-ADHD symptoms. Preliminary results from an RCT in Frankfurt (Leuzinger-Bohleber and Fischmann, 2010, also reported in this issue) support this conjecture. Significant effects favoring two-year-long psychodynamic therapies were obtained on anxiety and aggression but not on hyperactivity.

A further reason for analysts to step back from ADHD children is a resentment toward any wholesale thinking about individual beings (Gilmore, 2002). Analysts dislike bringing together patients into diagnostic entities that are based on manifest symptoms but exclude unconscious influences. From a psychoanalytic perspective this attitude is legitimate, but we might turn it into a constructive scientific effort. An important issue for future research is, I suggest, whether subgroups among ADHD children might be affected differentially by medication and/or psychodynamic therapy and/or behavioral interventions. My experience, which thus would need to be corroborated by systematic studies, is that psychotherapy should not be instituted with the primary aim of improving attention and activity problems. Here, medication seems more efficacious. Rather, it should be suggested when a child displays that he wants to learn about and handle the emotions behind his ADHD symptoms. Note, however, that the analyst must read between the lines of the child's communication, since no child will seek help with the explicit aim of "help me to understand myself better." He will rather express his interest by a smile or a comment about the analyst's office, such as "this window is cool . . ."

My position is that psychoanalysis may contribute in two ways to ADHD treatments. It might complement standard treatments by helping the child to grow emotionally, and it might increase our understanding of the internal world of these children. These goals can be achieved only via lengthy and high-frequency psychodynamic therapies. The many therapies that have emerged over the years (for a summary, see Barkley, 2006) aim at regulating and correcting behavior, sometimes also emotions. Psychoanalysis aims at something different, namely, to help the child learn about his inner world within the therapeutic relationship. The varieties of this relationship may also help him understand his behavior with classmates and family members. Last but not least, analysis may reveal how his symptoms are connected with varying feelings.

This article is a contribution toward understanding the links between the child's internal world and his overt symptoms. It focuses on the child's internal object, that is, how we may reconstruct its origins and observe its manifestations during sessions. In brief, to the child this object seems inaccessible, dismissive, and contemptuous. When he tries to get in contact with it, it rejects and derides his efforts. Such experiences may unleash impulsivity, hyperactivity, and emotional outbreaks. When this occurs within the transference, it opens up possibilities for psychoanalytic reflection together with the child.

PSYCHOANALYTIC MODELS OF ADHD

I want first to underscore what I regard as the legitimate and nonlegitimate claims of psychoanalysis, respectively, in treatments of ADHD. The psychoanalytic method cannot establish any *general* causality behind symptoms. If such explanations exist, they belong to the realm of natural sciences. The analyst cannot reject or confirm, for example, that "evidence points to neurological and genetic factors as the greatest contributors to this disorder" (Barkley, 2006, p. 219) or that "ADHD cannot and does not arise from purely social factors" (p. 220). Anyone who states that ADHD arises solely from social or, for that matter, neurological or genetic factors should recall Freud's (1895) etiological equation of mental disorders. He suggests that when a disorder appears we should differentiate between its precipitating causes, the necessary preconditions, the specific cause and, finally, "the concurrent causes, which are not necessarily present every time, and which cannot produce the effect by themselves alone" (p. 135).

No research, whether psychological or biological, has provided evidence for any *specific* cause of ADHD. Truly, psychological factors like early attachment patterns or family environmental factors have been shown to associate with conduct problems (Erikson et al., 1985; Lyons-Ruth, 1996; Fearon and Belsky, 2011). It is also known that conduct problems and ADHD have a high comorbidity (Jensen, Martin and Cantwell, 1997; Spencer, Biederman and Mick, 2007). The only conclusion we can draw is that psychological factors might be *concurrent* causes of conduct disorder and ADHD. Therefore, when Barkley (2006) writes that "social factors do not create ADHD or contribute through some social mechanism to causing this disorder" (p. 220), I agree with the first statement and disagree with the second. As we understand the unconscious meanings of a symptom, they might include the child's *experiences* of, for example, an unavailable mother or a vacillating father. If so, these factors are concurrent causes. This does not imply that all such mothers or fathers have ADHD children. Neither does it imply that all such children experience their parents this way or that they have such parents in "reality."

I will now briefly summarize the rather scarce psychoanalytic studies on ADHD. To Rainwater (2007), ADHD symptoms represent a manic defense by which the child seeks to avoid his "emotionally intense inner reality" (p. 74). He quotes Klein (1935) in that these excruciating emotions arise after the child has projected aggression on the object and then fears retaliation from it. In the next step, depressive guilt and remorse indicate to the child that he must restitute the object. The resulting hyperactivity is the child's effort to control the object and to avoid "the pain of internal reality" (Rainwater, 2007, p. 80). Hyperactivity is thus a manic defense (Winnicott, 1935) which aims at preventing the child from mourning. Rainwater summarizes that ADHD behavior may express the child's defense against "unconscious depressive and perhaps terrifying forces in his inner or outer experience" (Rainwater, 2007, p. 82).

Leuzinger-Bohleber and Fischmann (2010) also apply an object relations model based on Klein's and Winnicott's concepts. They contend that the child harbors negative affects which produce "extreme images of a hateful being" (p. 148) in the child. This triggers a process whereby aggression is projected onto the Other who, in consequence, is experienced as a persecutor. In contrast to Rainwater, they bring out ADHD symptoms as a result of schizo-paranoid anxieties. They emphasize, however, that one may observe different structural levels and a wide range of object relations among ADHD children. Therefore, they refrain from assuming a monocausal etiology in ADHD and from proposing a singular psychoanalytic model. This is the Frankfurt group that is conducting the RCT referred earlier on psychoanalytic therapy versus a comparison group.

In contrast to these studies, Gilmore (2000) applies an ego-psychological perspective. She views ADHD as a "disturbance in the synthetic, organizing and integrative function of the ego" (p. 1260), the sum of which constitutes the disorder. To her, ADHD is a "complex mixture of neuropsychiatric and neurotic components . . . [which is] often improved by medication but in many cases optimally treated with concurrent psychoanalysis' (Gilmore, 2000). The analyst's interpretations contribute to treatment in that they address the ego impairment. She insists that psychoanalysis should be combined with parent counseling, remediation and medication (Gilmore, 2002), while emphasizing that "the underlying disturbance in synthetic and integrative capacity is not treated by medications" (p. 387).

Akin to Gilmore's formulations are those by Sugarman (2006) who describes ADHD children's problems with self-regulation in that their regulation of affects and narcissism, as well as their self- and object relations, are faltering. "Consequently, their minds have difficulty balancing and maintaining a homeostatic equilibrium between the many mental processes and contents necessary for adequate self-regulation" (p. 237). Carney (2002) also brings out problems with self-regulation, which he defines as an "interpersonally developing capacity to modulate states of arousal and to organize behavior in meaningful, predictable ways" (p. 299). Sugarman (2006) emphasizes that whether the children have constitutional regulatory limitations or have suffered trauma, they "develop unconscious fantasies to account for their functional difficulties" (p. 237). These fantasies, he suggests, must be psychoanalyzed.

Palombo (2001) conceptualizes ADHD in self-psychological terms. The child's interactions with family and friends tend to be negative. This prevents the child's "self-object functions" (p. 153) to develop favorably, especially the idealizing function. As a result, the capacity to self-soothe and regulate is compromised and cannot be internalized by these children. Palombo points to their often miserable self-esteem. This makes them vulnerable to "disjunctive moments . . . when the child ceases to feel understood by the therapist" (p. 276). For example, the therapist may not acknowledge a significant event in the child's life or refuse to respond to questions. This may insert "an element of artificiality" (p. 266) in treatment that is painful to the child.

In previous articles, I have addressed the ADHD child's thought processes (Salomonsson, 2004) and his hypersensitivity to analytic interventions (Salomonsson, 2006). I link the child's problems with thinking about affective experiences to the fact that his internal object cannot contain his wishes and affects. Similarly to Leuzinger-Bohleber and Fischmann, and perhaps also to Rainwater, I argue that the child easily interprets faltering containment as a punishment for his sadistic attacks. My model adds that such containment jeopardizes the child's thought processes in that the transformation (Bion, 1965) of beta-elements into alpha-elements is blocked. The result may be that bizarre objects accumulate in the child's internal world. They may appear in drawings, in words or in actions. In ego-psychological terms, the child is fragmenting his thoughts and deteriorating in his communicative abilities.

Sometimes, the child projects the bizarre objects onto the analyst who suddenly may appear frightening or alien. In such instances, one may witness unruly attacks by the child. In addition, his memory function is compromised, which prevents him from recalling a satisfying object when he meets with a frustration. This idea is reminiscent of Palombo's notion of difficulties in self-soothing functions. As a result of his "temporal myopia" (Barkley, 1998, p. 247) the child easily panics when he fails to access the real satisfying object or his memory traces of it. In treatment, one may see how the child suddenly forgets a recent experience of the analyst as a supportive figure.

My model of ADHD thus combines object-relational and ego-psychological perspectives. In this article, I focus on a phenomenon that I have discovered when treating several ADHD children: a bad, uncontaining internal object, which is easily awakened in the analytic interchange and exhorts the child to expel the analyst's words. This object is affected by the present transference relation. It also has direct repercussions on the child's ego-functioning, and I will focus on one aspect not listed among the common ADHD symptoms: the ego's semiotic capacity, that is, its ability to use signs for thinking and communicating thoughts and feelings. This capacity may suddenly crumble in an ADHD child. In treatment, one can observe how his semiotic capacity is continuously influenced by the emotional state within the transference. This will affect how he receives analytic interventions. The exploration will be illustrated by the following case vignette.

THE CASE

Nicholas is six-and-a-half years old when his parents first ask me to see him. He has been diagnosed with a severe ADHD at a Child Psychiatric Unit some one and one-half years earlier. The psychologist worries about his impulsivity, his anxiety in the test situation, and his unhappy demeanor. She recommends the parents contact me to discuss psychoanalytic treatment. I first meet the mother alone, since the father is busy at work. She relates an excruciating home situation dominated by Nic's unruliness, impulsive behavior, and outbursts against his younger brother, as well as her difficulties in reaching him emotionally. Looking back, she had a strange feeling already at delivery. She cannot explain it. Nic is her first child, so then she had nothing with which to compare. She does not associate this feeling to Nic's appearance or behavior. Rather, it was an alien feeling about herself that overpowered her. She would not call it a depressed sentiment. I wonder to myself if she is addressing a break of contact that, for unknown reasons, started very early between her and Nic.

Nic's symptoms started when he was slightly older than one year. "He just couldn't be still! He was everywhere all the time. He crept around in the apartment, we had to watch over him constantly, one was always on the alert." When his brother was born, Nic was one and one-half years old. This unleashed strong and continuous jealousy reactions. Today, the home situation is strained, and meal times are an ordeal. Nic has to be watched so that he will not turn the table into a mess or hit or harass his brother.

First Encounter With Nic

I set up an appointment with Nic and his parents. I meet a boy with a windblown and greyish complexion and a pair of unhappy, unsteady eyes constantly fluttering across the room. He runs into the consulting room with his parents and immediately starts investigating it.

Nic: These pipes in the ceiling, there are rats in them, where do they go, to the swimming-pool? Where are the sprinklers, you need them don't you understand, in case there's a fire! There's a key hanging, what's it for? Wow, a cupboard!

Nic tries to open but it is locked. He looks at another cupboard.

N: Maybe there's a million inside that cupboard. Somebody ate it up. You know, in shops they eat money, and then they do a poo-poo. Maybe you put a million there! Then you're a millionaire.

He plays with two dolls, one a little child and the other a leopard. The leopard eats the child and then defecates.

I ask Nic: What happened to the doll?

N: It probably got terrified.

Analyst: Maybe you are terrified sometimes?

N: Yes, in the public swimming-pool. I didn't get out of the water, I almost drowned but Dad rescued me . . . Sometimes I get volcanic eruptions, I can't stop myself from scribbling at the walls at home. I did this to Mom.

He points at Mom. He has cut off a tuft of her hair.

Mother: Nic was upset with me yesterday.

N: Yeah, I put a fork on her chair, it's a pity she didn't sit on it, then she would have flown up to the ceiling. Come on, let's play with the cars. Dad, come play with us.

The car game has barely started when he wants to draw instead. He tries to make a drawing of a toy but does not succeed. He places it on the paper to copy it. After some seconds he gives up and says the back of the sketch-block is boring.

It is difficult to discern Nic's words, especially when he seems worried about my comments. Often, he does not respond. I tell Nic I need time to think and that I would like to get to know him better. He willingly agrees and I tell him that his parents and I will find another appointment.

After some days, the mother calls and says they want to think. Certainly, Nic needs help but they are not sure about analysis. And, how will they manage to bring him to sessions? We agree that she will call me again when they have discussed it further. After three months they call me again and this time, mother and father come together. The home situation is deteriorating, and they want to give analysis a try. Especially, they mention an event when Nic saw a stuffed bird lying in a trash container. He was dead-scared and just could not shake this fear off himself. It lasted week after week, which deeply worried the parents.

We agree that I will see Nic three times weekly which later, when possible, will be increased to four times. I will stay in contact with the child psychiatrist who is in charge of Nic's medication (Strattera®, atomoxetine). The family will get help by a family therapist who now and then visits the home. I will also see the parents monthly.

Comments

Nic reveals many typical ADHD features. There is the hyperactivity; he is always on the go and never completes a task or a theme he has started. Impulsivity is illustrated by his blurting out responses to my comments and questions. Though the interview situation does not raise any scholarly demands, his inability to concentrate is obvious.

I would add that, though it does not belong to the typical ADHD symptoms according to the DSM-IV-TR, the contact between Nic and me is queer. We do not get in touch and our eyes never really meet. As for his mood, he is neither happy nor sad. The only one who seems to have strong emotions is me. I feel unhappy, powerless, and lonesome as I watch him move about and listen to his comments. When he asks me technical questions, for example, about the fire sprinkler, he does not seem interested in an answer. The questions rather seem like efforts at escaping from anxiety. As is to be confirmed later in treatment, they express his dread of being overpowered by strong feelings. The only method he seems to master of extinguishing the "fire" inside him is hyperactivity. My main value to him during our initial contact seems to be as a potential millionaire. This view reflects, I hypothesize, a manic defense (Rainwater, 2007) against his own feelings of impotence.

Beneath the manic defense, there exists a terrible world in which the leopard eats the terrified little doll only to defecate it. He transforms it into an omnipotent and manic poo-poo world where everything disagreeable is defecated. His fear and aggression seems to center around the maternal object. Here, I refer to his cutting Mom's hair. In contrast, the paternal object is portrayed as a life saver in the story of the swimming pool and the car game. However, as the interrupted car game indicates, Nic cannot use a paternal figure to dissolve anxieties. They are too strong, or his ego is far too weak and splintered for it to have much chances of helping Nic. As for Nic's real parents, they are sincere and responsible in their concern about the boy. They have obviously used the months of reflection to decide to do their utmost for Nic. Thus, psychoanalysis starts.

VIGNETTE I – KISS THE WALL

As the analysis gets started, I find ways of working with Nic that basically are the same as I use with other child patients. Simply put, I link what he is saying and doing to what I assume he is thinking and feeling. However, typical for my work with Nic and other ADHD children is that I must constantly watch on which semiotic level he is functioning for the moment. That is, at what level of signification does he receive my words? To what extent is his understanding of them colored by how he experiences the tone of my voice, my demeanor, my clothes, and so forth? These levels shift swiftly. My assessments are often made instantly and under heavy countertransference pressure, and they have important repercussions on the progress of treatment. I agree that language, both as internal "self-talk" and as external communication, is necessary for regulating affects and inhibiting impulses (Barkley, 1998). Analysis reveals that the child's linguistic ability and emotional state are interconnected. Both the analyst and his patient must learn that a word may have quite different emotional impacts, sometimes even from one second to another. Alternatively, we might say that his symbolic capacity is fluctuating. I prefer, however, to use the Peircean terms sign and semiotics (Kloesel and Houser, 1992), since they incorporate *all* elements in communication and do not make any conceptual difference between unconscious and conscious levels (Salomonsson, 2007b).

The ensuing vignette demonstrates his vacillating semiotic capacity and ability to make use of my interventions. He has given instructions to prepare a "flea," that is, a sheet of paper folded into a rhombic shape, and then to have secret messages written under its flaps. He asks me to point at one flap, whereupon I should execute what is written beneath it. I read out to him:

Analyst: It says "Kiss and hug the wall!"
Nic: Then you must do it! Do it now!
A: I am thinking about these words . . .
N: Do it! Kiss the wall!
A: I am thinking what it would feel like to kiss and hug a wall, and what people around me would say. I guess they would tease me . . .
N [looking sad]: My little brother teases me. He calls me stupid . . . Kiss the wall! . . . I must go to the loo.

When Nic ordered me to kiss the wall, I felt tempted to address how he felt standing before an unapproachable wall-like person while being teased about his urge to get in contact with him/her. This impression was nourished by my countertransference, in which I identified with a passionate, yearning human in front of an inanimate, unyielding thing. However, I feared that he would react vehemently if I spoke with him directly about it. Instead, I spoke of myself and my feelings in front of the wall. This detour enabled Nic to briefly touch upon humiliating feelings aroused by his brother. Immediately thereafter, he had to evacuate them via his urine. After visiting the loo, he did not want to speak about the flea game or his feelings.

Events like this one made me realize his varying ability to play with signs, for example, to transfer the meaning of a word from one situation to another, as in metonymy, or to understand the meaning of a metaphor. Furthermore, it made me aware that this ability varied in relation to the present state of the internal object. I will submit a second vignette to illustrate this idea and then discuss it theoretically.

VIGNETTE II – MRS. DESERT

At the time of vignette II, ten-and-a-half-year-old Nic has been in analysis for slightly more than three years. Recently, he has been transferred from his remedial class with just a few pupils to an ordinary class. Nic is nowadays more of an ordinary boy with friends, though he has difficulties sleeping and concentrating on his homework. He is still on Strattera. He is fond of computers and technical things, as well as of the family pets. Last spring has been marked by Nic's growing resentment coming to his "boring sessions" instead of being with his friends. Old themes reoccur; his contempt of grown-ups, his sense of the unfair impotence of children, and his ridiculing me when I addressed his affects about these matters.

During one session in which the parents also take part, Nic reveals that he does not know how to tell the time. The parents are shocked and feel sorry for him as he is fighting with his shameful disclosure: "Oh, Mom, get me your Chapstick, my lips are so dry," he says while barely managing to refrain from crying. Once again, like in the kiss-the-wall scene, an excruciating emotion is met with a concrete request. There would be no point in speaking with Nic about the sadness, shame, and resentment he feels in this situation.

Shortly after this session, his father brings him to his Monday morning session. Nic looks tired but content. As he takes off his jacket, he shows me his new ball pen.

Nic: I found it in the street. It's cool.

Analyst: Yes, it looks nice.

He enters my consulting room after me. He closes the door spontaneously, something he often resists because it is a "stupid" and "unnecessary" thing to do.

N: (with some surprise and perhaps admiration) Wow, it's heavy, this door!

After a while, he continues.

N: You know, some ball pens you can use under water or upside down! Why? It seems an unnecessary field of application. (Nic often uses such adult expressions).

A: You wonder why people would want to write upside down.

N: (with a smart smile) I know! If you're hanging in a jungle tree, and you want a parrot to fly with your message to the other side of the earth, then you'd have to use such a pen!

A: Yes, that would be practical . . .

He sits silently with the pen in his hand. Suddenly, he pretends to throw it in my face. Inadvertently, I blink.

A: I blinked when you pretended to fling the pen at me. It was a reflex. I did not feel afraid. You are friendly today, so I need not be afraid.

N: Some 6-year old chaps hunted me at school. I had to escape up along a fence.

A: So you got afraid.

N: Bah!

He hands me a paper where he has written: "How B." Next: "Boring" (in English). Finally: "B = Boring = tråkigt," that is, the word in Swedish.

A: You think I'm boring when I said you got afraid. But you know, feelings are practical. They are like signals. You got afraid of the kids so you had time to escape.

N: Well, I don't think so. There was no time for being afraid! I just thought, "I've got to run for my life," like when older boys chase you and you've got to run.

A: Is it that way for you? As for me, I'd think "These are dangerous guys, I have to run" and "I'm afraid," all at the same time! Then I'd run.
We speak of this for a while. He does not admit he is afraid sometimes. He says:
N: Haven't you got it yet? B = Björn = Boring?
A: Yes, you think I am boring when I speak with you about your feelings.
N: Ah, worthless!
A: You think I am worthless and boring.
N: Well, not worthless, really. Here is another paper: 'B = Björn = can be boring.'
A: So you think I can be boring; sometimes but not always.
No protests. After a while he mentions "desert." I am reminded of this recurring image of drought and helplessness, like when he asked his mother for the chapstick.
N: My headmistress is called "Mrs. Desert." I don't know why. She is so strict! She does not allow the pupils to skip class. They are allowed to cut class in my brother's school. That'd be nice, to get away during a lesson and buy candy!
A: You wish Mrs. Desert would allow it in your school, too.
N: No no, that's not it! I want it to be fair! Either every school should allow skipping classes or none . . . You know, in some school yards there's a war. The children throw stones at each other.
A: Then they must be very afraid.
N: No, they just keep indoors!
A: You don't agree that one can get afraid in the schoolyard. But if one gets afraid, one can run inside not to get hurt by the stones.
He turns silent and gets out in the waiting room. He returns with a water pistol.
N: Guess which brand is written on it!
A: It's the Simpsons. You like them. Once, you called them an ADHD family.
Nic wants, and I allow him, to squirt some water on me. He is gentle with me.
A: It's OK. I can see you don't want to be rude on me, so I don't have to be afraid.
He now turns the mouthpiece into his mouth and sips some water. I am reminded of the desert again, and of a baby thirstily sipping from his mother's breast or from a bottle.
Time is up. As he puts his jacket on, he babbles about events at school. He leaves with a friendly "See you."

COMMENTS TO VIGNETTE II

James Gammill (1998) quotes Aulagnier (1977) in that the analyst's pleasure is essential to his investment in the patient's material and to his interpretative activity. This gives the patient a living model with whom he can identify. This atmosphere was evident in the session. I felt relaxed, amused by his parrot story and moved by the tale of Mrs. Desert. These sentiments increased "the associative activity and the inventiveness of the analyst [which may] contribute significantly to the child's capacity to associate and to elaborate his fantasies" (Gammill, 1998, p. 232).

If we follow Gammill's (1998) differentiation between "dramatic play" and "enactment of massive projective identifications" (p. 221) in child psychoanalytic work, vignette II mainly consisted in the first type. In contrast, when Nic ordered me to kiss the wall in vignette I, he sought to project his distress into me. In that situation, analytic work had to center on containing Nic's projections of an outcast boy. Vignette II demonstrates that I now have better opportunities to investigate Nic's symptoms with my psychoanalytic instrument. I may query in what ways his behavior and words express inner conflicts and defenses. I also address the affects that crash inside him and build up the psychic conflict, as when I am speaking about being afraid. Nic expresses his resistance mostly by "Bah"' and writing paper notes. As the session unfolds, however, he remains calm and by the end he also shows signs of friendly acceptance of what I suggested.

What determines at which communicative level a child receives the analyst's interventions? My main argument is that it is determined by the state of the child's internal object. I will first define this term and then show how it relates to the variations of the child's semiotic ability.

The Internal Object

The first internal object to be described was the super-ego (Freud, 1923). However, this "single differentiated function of our mental make-up" is not the same as the "'personal relations,' however primitive and fantastic, we have had with the figures who people our inner worlds" (Riviere, 1955, p. 347). These psychic inhabitants correspond to the Kleinian concept of internal object. This term refers to "an unconscious experience or fantasy of a concrete object physically located internal to the ego (body) which has its own motives and intentions towards the ego and to other objects" (Hinshelwood, 1989, p. 68). One's experience of it depends on how one experiences the external object. In this sense, internal objects are mirrors of reality, "but they also contribute significantly, through projection, to the way the external objects are themselves perceived and experienced" (Hinshelwood, 1989, p. 68). Our object relations are thus molded by an "interaction between introjection and projection, between internal and external objects and situations" (Klein, 1946, p. 99).

Internal objects are the bricks with which the child builds up his inner world. He does this by introjecting his experiences which are colored by hereditary factors, earlier physical and emotional experiences and, last but not least, projections. Internal objects may contribute either to ego- or to super-ego-formation (Heimann, 1989). The outcome is determined by "the attributes of the introjected parent with which the child is predominantly concerned at the moment" (p. 137). In the analytic situation, this formulation is valid also for the characteristics of the introjected analyst. In moments when the child focuses on his parents or analyst's "intelligence, skill, manipulation of things – functions belonging to the intellectual and motor sphere of the ego – the introjected object is mainly taken up into the child's ego" (Heimann, 1989). In contrast, when love and hate are in acute conflict, the introjected object will contribute to forming the super-ego.

A problem with super-ego formation is that it might acquire an unyielding, strict authority. Second, it might quench the formation of the internal good object, which then cannot function "as a focal point in the ego" (Klein, 1946, p. 101). In such instances, the child will identify with the bad internal object (Hinshelwood, 1994), for example, with the "devil inside" (Freud, 1929, p. 33). The question is, of course, when and why this negative outcome occurs. To answer this, we must refer to the state of the internal object and of the child's semiotic abilities, and how the two are inter-related.

SIGNIFICATION AND THE INTERNAL OBJECT

Let us suppose a child has an experience of something aching inside. Everything and everyone connected with this experience is automatically experienced as "bad," and thus a bad, internal object is created. What needs to be investigated to fully understand the nature of this object is the child's concomitant vision of the container. On the one hand, the child might feel that he is alone with the ache or feel ridiculed or dismissed because of it. On the other hand, he might feel someone is there to share the ache with him. Containment implies providing "the word or phrase which binds this experience" (Segal, 1957, p. 63) or to "translate" (Salomonsson, 2007a) the child's nameless dread (Bion, 1962).

Anzieu (1990) expresses it similarly in that we cannot speak of the child's thoughts and feelings in isolation. We must also include the child's notion of the container/form. For this combination of emotion and its container, he coins the term "formal signifier." When Nic is ruled by the kiss-the-wall-object, his formal signifier expresses pain plus the faltering containment. He then gets problems in moving freely between words and more primordial demarcating signifiers, that is, "the gestures, the mimic and the prosody, which complete the functions of the word" (Rosolato, 1985, p. 14). Therefore, in the kiss-the-wall session, it was impossible for me to suggest a link between his urinating and the pain in the flea game. I rather addressed what awful feelings *I* would have had if I were forced to kiss a wall.

Internal objects are based on concrete and sensuous interpretations of the world (Heimann, 1989). For example, "I have a tummy-ache" = "Everything and everyone is bad." In addition, they are concrete in their modes of cognitive functioning. For example, Nic was once speaking about a row with his brother. That is, one of the bad internal objects, his envied little brother, was in the forefront. Nic described the row: "It was awful, I ran out of words . . . look, my vocal chords are here!" He pointed as if to show me where he had run out of words. In that situation, I could not address his emotional pain while fighting with his brother. I just commented "It is not nice when one runs out of words."

Nevertheless, sooner or later the momentary affect needs to be talked about in psychoanalysis. After all, "it always means progress when the child has to acknowledge the reality of the objects through his own words" (Klein, 1927, p. 314). I suggest that the internal object provides us with a guideline when we may address the affect or when we have to remain in the background with interpretations. Vignette I demonstrates the second alternative, that is, addressing his feelings only indirectly by referring to myself or to "One may feel this way when one stands before a wall . . . "

At other times, Nic feels my words are dangerous things or weapons that he must physically fend off by spitting or fighting. This creates a countertransference problem in that while his attacks inflict pain and humiliation on me, my task is to understand *his* pain and humiliation. Such problems have to be overcome in order to understand the child's basic problem in receiving and integrating analytic interventions. He dismisses or fends off my interventions when I represent a bad, uncontaining object thrusting interpretation-things at him. This conclusion brings together my essential point: *the relation between the momentary state of the internal object and of his semiotic ability*.

When the bad, kiss-the-wall-object is predominant, the child's semiotic ability capsizes. Nic then experiences words as real things rather than messages about his feelings or thoughts. Words can never completely portray what an affect means or how it is experienced because, as Freud

(1915) says, word-presentations are closed and their number of meanings is finite. This applies to human communication in general, but to a child who is semiotically fragile this fact is unbearable. He is afraid to get in contact with his feelings and to deal with the words with which the analyst portrays them. He cannot receive an interpretation as it was intended by the therapist, as a suggestion of what is going on inside him. In addition, the ADHD child often experiences the nonverbal tributaries to the analyst's words as equally threatening. He may see a frown on the analyst's forehead, a reflex in his glasses, a color of his teeth, and so forth. He may be terrified by such an observation rather than be interested or consoled by what the analyst actually is saying.

One might dismiss this conceptualization of the semiotic fragility and its relation to the internal object, and maintain that the phenomenon simply reflects the cognitive difficulties in ADHD children. Evidently, Nic has many cognitive difficulties. What is emphasized here is that they are influenced by emotional factors and that psychoanalysis may help in uncovering them. Furthermore, Nic's cognitive and linguistic capacities are sometimes stunning, that is, when he is in a good mood. To be able to speak of "an unnecessary field of application" in connection with the ball pen is not bad for a ten-and-a-half-year-old boy.

Why does the bad internal object have such a disastrous impact on Nic's semiotic agility? One reply is that verbal thinking is connected with the individual's "awareness of psychic reality" (Bion, 1954, p. 114). Words make the child aware of his rage and the ensuing risk of loosing the good objects. Thus, words make Nic sad because they remind him of his destructiveness. Sadness is then connected with an experience that the container does not understand, is not interested in him, or is even contemptuous. In other words, he feels sad, lonely, and ridiculed. No wonder that he hates the words that remind him of those feelings. To him, they are "interwoven with catastrophe and the painful emotion of the depression" (Bion, 1954, p. 117) and thus, he must get rid of their impact. He does this via projective identification into me. The formula is: "Bad feelings? Eject them into the analyst!" The point is that the analyst should feel as lousy and ridiculous as he did. Alternatively, the feelings need to be evacuated, for example, via urine in the kiss-the-wall scene.

In our conversation during vignette II about the six-year-old madcaps on the schoolyard, the perspective is first dominated by this evacuation philosophy. Nic speaks of his running away from the boys as a technical problem, not as a sign that he was afraid. I insist, however, by comparing with what I probably would have felt in a similar situation; I would have been afraid. At first, he protests and considers me boring. Then he introduces Mrs. Desert and the atmosphere changes. To be true, she is strict and does not allow free access to candy. In this sense, she lives up to her name. However, she also represents the daily frame of school work. Influenced by this object, Nic starts an interesting discussion about justice. He wants things to be fair. Either, every kid should live in paradise, that is, be allowed to cut class. Or, none should have that privilege, especially not his brother! The point is that he is now talking with someone he feels is interested in a discussion rather than slamming the door in his face. In the final scene he is squirting and playing with me, and then sipping from the Simpsons pistol. I interpret this, however silently, as his playing with a breast that confers nourishment and containment. This game, as well as his friendly "see you" upon leaving me, confirms that he has largely retracted his negative projections. I am no longer boring or stupid. Rather, I seem to be an interesting guy he can chuckle and discuss with.

By the end of the session, the good internal object is acting as "a focal point in the ego" (Klein, 1946, p. 101). Such an object "counteracts the processes of splitting and dispersal, makes for cohesiveness and integration, and is instrumental in building up the ego" (Klein,

1946, p. 101). Klein's formulation illustrates the old adage that nothing is new under the sun. The ideological differences between today's conventional ADHD treatment and child psychoanalysis are partly inescapable, but in some aspects both approaches share the same treatments aims. Child psychiatrists and pedagogues try to help the child acquire more adaptive ways of paying attention to his tasks. They also assist him in refraining from impulsive motor behavior and emotional outbreaks. In psychoanalytic terms, they aim at a better ego-functioning in the child, an aim to which any psychoanalyst would subscribe. In this article, I have suggested that psychoanalysis can be of help in this process. In addition, it emphasizes the links between emotions and ego-functioning in the child. The more we understand that the child's comprehension of interventions is influenced by his present internal object, the better are our chances of helping the child. Actually, I think this applies both to a psychoanalyst who intervenes in a session, a teacher who speaks with the child in the classroom, and a doctor who prescribes a drug.

ACKNOWLEDGMENTS

I wish to thank Nic's parents for giving me permission to submit the clinical material in a de-identified form. The article was supported by grants from the Ax:son Johnson, Engkvist, Groschinsky, Kempe-Carlgren, Mayflower Charity, and the Wennborg Foundations.

REFERENCES

Abikoff, H. P. D., Hechtman, L. M. D., Klein, R. G. P. D., Gallagher, R. P. D., Fleiss, K. P. D., Etcovitch, J. M. A., Cousins, L. P. D., Greenfield, B. M. D., Martin, D. M. A. & Pollack, S. P. D. (2004a), Social functioning in children with ADHD treated with long-term methylphenidate and multimodal psychosocial treatment. *Journal of the American Academy of Child & Adolescent Psychiatry*, 43: 820–9.

_____ Hechtman, L. M. D., Klein, R. G. P. D., Weiss, G. M. D., Fleiss, K. P. D., Etcovitch, J. M. A., Cousins, L. P. D., Greenfield, B. M. D., Martin, D. M. A. & Pollack, S. P. D. (2004b), Symptomatic improvement in children with ADHD treated with long-term methylphenidate and multimodal psychosocial treatment. *Journal of the American Academy of Child & Adolescent Psychiatry*, 43: 802–11.

Anzieu, D., ed. (1990), *Psychic Envelopes (Les Enveloppes Psychiques)*. London: Karnac Books.

Aulagnier, P. (1977). Le travail de l'interprétation. La fonction du plaisir dans le travail analytique (The work of interpretation. The function of pleasure in analytic work). In: *Comment l'interprétation Vient au Psychanalyste (How Interpretation Arises in the Psychoanalyst's Mind)*, N. Major (ed.). Paris: Aubier-Montaigne.

Barkley, R. A. (1998), *Attention-deficit Hyperactivity Disorder*. New York: Guilford Press.

_____ (2006), *Attention-deficit Hyperactivity Disorder*, 3rd ed. New York: Guilford Press.

Bion, W. R. (1954), Notes on the theory of schizophrenia. *International Journal of Psycho-Analysis*, *35*: 113–8.

_____ (1962), The psycho-analytic study of thinking. *International Journal of Psychoanalysis*, *43*: 306–10.

_____ (1965), *Transformations*. London: Karnac Books.

Carney, J. K. (2002), Prologue to an issue on self-regulation. Issues of attention and attachment. *Psychoanalytic Inquiry*, *22*: 299–306.

Erikson, M. F., Sroufe, L. A. & Egeland, B. (1985), The relationship between quality of attachment and behavior problems in preschool in a high-risk sample. *Monographs of the Society for Research in Child Development*, *50*: 147–66.

Fearon, R. M. P. & Belsky, J. (2011), Infant-mother attachment and the growth of externalizing problems across the primary-school years. *Journal of Child Psychology & Psychiatry*.

Freud, A. (1929), On the theory of analysis of children. *International Journal of Psycho-Analysis*, *10*: 29–38.

Freud, S. (1895). A reply to criticisms of my paper on anxiety neurosis. In: *The Standard Edition of the Complete Psychological Works of Sigmund Freud, vol. 3*, J. Strachey (ed.). London: Hogarth Press.

_____ (1915). The unconscious. In: *Standard Edition of the Complete Psychological Works of Sigmund Freud* vol. 14, J. Strachey (ed.). London: Hogarth Press.

_____ (1923). The ego and the id. In: *The Standard Edition of the Complete Psychological Works of Sigmund Freud*, J. Strachey (ed.). London: Hogarth Press.

Gammill, J. (1998), *A partir de Melanie Klein (From Melanie Klein and onwards)*. Meyzieu: Césura.

Gilmore, K. (2000), A psychoanalytic perspective on attention-deficit/hyperactivity disorder. *Journal of the American Psychoanalytic Association, 48*: 1259–93.

_____ (2002), Diagnosis, dynamics, and development: Considerations in the psychoanalytic assessment of children with AD/HD. *Psychoanalytic Inquiry, 22*, 372–390.

Hechtman, L. M. D., Abikoff, H. P. D., Klein, R. G. P. D., Greenfield, B. M. D., Etcovitch, J. M. A., Cousins, L. P. D., Fleiss, K. P. D., Weiss, M. M. D. & Pollack, S. P. D. (2004a), Children with ADHD treated with long-term methylphenidate and multimodal psychosocial treatment: Impact on parental practices. *Journal of the American Academy of Child & Adolescent Psychiatry, 43*: 830–8.

_____ Abikoff, H. P. D., Klein, R. G. P. D., Weiss, G. M. D., Respitz, C. M. A., Kouri, J. M. A., Blum, C. M. A., Greenfield, B. M. D., Etcovitch, J. M. A., Fleiss, K. P. D. & Pollack, S. P. D. (2004b), Academic achievement and emotional status of children with ADHD treated with long-term methylphenidate and multimodal psychosocial treatment. *Journal of the American Academy of Child & Adolescent Psychiatry, 43*: 812–9.

Heimann, P. (1989). Certain functions of introjection and projection in early infancy. In: *Developments in Psychoanalysis*, J. Riviere (ed.). London: Karnac Books.

Hinshelwood, R. D. (1989), *A Dictionary of Kleinian Thought*. London: Free Association Books.

_____ (1994), *Clinical Klein*. London: Free Association Books.

Jensen, P. S. M. D., Martin, D. B. A. & Cantwell, D. P. M. D. (1997), Comorbidity in ADHD: Implications for research, practice, and DSM-V. *Journal of the American Academy of Child & Adolescent Psychiatry, 36*: 1065–79.

Klein, M. (1927). The importance of words in early analysis. In: *Envy and Gratitude and Other Works, vol. 3*, M. Klein (ed.). London: Hogarth Press, p. 314.

_____ (1935). A contribution to the psychogenesis of manic-depressive states. In: *The Writings of Melanie Klein*, vol. 1, R. Money-Kyrle (ed.). London: Hogarth Press, pp. 262–289.

_____ (1946). Notes on some schizoid mechanisms. In: *The Writings of Melanie Klein, vol. 3*, R. Money-Kyrle (ed.). London: Hogarth Press, pp. 1–24.

Klein, R. G. P. D., Abikoff, H. P. D., Hechtman, L. M. D. & Weiss, G. M. D. (2004), Design and rationale of controlled study of long-term methylphenidate and multimodal psychosocial treatment in children with ADHD. *Journal of the American Academy of Child & Adolescent Psychiatry, 43*: 792–801.

Kloesel, C. & Houser, N., eds. (1992), *The Essential Peirce, vol. 1: 1867–1893*. Bloomington, IN: Indiana University Press.

Leuzinger-Bohleber, M. & Fischmann, T. (2010). Attention-deficit-hyperactivity-disorder (AD/HD): A field for contemporary psychoanalysis? Some clinical, conceptual and neurobiological considerations based on the Frankfurt Prevention Study. In: *Assessing Change in Psychoanalytic Psychotherapy of Children and Adolescents. Today's Challenge*, J. Tsiantis & J. Trowell (eds.). London: Karnac.

Lyons-Ruth, K. (1996), Attachment relationships among children with aggressive behavior problems: The role of disorganized early attachment patterns. *Journal of Consulting & Clinical Psychology, 64*: 64–73.

MTA Cooperative Group. (1999), A 14-month randomized clinical trial of treatment strategies for attention-deficit/hyperactivity disorder. *Archives of General Psychiatry, 56*: 1073–86.

Palombo, J. (2001), *Learning Disorders and Disorders of the Self*. New York: Norton.

Polanczyk, G., De Lima, M. S., Horta, B. L., Biederman, J. & Rohde, L. A. (2007), The worldwide prevalence of ADHD: A systematic review and metaregression analysis. *The American Journal of Psychiatry, 164*: 942–8.

Rainwater, J. B. (2007), A psychoanalytic contribution to the understanding and treatment of attention deficit hyperactivity disorder. *Dissertation Abstracts International: Section B: The Sciences and Engineering, 68*(3-B): 1940. viewed 6 Feb. 2011, <http://gradworks.umi.com/3255212.pdf>

Riviere, J. (1955). The unconscious fantasy of an inner world reflected in examples from literature. In: *New Directions in Psycho-analysis*, M. Klein, P. Heimann & R. Money-Kyrle (eds.). London: Maresfield Library.

Rosolato, G. (1985), *Éléments de l'interprétation (Elements of Interpretation)*. Paris: Gallimard.

Salomonsson, B. (2004), Some psychoanalytic viewpoints on neuropsychiatric disorders in children. *International Journal of Psycho-Analysis*, *85*: 117–35.

_____ (2006), The impact of words on children with ADHD and DAMP. Consequences for psychoanalytic technique. *International Journal of Psycho-Analysis*, *87*: 1029–47.

_____ (2007a), Semiotic transformations in psychoanalysis with infants and adults. *International Journal of Psycho-Analysis*, *88*: 1201–21.

_____ (2007b), "Talk to me baby, tell me what's the matter now." Semiotic and developmental perspectives on communication in psychoanalytic infant treatment. *International Journal of Psycho-Analysis, 88*: 127-46.

Segal, H. (1957, with 1979 postscript). Notes on symbol formation. In: *The Work of Hanna Segal* (1981). Northvale, NJ: Aronson.

Spencer, T. J., Biederman, J. & Mick, E. (2007), Attention-deficit/hyperactivity disorder: Diagnosis, lifespan, comorbidities, and neurobiology. *Journal of Pediatric Psychology*, *32*: 631–42.

Sugarman, A. (2006), Attention deficit hyperactivity disorder and trauma. *International Journal of Psycho-Analysis*, *87*: 237–41.

Winnicott, D. W. (1935). The manic defence. In: *Through Paediatrics to Psycho-analysis*, M. M. R. Khan (ed.). London: Hogarth Press.

Trouble Paying Attention

Daniel Gensler, Ph.D.

Attention can be compromised by various factors, including ADHD, emotional trouble, learning disability, language disorder, and executive function problems. When these factors are present they interact, each influencing the other. Therapists also have trouble maintaining a consistent, even focus because of selective inattention, countertransference, and pressure from parents and school. To illustrate, this article presents the background of a case of a seventh grade boy with attention problems. Neuropsychological and psychoanalytic concepts relevant to attention are then reviewed, before returning to a description of the treatment of that case. A summary uses the case to demonstrate a contextual, psychodynamic approach to the children with attention problems.

People who have trouble paying attention in school, at home, at work, or in therapy are not all suffering from attention deficit hyperactivity disorder (ADHD) and are not all in need of psychostimulant medication. There are other explanations for having trouble paying attention. These include the distractions of medical or physical trouble, extremes of intelligence, trauma, life crisis, language trouble, poor instruction, learning disability, or executive function disorder. Trouble paying attention also occurs because of emotional trouble, personality disorder, and developmental difficulties in affect regulation and self-soothing. These situations can lead to high levels of anxiety that are distracting.

Psychotherapists also have trouble paying attention. Despite Freud's recommendation, we are not able to bring an evenly suspended attention to our work. Selective inattention operates as the patient's character structure and defenses distract us, and through countertransference.

For a child and a therapist, attention is influenced by the entire context of therapy, including factors that are personal to the child, pressure from school and parents, and therapist preoccupations. Attention to the variety of factors affecting a patient's and a therapist's attentiveness keeps the focus on the real complexity of what is going on, and allows more flexibility in intervening helpfully.

CASE BACKGROUND

This is a case (still ongoing) of an adopted boy with attention deficit hyperactivity disorder (ADHD), disorganization, academic underachievement, oppositionalism, a tendency to lie, and a father in jail. Tom was 12 years old and in the seventh grade when I met him. When he was born, his biological mother already had five children, whom she had kept and raised as a single mother. She arranged to have him adopted. His adoptive mother had had several miscarriages before she and her husband adopted Tom at ten days old. Tom knew about his biological mother and biological siblings: he had a long letter from his birth mother, wishing him well.

At 18 months, his adoptive parents adopted another baby, a little girl. By that time, tension was increasing between his adoptive parents. In one incident when Tom was three, he witnessed his father acting violently toward his baby sister and his mother, including police coming to the home and speaking to both his parents. Marital tension continued until Tom was in first grade. His father was then hospitalized in a psychiatric facility, and the parents remained separated after that point, divorcing later that year. Prior to the divorce, Tom had not seen much of his father, who was staying away from the house more and more. After the divorce, Tom actually saw more of his father due to the regularity of visitation. His father was the more lenient parent and his mother was stricter, but in fact it was never easy for his mother to exercise authority. She tended to talk too much and to go on too long, and she would lose Tom's attention after a minute.

After his father moved out when Tom was six, Tom tended to get his way with his mother more than before. He lived with his mother and sister and had weekly visitations with his father. His visits with his father were described as low key and pleasant—hanging out, playing video games, eating pizza. Tom enjoyed these visits. He began psychotherapy with a female therapist six months after his father left. The therapist saw him in an unusual arrangement in which the therapist came to the home and split the time between Tom and his sister. Tom saw her for years.

By second grade, Tom was having difficulty completing reading and writing assignments and sustaining his attention in group activities. He was poor with his management of time and organization of materials. He was inconsistently attentive, impulsive, and needed frequent redirection. Psychological evaluation found him to be superior in verbal skills but only average in visual-motor areas. His auditory attentiveness was also weak. He was found to tire easily, to be underaroused, and "zoned out." When frustrated, he rushed, responded minimally, became passive, or gave up. Relations with peers were mildly difficult, and by fourth and fifth grade he suffered from being teased.

When Tom was in the middle of sixth grade, his father was sent to prison for a crime committed several years earlier (embezzling several million dollars). He left Tom's mother with a great deal of debt. The prison sentence was for a year and a half, and so his father was expected to be released from prison when Tom was in the eighth grade. Tom received letters from his father about once a week from jail; they were typically a few lines long, accompanying a picture or an article from a newspaper. His father said prison life wasn't so bad; there was even a golf course there.

At the beginning of seventh grade, in the middle of his father's time in jail, Tom had another psychoeducational evaluation, done by me. In the evaluation, he again was found to be nearly superior in verbal-expressive abilities but only average in most other areas. There was no sign of an earlier difficulty in auditory or phonological processing. Many weaknesses were apparent in executive functioning. He was inconsistent in his visual and auditory attention, even with medication (by this time he was taking Concerta). He tended to be impulsive, and had difficulty inhibiting responses that were not appropriate for the task at hand. His working memory was inconsistent as well, and he had trouble maintaining an appropriate response set as he went through tasks. He also became overwhelmed by tasks requiring him to engage in deductive reasoning without much guidance. His abilities in reading, writing, and math were average or better. In reading passages in order to answer questions about them, Tom was usually too impatient to go through the entire passage first. Instead, he developed a strategy of priming his attention by reading the questions and then scanning the text for the answer.

Projective testing found that Tom wanted to do well. But he was angry, sad and frustrated when he tried unsuccessfully to get what he wanted, academically and interpersonally. The interference of his various executive function difficulties was particularly frustrating, given his preference to work quickly and do well. He also felt teased by peers, uncomfortable with how his mother was trying to help him with his homework, ashamed over not having a father he could talk about and introduce to other kids, and worried about his father in jail. He coped with the intensity of his feelings by becoming oppositional, disdainful, and argumentative. He tended to externalize responsibility, blame others, and avoid matters that made him uneasy. Sarcastic humor helped him organize many of these feelings and ways of coping. These various coping styles were consolidated into a somewhat narcissistic sense of identity in which he felt entitled to see things his way and to behave as he pleased. While his capacity for social judgment was good, his actual responses socially were rigidly self-justifying, as if his way was the natural way and nothing else counted. He kept himself from paying attention to the self who wanted to do well in school and who knew he had trouble there. The overall DSM-IV diagnostic impression was of ADHD (Predominantly Inattentive Type), other executive function weaknesses, and oppositional defiant disorder.

By the time of the evaluation, Tom and his mother had decided to stop meeting with his therapist (although she continued to come to the home to see his sister), feeling dissatisfied with the results of the therapy. I recommended that his mother resume Tom's psychotherapy. She did not want to return to the former therapist, preferring a male therapist for her son. I gave her several names, but she wanted him to see me, and I accepted him into therapy.

CONCEPTS

Before going on to discuss the treatment in this case, I want to look at what neuropsychology and then psychoanalysis have had to say about paying attention. Within the limits of this presentation, I will not look at the literature on attention from experimental psychology (Kahneman, 1973), hemineglect (Ramachandran and Blakeslee, 1998), or Buddhism (Epstein, 1984, 1988). First, ADHD is partially genetic. Hallowell and Ratey (1994) state that 30 percent of parents of children with ADHD have ADHD themselves. Thirty-three percent of fraternal twins who have ADHD also have ADHD, and 51 percent of identical twins with ADHD also have ADHD.

The biological function of attention is to adapt to a current need by processing information selectively and in an orderly way (Fuster, 1995). This process is guided by long-term memory of related information, situations, and context. The ability to pay attention is one of the executive functions, which control the ability to maintain an appropriate problem-solving orientation for attainment of a future goal. Paying attention involves withdrawal of attention from other things to focus on one thing. It requires a minimal level of alertness, along with the ability to suppress associations that are not relevant. Attention occurs in two steps. First, there is a rapid, unconscious scrutiny and screening. In this unconscious review, material is retrieved selectively from messages that have not yet been consciously attended to, if those messages contain cues that are relevant to the adaptive context. Then this material is consciously analyzed and categorized.

To pay attention well, a person must be able to maintain control over mental energy, over intake of information, and over performance. Levine (2002) details many of the abilities necessary for effective attention in each of these areas. Regarding control over mental energy, effective attention requires being awake and consistently alert. Regarding control over intake of information, effective attention requires selecting what is significant for the task, not being distracted by what is insignificant, looking deeply and in detail while not missing the whole picture, associating to relevant connections, and alternating between relevant topics appropriately over time.

Regarding control over performance, effective attention requires previewing the likely consequences of a response, weighing options for a response, suppressing responses irrelevant to the task, and responding at the right rate. When controls over these performance abilities are poor, a person appears impulsive. Other areas in which attention is involved in performance are in synchronizing multiple responses, evaluating the quality of a response, and modifying it appropriately.

To bring attention to bear effectively on a problem, working memory is needed. Working memory, which is another executive function, is the ability to hold information in mind in the absence of an external cue and to use that information while performing operations on the information. Such operations include rearranging, categorizing, doing math, or doing logic. In this way, working memory joins with attention as mental functions needed for the voluntary control of behavior based on internal plans.

Goldberg (2001) offers a flashlight metaphor to explain the neuropsychology of attention. Using a flashlight requires three objects: the hand that holds the flashlight, the flashlight, and the target that the flashlight illuminates. In the brain, the capacity for paying attention—the basis for arousal, alertness, and vigilance—is in the reticular activating system, ascending from the upper brain stem; this is the flashlight. The control over this capacity for attention is in the prefrontal cortex; this is the hand that sets goals for looking, chooses to pick up the flashlight in order to look, and shines the light in certain directions and not in others. Finally, the target for this attention (what the light is aimed at) is often in posterior cortical areas, brain areas that underlie the parts of the mind that receive information from the external world.

Problems in many areas of the brain can interfere with attention. If the problem is in the prefrontal cortex (in Goldberg's metaphor, the hand that holds the flashlight), then the person might be said to have executive function disorder. If the problem is in the ventral brain stem or the ascending reticular activating system (in the metaphor, the flashlight), then the person could be said to have an attention deficit disorder. If the problem is in the posterior cortical areas that receive information from the world (in the metaphor, the target of the light), then the person could be said to have a sensory impairment or a learning disability.

Motivation is another critical component of attention. To attend effectively, someone must want to attend to the matter at hand in the first place. A person must attend despite delayed gratification or low levels of gratification, and must care to produce a good response. Barkley (1990) describes ADHD as a deficit in the motivation system of the brain, where inadequate ability for goal-directed behavior makes it hard to stay on task without constant feedback or reward. He locates the deficit in the connections between the prefrontal cortex, the limbic system, and striatum. These are areas of the brain that underlie our mind's abilities to inhibit responses, to feel the incentive to learn, and to react to reinforcement as plans are made to respond to situations.

DSM-IV distinguishes ADHD, Predominantly Inattentive Type, from ADHD, Predominantly Hyperactive-Impulsive Type. Barkley (1997) distinguishes two types of inattentiveness, one belonging to each type of ADHD. For people with the primarily inattentive type of ADHD, automaticity is weak. Automaticity is knowing how to do something so well that you do not have to think about it while doing it (Goodyear and Hynd, 1992). In addition to weak automaticity, there is also a generally slow speed of information processing and trouble maintaining a focused, selective attention. Such individuals have symptoms of daydreaming, spacing out or staring off, being in a fog, being easily confused, and generally being lethargic, hypoactive, and passive (Barkley, 1997, p. 67).

In the other kind of ADHD, the primarily hyperactive-impulsive type, deficits in attention derive from difficulty in self-regulation and in behavioral inhibition. This term, behavioral inhibition, refers to the ability to inhibit impulses to act, to stop ongoing responses, and to prevent interferences with responses. In this second type of ADHD (the hyperactive-impulsive type), attention is intact as long as immediate and frequent reinforcement is available for persisting in performing responses. However, attention is impaired when there is no immediate reward for attending—when attention must be maintained over longer, more complex responses, when tasks have to be strung together to achieve more distant consequences (Barkley, 1997, p. 84). This kind of attention is inefficient in the second (hyperactive-impulsive) type of ADHD.

I want to take a closer look at the selectivity of attention in this second type of ADHD (hyperactive-impulsive type). Here, attention is unreliable and troublesome regarding uninteresting activities but reliable for interesting activities. From the point of view of the flashlight metaphor, the selectivity of attention in this kind of ADHD is because of the "hand" part of Goldberg's flashlight metaphor. That is, the hand that holds the flashlight must be motivated to pick up the light and to keep on shining it. In the brain, the amygdala (part of the limbic system) is involved in recognizing the motivational significance of a stimulus. Damasio (2002) describes how the amygdala rapidly assesses incoming information for its emotional implications—whether the situation suggests the need to attack, escape, have sex, eat, or any of the derivatives of these motivations. The amygdala is involved in preparing an individual for an emotional response, and it makes this assessment more rapidly than the brain centers that control consciousness and attention. Even if the prefrontal cortex is working well, with good ability for goal setting, volition, and delayed gratification, these good abilities are compromised when the amygdala comes online strongly and primes a person for an immediate emotional response. Other motivations are compromised, and the effort to pay attention to these other motivations is weakened.

The psychology of drive and ego is familiar with this conceptual territory. The amygdala mediates tendencies that psychoanalysis calls drive, drive derivatives and the ego's defensive responses to danger. The prefrontal cortex mediates abilities that psychoanalysis calls ego functions, such as planning and intention. Posterior cortical areas mediate abilities that psychoanalysis calls other ego functions, such as sensation.

A clinician is faced with a wide array of contexts that may compromise the ability to attend. These include illness, disability, sleepiness, intelligence, language delay, or learning disability. It is hard to have control over mental energy and pay attention effectively when someone is having a seizure or dealing with hypothyroidism or the tics of Tourette's syndrome; or when dealing with impairment in hearing or vision; or when sleep deprived. It is hard to have control over intake of information, and to pay attention effectively, when someone is not intelligent enough to pay good attention. Sufficient intelligence is needed to select what is significant for the task, to screen out what is insignificant, to look deeply and in detail while not missing the whole picture, to associate to relevant connections, and to alternate between relevant topics appropriately over time. At the other end of the intelligence spectrum, a gifted individual may not feel motivated to do all this when the object of his or her attention is boringly simple and unchallenging. Further, if English is a second language, the flow of language may be too hard to attend to, compared to the ease of understanding one's native tongue.

Other compromises to attention come from within the school or work situation itself. Instruction may be inadequate or missing. There might be a poor match between a student and a teacher or between a worker and a supervisor trying to teach something. Under such circumstances, anxiety, resentment, guilt, and helplessness reverberate between student and teacher or between worker and supervisor, and these feelings distract the individual from attending and learning.

Internal emotional issues interfere with the ability to pay attention and to learn from experience. In school, a student may be afraid to compete, afraid to try and fail, or afraid to try and succeed. Focusing on a subject can be associated with anxiety over competition, when focusing increases the chance of doing better than someone else. Alternately, a student may be afraid of moving forward in school and graduating, because of separation anxieties, and for such a student, losing focus is motivated by a fantasy that she or he could stay back in school and never have to grow up. Students can actually fall asleep to avoid dealing with overwhelming feelings of rage or helplessness. Many psychiatric syndromes, autistic spectrum disorders, and substance abuse, can contribute to a loss of focus.

Further, developmental difficulties in affect regulation and self-soothing can lead to levels of anxiety and agitation that distract someone from paying attention at school, in the workplace, or at home. Take, for example, a disorganized and spacey student. It would be valuable to know, in understanding this student, that his mother has been deeply distracted for years, that the student is in the care of his father, and that the father is unpredictably explosive. Under such circumstances, with all these issues, organization can seem impossible, and the teacher's talking can sound like a background hum. Once emotionally based difficulties in focusing, attending and learning last long enough, they can look like ADHD (predominantly inattentive type).

Other compromises to attention come when recent external life circumstances distract someone from attending to the task at hand. The list is familiar: abuse, death, an accident or illness, disaster, a new baby, divorce, remarriage, moving, job loss, a family member in the armed services or prison, and so forth. Take the experience of trauma. The experience of trauma is often followed by traumatic reminders, and traumatic reminders lead to an activation of the autonomic nervous system that would not have occurred before the trauma. These reminders can be unexpected and can completely distract someone from what was being attended to. Instead, the person is flooded with flashbacks, or becomes numb, avoids the situation, and has trouble concentrating on it (Pynoos, Steinberg and Goenjian, 1996).

Other compromises to attention come from the nature of family interaction. When parents have never spent time with a child in reading or focusing on homework together, the experience of homework can be so lonely and unrewarding that the child can lose interest. Or when a student is used to cold, unresponsive parents, the student can learn that becoming agitated and going off-task gets some kind of response, although a negative one.

In sum, inattentiveness is like fever, a symptom of many disorders rather than a sign of just one.

PSYCHOTHERAPISTS' ATTENTION

I want to shift our attention now to psychotherapists. How do we pay attention to our patients? I do not want to talk here about an analyst's formulation of interventions and interpretations. That kind of cognitive activity on the part of the therapist derives from something prior, namely, the process of paying attention to the patient in the first place.

There is a history of efforts to describe a therapist's attention. Freud (1912) recommended that we do so by maintaining an evenly suspended or evenly hovering attention as patients speak. However, the idea of evenly hovering attention was soon found to be untenable. Anna Freud (1936) urged analysts to focus their attention on the id and the ego, guiding their analytic attention in a more structured way than the idea of attention hovering evenly without conscious expectations. Rather, there were conscious expectations that an analyst should attend to conscious and unconscious anxiety, prohibitions and defenses. Years later, Pine (1990) advised analysts to be as evenhanded as possible as we make sense, find order, and discover meaning. He suggested we do so by keeping our theoretical possibilities as diverse as possible, hovering over experiences of drive, ego, object, and self. This point of view recognizes the inherent selectivity of attention, based on prior expectations and current cognitive templates for organizing experience. Similarly, Spence (1982) noted that passive, evenly suspended attention cannot occur in reaction to the ambiguity of patient's comments and efforts at free association. These kinds of communication by the patient require an active and constructive listening, where an analyst supplies meaning and imposes context. By this time in the development of psychoanalytic theory, the concept of evenly hovering attention was hardly in use. From a modern point of view, evenly hovering attention seems impossible because of the uneven qualities of attention: its effort, selectivity, intensity, and dependence on context.

The terms selective inattention and dissociation are more useful in explaining compromises to a therapist's attentiveness. Sullivan (1956) noted some of the ways in which the content of consciousness, what we are aware of, can become narrow and focused. In one kind of selective inattention, people who are trying to do something well, something which is difficult to do, have to focus on the relevant and ignore the irrelevant. They also have to focus their memory selectively, recalling what is significant and relevant in understanding the present situation.

Yet in another kind of selective inattention, that which is significant is not attended to. Here, we do not profit from experience; we do not note its meaning, we overlook its implications, and we do not draw conclusions from it. This process of inattending occurs as part of the self-system's efforts to avoid the experience of anxiety. If we anticipate that realizing the significance of events will make us anxious, we do not attend to the significant details in those events. We gloss over that part of the account of events, and we do not let events mean to us what they would have to mean if we were to notice their details more carefully. The self-system moves the experience of those events rapidly into memory without developing any significant implications from them, making them seem so unimportant that we may not think to recall them. In Sullivan's words, we maintain a feeling of self-respect and calm by hurrying through any evidence to the contrary.

Dissociation, in Sullivan's view, starts with selective inattention but goes beyond it. In dissociation, we avoid seeing parts of an event we do not want to see or avoid knowing about impulses we do not want to have, or are never even aware of a troublesome event when it happens and have no later recall of it. We get no warning as to what we missed. In dissociation, instead of being aware of the experience, we spend time attending to it for the express purpose of finding ways not to notice it. We do so by devising fantasies that replace the experience, substituting it with something less anxiety provoking and more satisfactory to the self system.

Levenson (1982) taught supervisees that one of the steps in the algorithm of doing psychoanalysis was to look for gaps in the continuity and coherence of the patient's life story and to inquire further in order to fill those holes (p. 118). In a similar vein, Cooper and Witenberg (1983) focused on the process of stimulating curiosity in supervision. They urged supervisors to ask analysts in training to attend to gaps in the patient's story, or to parts of the story that the analyst could not quite picture, or to unlikely details in the story, or to discrepancies between how the patient reacted and how the therapist might have reacted in a similar situation. In the kind of therapeutic attention they recommend, a therapist needs to summon curiosity when confronted with such holes in the narrative. Paying attention to such discrepancies can then lead a therapist to formulate reasons for the missing or unexpected information. This formulation can then guide further inquiry or interpretive remarks.

Stern (1997) noted that in Sullivan's view, selective inattention is a security operation performed by the self-system to prevent intolerable levels of anxiety in the interpersonal world. Critiquing this point of view, he uses a broader definition of the interpersonal field than one defined only by anxiety and the self-system's security operations. Rather, we make unconscious invitations to other people to interact in various interpersonal ventures. Interpersonal life develops as we issue and respond to such invitations, imagining how others will respond to us and how we will feel about them. The resulting interpersonal field offers freedom, and limits, for interaction.

Stern writes that "each interpersonal field is defined by both dissociation and imagination, by what it illuminates and what it keeps in the darkness" (p. 155), using the same metaphor of light that Goldberg used. Looking at attention neuropsychologically, the influences on the prefrontal cortex (the hand that aims the flashlight of attention) include the amygdala's evaluation of the emotional significance of the context. In Stern's view, however, the context is now seen as an interpersonal field that defines at least some of the limits and possibilities of the illumination that a person can bring to bear as he or she shines the flashlight of attention.

Stern goes on to consider how therapists can attend to a patient's unformulated experience at all. If it is not conscious, what is there to attend to? He offers a sequence in which the therapist is embedded in the grip of the interpersonal field with the patient; the therapist emerges from this embeddedness and formulates his experience of the patient, and the grip of the field is broken (p. 199). To go through this sequence, the therapist looks for "absences, gaps, contradictions, stereotypes, repetitions, and dead spots in the material" (p. 99). Here Stern is in line with Levenson and with Cooper and Witenberg. Stern goes further, describing how a therapist thinks to look for such gaps, how the therapist becomes aware that there is something to be curious about and to pay attention to (p. 174). He describes curiosity as developing often out of awareness of countertransference, in a movement from unconscious experience to conscious focus on the countertransference. First, the analyst might feel a discomfort with a patient's comment or pressure to respond in a way that would not feel right. Then he or she might realize some frustration or resentment with the patient, or self-criticism in the face of the patient, or hazy wishes to accommodate or resist or argue with the patient. As the analyst realizes this, he can bring a sharper attention to the fact of this discomfort, pressure, resentment, self-criticism, or wish (pp. 189, 197–198), with now-clear curiosity as to how all this is happening. Sometimes this process is facilitated when the therapist can start to imagine feeling differently toward the patient. Thinking this way then turns the therapist toward a more clear attention to how he or she actually *is* feeling. Analysts try to pay attention to discrepancies between what they expect to occur, based on prior experience with the patient, and what actually happens with the patient (p. 244). Through realizing such discrepancies, an analyst can become curious and pay attention to what he or she already knows and had not been questioning, until that point (p. 250). Then the analyst can question the assumptions underlying what is known. At that point, gaps in the material are knowable, and new phenomena become evident in those gaps (p. 240).

CASE TREATMENT

With these considerations in mind, I return now to the case of Tom, the boy whose father was in prison, and describe the course of therapy. We met once weekly because of financial and scheduling considerations. From the start, Tom was outspoken in his resentment of his mother for trying to manage his homework for him. He claimed he did not care about school. Rather, he cared about concealing the true whereabouts of his father from the other students. His father had actually told Tom not to tell other students where the location of his father. When kids asked where his father was, he told them that his father was away on assignment, working as a spy for the government. He made up a badge that supposedly identified his father as a federal agent and showed it to other students when he could not get them to change the subject.

Tom also cared about appearing cool. He had only a few friends, but he exaggerated his popularity. Because of the debt his mother was dealing with since her ex-husband's imprisonment, the family had no extra money and could not compete with the wealth in some of his friends' families. Nonetheless, Tom wanted to get the best cell phone, to be the best trick bicyclist, and to show how much he knew about weapons and military video games. He exaggerated to make himself appear cool and was not interested in paying attention to the truth regarding the extent and limits of his actual knowledge or abilities.

Tom's tendency to be flexible with the truth extended to his schoolwork. He lied frequently and easily about his homework, not doing it or not handing it in, and then telling his mother that he had completed it and that he had handed it in to the teacher. Tom's mother had already started to communicate regularly with the school regarding Tom's schoolwork and class attendance, exposing his lies on these subjects. However, her efforts to control his homework through rewards or punishments all failed. The mother-son relationship was deteriorating, and they were enmeshed in fighting over homework. The enmeshment served multiple psychological functions. It was a way for a single mother and 12-year-old boy to feel an oedipal closeness while also creating a safe distance between them. Further, it was a way for Tom to feel some control and to express some anger to his mother over his father's absence, in a sadomasochistic way. His provocativeness also served to test her commitment to him, unlike his biological mother, who had kept five children but had arranged to have him adopted. In addition, his provocativeness and lying helped him identify as a young man who was breaking the rules, as his father had. Lying also helped him avoid knowing his feelings of shame over his father's imprisonment, and it helped him avoid knowing his feelings of shame over his executive function weaknesses.

Tom and his mother needed to separate before he could face these issues because the enmeshment with his mother over schoolwork allowed him to avoid facing these feelings and to avoid facing his defenses against them. A projective identification was occurring, in which the mother was induced into feeling and behaving like the kind of punitive authority that had imprisoned the father. In this context, she also exaggerated, making Tom's misdemeanors into severe violations of basic codes. When I first met her, she was afraid Tom could become a mass killer, like the perpetrators of campus shootings then in the news. Later she called him the scam artist and liar of the century.

In order to help bring about a lessening of their enmeshment, I intervened at family, systemic, and individual levels. At the family level, I spoke with his mother frequently on the phone and saw her either alone or with Tom about once a month. For a while she flooded me with e-mails expressing her anxiety about Tom and with copies of anxious e-mails to and from his teachers. I tried to help her to see Tom's lying and ignoring responsibility as not necessarily falling in his father's criminal footsteps. Rather, I urged her to understand Tom's lying and irresponsibility and oppositionalism in their own terms, as arising out of all the motives I just described (i.e., motives to enmesh, to provoke, to control, and to avoid feelings). If the mother could contain her fear that Tom would turn out to be a criminal like his father, and if Tom could see her fear as just a fear, rather than a likely truth, then Tom would have a chance to keep open the possibility of identifying with his father without having to develop a sociopathic identity.

At the level of the school, I got the mother's permission and then initiated a request to the school psychologist for the school to change its attitude toward Tom and his mother. Specifically, I asked the school psychologist if the school could take over from the mother the responsibility of monitoring and setting negative and positive consequences for homework and class attendance. The school psychologist agreed, and actions were taken to put this change into effect. For example, the school started to require Tom to attend more resource room periods, to go to more periods of homework help, and to have lunchtime detention when he did not attend these periods. I urged the mother to limit the imposing of negative consequences at home to matters that had to do with the home, such as lying and not doing chores, rather than to punish him for matters that had to do with school.

Tom continued to take Concerta for ADHD. In school, he was allowed to have preferential seating, refocusing and redirection during class, repetition of directions during tests, permission to finish testing in a separate location, an additional set of books, homework help, and daily resource room. Mother and I attended together more than one meeting of his school's Committee on Special Education in order to coordinate school, home, and therapy in working with Tom. These meetings reduced the resentment and helplessness that the school and mother were feeling about Tom for a while, providing instead a sense of collaboration.

These systemic interventions had distracted me from attending more carefully to the individual therapy. With the changes at home and school, tension eased somewhat. As I felt less flooded by the mother's and school's anxiety, I could concentrate more on the individual therapy. I noticed the discrepancies between the description of Tom as a lying sociopathic deviant and how I saw him in my office. His different self-states (Bromberg, 1998) became more clear—a delightful though silly and immature boy who cuddled under a blanket and showed off his electronic toys; a bored sullen boy who did not want to be with me in therapy and wished that he could leave early; an anxious boy who missed his father and felt deprived; a boy who lied and made up stories; and so forth. I told Tom about the different ways he could be; he paid attention and seemed interested. He told me he wanted to be a policeman when he grew up or a thief who would steal things, and we spoke about ways in which he could be like his father and ways in which he could be different from his father.

However, he steadily avoided paying attention to his feelings. I realized how he changed the subject in order to protect himself from knowing his feelings. We explored his ways of changing the subject and even listed them: pretending to sleep, stating how bored he was, blaming the teacher, trying to leave, lying or denying the facts, mentioning random facts, insulting the other person, and so forth. Soon we both were labeling his avoidance maneuvers, as they occurred.

This kind of opening in therapy was probably facilitated by the shifts that were taking place at the level of the family and the school, shifts which had relieved tension at home enough for Tom to feel room to do something other than to complain. The shifts also let me feel freer to pay closer attention to Tom in therapy. Also, they made him pay better attention to me as someone who could potentially get things done for him or get things done to him. The changes in the family-school system were ostensibly the responsibility of the school and his mother, but he knew that I had had a hand in bringing them about. From his point of view, I had potential for helping him or for getting in his way. The shift had a further meaning, in which the school and I took on structuring and limit-setting roles that a second parent may have assumed (although Tom's father never had), freeing Tom and his mother to relate in a different way.

I started to examine Tom's feeling of ending with his former therapist even while she continued to see his sister in the home. This arrangement had a little of the same structure as his biological mother putting him up for adoption while keeping his five older siblings in the home—except that here, Tom was the one doing the rejecting, reversing what happened when he was a baby. However, noting this pattern was not of interest to him. Nor was he interested in considering the evidence that he was lying to the teachers and his mother about not attending extra help classes at school (as he said, "they're all stupid, they don't know what they're talking about"). Nor was he interested in considering the likelihood that it really was he, Tom, who broke a window or took money at home. Nor was he interested in considering whether or not the stories he told people had really happened. For example, he told other students that a sonic boom had been caused by planes flying around the Empire State Building after a supposed terrorist threat there. I brought his attention to evidence that contradicted or brought doubts upon his story and suggested that telling such stories provoked other students to tease him. He maintained his story to me and added that he had told the students that he knew the story was true because of knowledge from his father, the supposed FBI agent.

At one point, another boy created a false bomb scare at school and was removed from school for a while. Through this incident we were able to consider Tom's own feeling of shame and stigma. He swore that if he were that boy, he would never come back to school and face what everyone would be saying about him. He could feel and admit his shame over his father. After this, Tom started to play with his lacrosse stick and ball during sessions, as he used to play with his father. Once, a ball hit a ceramic tile in my office and broke it in two. As I considered how we could glue it back together, he ignored me, criticized how precariously the tile had been placed, and urged me to keep playing ball with him. Quickly I could let him see how he avoided the truth (that he had broken the tile) and how he avoided his likely feelings about the truth (that he probably felt guilty). Then he helped me glue the tile together. This sequence led to a new attention to things that were broken in the office, whether by him or not by him. For example, once, he dunked a Nerf ball into a basketball net in my office and loosened the connection of the net to the wall; at another time, he noticed a stuffed tiger whose eye had fallen off. We worked together on fixing these things, enacting a reparation for activity that felt criminal while also creating a relationship involving shared attention to common experience. At one point I wondered whether it was worth making kids tease him for passing wild stories (e.g., about the terrorist threat to the Empire State Building) because here he was responsible for getting himself teased, rather than suffering teasing without meaning to provoke it. I got his attention here.

SUMMARY

Here is a case of a seventh grade boy who was said to have longstanding ADHD and was medicated for this condition. This condition could have been genetic (he was adopted and the ability of his biological parents to pay attention was unknown). His inattentiveness could have been influenced by his early delay in receptive language. It could be a defensive reaction, screening out his mother's tendency to go on and on. It could have also stemmed from dysregulation of his emotional life because of traumatic experience (i.e., knowledge that his biological mother kept her first five children but put him up for adoption; his father's violence, breakdown, hospitalization, and later imprisonment; the police being called to the house; his parents' divorce). Most of the individual therapy involved trying to get his attention, despite the (possible) biological, trauma-based, and psychodynamic reasons and ways he had learned not to pay attention. In lying and avoiding, he ignored and did not attend to the facts regarding his limited popularity, his limited ability to do bicycle tricks, his not doing homework and not going to study center, and his embarrassment and upset over his father being jail.

On the other hand, through the therapy he started to pay better attention. Doubting that there really was a golf course in the prison, he noticed that his father indeed lied. He paid attention to the influence I had over his mother and the school, he paid attention to the boy who started a bomb scare, and he used that story to express his shame over his father being in prison. When he broke my tile, he paid attention to my description of him as someone who avoided admitting the truth, and who avoided thinking about his feelings about what happened.

I also developed in my attentiveness. I was distracted by the flooding of anxiety from the mother and the school, and had to resolve that distraction by doing something in the family and school system, before I could attend more effectively to Tom and to our individual therapy. Before that, I had not noticed all of his different self-states, and so I had not brought his attention to them either.

To conclude, I have paid attention to one particular element in our work as therapists, namely, attending. Attentiveness is a building block, a facilitator, a way to realize significance, which then allows more global interventions such as empathizing, formulating and interpreting, once the significance is noted. I have tried to describe neuropsychological and experiential aspects of paying attention and of compromises to paying attention. The case of Tom demonstrates multiple sources of inattentiveness, and the need to use multiple interventions to deal with it (including psychopharmaceutical, school intervention, family intervention, and psychodynamic therapy).

The most important basis for these interventions is a recognition of the full interpersonal context of a child's life rather than to focus only on a biological vulnerability.

REFERENCES

Barkley, R. (1990), *Attention Deficit Hyperactivity Disorder: A Handbook for Diagnosis and Treatment*. New York: Guilford.

——— (1997), Behavioral inhibition, sustained attention, and executive functions: constructing a unifying theory of ADHD. *Psychological Bulletin*, *121*: 65–94.

Bromberg, P. (1998), *Standing in the Spaces: Essays on Clinical Process, Trauma, and Dissociation*. Hillsdale, NJ: The Analytic Press.

Cooper, A. & Witenberg, E. (1983), The stimulation of curiosity in the supervisory process. *Contemporary Psychoanalysis*, *19*: 248–64.

Damasio, A. (2003), *Looking For Spinoza: Joy, Sorrow, and the Feeling Brain*. New York: Harcourt, pp. 60–1.

Epstein, M. (1984), On the neglect of evenly suspended attention. *Journal of Transpersonal Psychology*, *16*: 193–205.

——— (1988), Attention and psychoanalysis. *Psychoanalysis and Contemporary Thought*, *11*: 171–89.

Freud, A. (1936), *The Ego and the Mechanisms of Defence: The Writings of Anna Freud, Volume 2*. New York: International Universities Press.

Freud, S. (1912), Recommendations to physicians practicing psycho-analysis. *Standard Edition of the Complete Works of Sigmund Freud*, *12*: 111–20.

——— (1923), Two encyclopedia articles. *Standard Edition of the Complete Works of Sigmund Freud*, *18*: 235–54.

——— (1925), An autobiographical study. *Standard Edition of the Complete Works of Sigmund Freud*, *20*: 7–74.

Fuster, J. (1995), *Memory in the Cerebral Cortex: An Empirical Approach to Neural Networks in the Human and Nonhuman Primate*. Cambridge, MA: MIT Press.

Goldberg, E. (2001), *The Executive Brain: Frontal Lobes and the Civilized Mind*. New York: Oxford University Press.

Goodyear, P. & Hynd, G. (1992), Attention deficit disorder with (ADD/H) and without (ADD/WO) hyperactivity: behavioral and neuropsychological differentiation. *Journal of Clinical Child Psychology*, *21*: 273–304.

Hallowell, E. & Ratey, J. (1994), *Driven to Distraction*. New York: Simon and Schuster.

Kahneman, D. (1973), *Attention and Effort*. Englewood Cliffs, NJ: Prentice-Hall.

Levenson, E. (1982), *The Purloined Self: Interpersonal Perspectives in Psychoanalysis. Contemporary Psychoanalysis Books*. New York: William Alanson White Institute, pp. 111–25.

Levine, M. (2002), *A Mind at a Time*. New York: Simon and Schuster.

Pine, F. (1990). Drive, Ego, Object and Self: A Synthesis for Clinical Work. New York: Basic Books.

Pynoos, R. S., Steinberg, A. M., & Goenjian, A. (1996). Traumatic stress in childhood and adolescence: Recent developments and current controversies. In: *Traumatic Stress: The Effects of Overwhelming Experience on Mind, Body, and Society*, A. Bessel, A. Van Der Kolk, A. C. McFarlane, & L. Weisaeth (eds.). New York: Guilford Press, pp. 331–58.

Ramachandran, V. S. & Blakeslee, S. (1998), *Phantoms in the Brain: Probing the Mysteries of the Human Mind*. New York: William Morrow.

Spence, D. (1982). Narrative Truth and Historical Truth: Meaning and Interpretation in Psychoanalysis. New York: Norton.

Stern, D. (1997), *Unformulated Experience: From Dissociation to Imagination in Psychoanalysis*. Hillsdale, NJ: Analytic Press.

Sullivan, H. S. (1956), *Clinical Studies in Psychiatry*. New York: W. W. Norton and Company.

Is ADHD a Real Neurological Disorder or Collection of Psychosocial Symptomatic Behaviors? Implications for Treatment in the Case of Randall E.

Burton Norman Seitler, Ph.D.

What we call something has consequences in terms of how we conceptualize and treat it. A multitude of names, all hypothesizing a neurological substrate, preceded the by-now-familiar "Attention Deficit Hyperactive Disorder" (ADHD) nosology. But what if the emphasis on its neurological origin was neither wrong nor irrelevant? How would this effect our approach to individuals so labeled? I contend that embracing a neurobiochemical conceptualization of ADHD has prematurely and mistakenly led us to believe that its solution must necessarily involve an *organic* remedy (such as medication), which often precludes psychodynamic approaches. I have worked psychodynamically with children for more than 40 years, including a host of those who have been independently diagnosed as ADHD (or many of its previous descriptors). I have concluded that this thing we call ADHD is typically related to a form of *agitated depression*, which *is* amenable to psychodynamic treatment. I have provided the psychodynamic treatment of Randall as an illustration of a child whose hyperactive symptomatology initially helped him stave off unbearable feelings of agitated depression. Even though his disorderly behavior caused Randall considerable trouble, it was the best he could do—until his underlying feelings could be analyzed, understood, and treated in a safe, human, and interpersonal interaction, sans medication.

Up to now, a reductionistic approach has been taken regarding attention deficit hyperactivity disorder (ADHD). Based on the extant belief that ADHD has a neurobiochemical origin, an increasing number of children, especially boys, who had been diagnosed with ADHD, have been treated with stimulant medications. However, many are now beginning to question whether ADHD can justifiably be classified (and thus treated) as a disease (Baughman, 1993, 2006; Furman, 2002, 2005; Rosemond and Ravenel, 2008; Seitler, 2006a, 2006b, 2008a, 2008b; Kaye, 1994).

A methodical review of the literature shows that the symptoms of ADHD listed in the *Diagnostic and Statistical Manual IV* of inattentiveness, forgetfulness, hyperactivity, and impulsivity are not unique to ADHD. In fact, most of us have exhibited one or more of the previous symptoms in our lives. Therefore, the terminology and description add nothing definitive that distinguishes ADHD from other behaviors. Moreover, no neuropsychological test results or physiological pathology have uniformly been found for ADHD (Rosemond and Ravenel, 2008; Furman, 2005). Also, no structural or functional neuroimaging studies have ever consistently identified a unique etiology for ADHD (Jackson, 2006; Furman, 2002; Weinberg and Brumback, 1992). In this regard, Flaherty et al. (2005), on behalf of the American Psychiatric Association, boldly asserted that the current state of neuroimaging does not warrant using such technology for diagnosing psychiatric disorders. Connors (1998) said as much in a paper he presented to the National Institute of Health (NIH) Consensus Development Conference: Diagnosis and Treatment of Attention Deficit Hyperactivity Disorder. In reviewing neuroimaging studies, he stated:

> The embarrassment of riches from neuroimaging studies reflects a poor understanding of any specificity for the neural basis of ADHD. The high levels of comorbidity of ADHD with oppositional, conduct, and mood disorders also call into question the specificity of the definition of the disease and whether current criteria are sufficient to allow further understanding of the neurobiology of the syndrome. (p. 23)

In addition, no genetic markers for ADHD have been identified. Even the definition of ADHD has been fuzzy, thus making studying "it" empirically, fraught with difficulty.

To date, most empirical studies have heavily relied on the Conners Rating Scale, which has questionable validity. Although supporters of the Connors Scale claim it has high inter-rater reliability, research only notes "high face validity" (Connors, 1998; Goldman et al., 1998), which is essentially how a test *looks* but not how well it answers the questions. For example, does it measure what it claims to measure and thus, test what it maintains it tests? When all is said and done, having face validity is really no better than having no validity at all. Even results of the Conners Revised Rating Scale, as well as teacher or parent "ratings" of school children have been highly discrepant. In addition, studies have shown that scales such as the Connors, ADHD Rating scale, the Brown, and the Wender Utah are "significantly easy to fake" (Jachimowicz and Geiselman, 2004). What this means is that an objective basis for the diagnosis of ADHD has been severely compromised by the use of subjective informant data derived from the above scales or from interview material.

Also, the use of stimulant medication has failed to distinguish any differential behavioral distinctions between children diagnosed as ADHD and children who were not so diagnosed. Also, proponents of the neurobiological model for the etiology of ADHD have not been able to successfully explain the huge differences in incidence of ADHD between girls and boys (Arnold, 1996; Gaub and Carlson, 1997). My own work (2006a, 2006b, 2007, 2008a, 2008b) suggests that such gender differences may be cultural manifestations having to do with the manner in which boys and girls are differentially permitted or able to express certain kinds of feelings, particularly sadness or depression. In our culture, it is perfectly acceptable for girls to cry. However, we seem to have a different standard for boys, who are often ridiculed if they cry or show tender feelings of one sort or another.

In short, the chant that has reverberated over a span of over four decades, namely, that ADHD (or any of the terms that preceded it) is a neurobiochemical disease, is simply not supported by a close analysis of the evidence. This is important because a consequence of holding to a strictly neurobiochemical substrate for ADHD is that it almost inexorably results in an organic solution to this purported but not supported "disease," one that involves the use of stimulant medications such as Ritalin, Adderall, Straterra, and so on. While these medications might be able to quell a child's excessive activity level in the short term, over a period of time they no longer are effective (Rosemond and Ravenel, 2008). In addition, neither children nor their parents typically learn that feelings underlie their overt behavioral manifestations, or what to do when those feelings are experienced. As a result, learning how to regulate or modulate affect may not occur or is severely compromised (Schore, 1991). This frequently results in a lifetime of dependence on the drug regimen rather than on their children's inner resources. Worse, medications have been shown to have serious after-effects (Baughman, 1993, 2006; Jackson, 2005, 2009; Breggin and Breggin, 1995; Barkley et al., 1990).

I use the term *after-effects* instead of *side-effects* because *side-effects* imply that the effects of the prescribed drugs are either rare or minimal. Research is now telling us a different, much more somber story about the after-effects of stimulants (Jackson, 2005, 2009; Lambert, 1998, 2005; Lambert and Hartsough, 1998; Raine, 2009, 2010). The Raine study longitudinally followed Australian children who were receiving stimulant medication for eight years. Among their findings, a few significant and alarming results stand out.

- The existence of long-term cardiovascular damage and significantly increased diastolic blood pressure, as compared to matched children who did not receive medication.
- School failure. Despite the long-held and, as it turns out, *mis*belief that children concentrate and achieve better when on a stimulant, they have a 10.5 times greater chance of being identified by a teacher as performing below grade level.
- Inattention and hyperactivity slightly *worsened* over the long term, contrary to what the public, as well as professionals in the field, have been told up until now. Drug advocates have made an argument that the above results occurred because the medicated children had more severe forms of ADHD. However, when children were first being included in the Raine study, the medicated group and nonmedicated group were compared with each other on developmental, behavioral, and health measures, producing **no** significant differences between the two groups at the outset.
- Other longitudinal research (Lambert, 2005; Lambert and Hartsough, 1998) has noted that children, who are on stimulants over the course of time, have a significantly greater chance of becoming addicted to cigarettes or cocaine.

There was a time when the idea of using medications and psychotherapy for working with patients who had been characterized by the term ADHD was considered to be the *moderate* position. After all, it was reasoned, if psychotherapy was effective and not harmful—and if medications had efficacy and did not do any damage—it would make sense to utilize both options together. Moreover, in doing so, the whole messy debate regarding whether or not ADHD had a "neurobiochemical" origin could be straddled by clinicians whose main aim was to help those under their care. That was before it began to become known, in some small circles and later on to an ever-increasing body of researchers and clinicians, that medications were neither as benign nor as efficacious in treating this "ADHD condition" as had previously been claimed. In fact, one of the initial "casualties" emerging out of the emphasis on the almost exclusive treatment of ADHD with medications was talk therapy, particularly uncovering treatments. This may explain, in large part, why there has been a relative dearth of published psychodynamic or psychoanalytic research or case studies in this area.

I have worked with children for more than 40 years, including many youngsters who were described as hyperactive or what we now refer to as ADHD. During that time, I began to question the neurobiochemical ideas that were beginning to take hold. My experiences with children who were diagnosed as exhibiting ADHD lead me to different conclusions. I have presented my experiences with such children elsewhere (Seitler, 2006a, 2006b, 2007, 2008a, 2008b).

The following is a case study of a young boy, who I have called "Randall," who was diagnosed by his pediatrician and neurologist as "hyperactive" and who had received psychotherapy treatment with me. It is offered here as a representative case illustrating that psychotherapy, in this case, psychoanalytically informed psychotherapy, can offer a parsimonious explanation for ADHD and a safe, effective, long-lasting treatment of children whom we have referred to with the term ADHD based on that understanding.

THE CASE OF RAMBLIN' RANDALL

Randall E. was brought to see me by his parents when he was six-and-a-half years old. Prior to their visit to me, R.E. had already begun establishing the rather dubious distinction of being asked to leave preschool for repeated misbehavior, such as pulling a girl's hair, impulsively getting up from his seat and roaming around the room, despite having been told to remain seated, and not heeding his teacher or adult in charge. Even attempts at enrollment in a fairly easy-going summer playgroup, which supposedly allowed the enrolled children some semblance of latitude and maneuverability, wound up with Randall being unceremoniously discharged. Randall's experience in Kindergarten was equally unsuccessful.

His parents were beside themselves. Not only were they frustrated with his seemingly uncontrollable behavior, but they were also embarrassed and more than a little bit worried that, in their words, " . . . something is wrong with our son."

Mr. and Mrs. E. were observed to be bright, articulate, and well-heeled individuals who lived in a tony suburb of New York. They were social-conscious and very active in their community. Mr. E. was an architect. His wife had a Master's degree in art history, although she did not work. They mentioned that they prided themselves on being relatively stable emotionally, although they were children of concentration camp survivors and could not help but wonder if their parents' experiences might have affected them. Despite their intuitive appreciation of the possibility that there might have been a transmission of their parents' trauma to them, when offered the opportunity to see someone for their own therapy, they demurred, preferring to exclusively focus their attention on their son, Randall, and his difficulties. Perhaps that in and of itself is an indication of the sensitive nature of this issue for Mr. and Mrs. E. and the likely delicateness required for delving into it.

Mr. E. struck me as low-keyed, mild-mannered, and thoughtful. He seemed to know that something was "amiss" but was not certain what it was or if it was extensive or severe. Mrs. E. seemed to be even more concerned than her husband and appeared more than a little bit on edge. Her distress seemed appropriate enough for our initial consultation, but it abated only slightly in our subsequent meetings over the years. By comparison, her husband seemed to grow less and less tense in the course of meeting on a monthly basis to discuss Randall's progress. More will be said about this somewhat later on in this discussion.

As thorough a developmental history as could be obtained was taken over several sessions. Even so, most clinicians are aware that a number of things are sometimes uncovered well after a history is taken that (for a variety of reasons) parents somehow did not mention initially. This turned out to be the case here as well. Under the section, "Generational Transmission of Trauma," parental memories that were uncovered, subsequent to the early history gathering, is discussed.

UNREMARKABLE DEVELOPMENTAL MILESTONES

Randall's developmental milestones did not seem to be out of the ordinary. If anything, he achieved most of his physical and cognitive landmarks considerably earlier than expected. He was, however, a very curious and inquisitive youngster, frequently exploring, getting into, or taking apart things. Somehow or other, Randall's active nature frequently wound up creating problems for him and correspondingly for his parents. His parents commented on one thing in particular they said both intrigued Randall and simultaneously frightened them. He loved tinkering with inanimate objects. Specifically, he was especially fascinated by the garage door opener, often playing with it—pressing the remote button over and over again to make the door go up and down—for extended periods of time. In addition, he was similarly interested in looking at and figuring out how fans, clocks, or other kinds of mechanisms operated.

His parents said that Randall's social skills were another matter altogether. They described him as being "short with other children" and explained that he seemed to have little or no patience if another child could not understand something as quickly as he preferred or was perceived by Randall as "slow moving," in their words. His parents thought the worst, fearing that their son might be autistic. Before they came in to seek my services because of their fears, they took their son for a pediatric and then a neurological examination. Both independently felt that Randall fit the description of a child who was hyperactive.

Although they complained that Randall was highly impatient, that his frustration tolerance was very limited, and that his activity level was exceedingly high, they were dead-set against his being on any kind of medication. They asked me if I would be willing to work with him in view of the history that they had provided and their strong opposition to the use of stimulants or any other form of medication with Randall. I agreed to do so.

PREPARING THE CHILD FOR PSYCHOTHERAPY

As is my custom, we discussed what they would tell Randall in order to prepare him for coming in to see me. I find that it is generally a good idea for the child to understand why he is being brought in to see "this strange doctor." When a child is not told why he is being taken somewhere, the potential for all kinds of fantasies to occur (some of which are not necessarily calming) may increase. Although fantasies are an integral, and arguably necessary part of growing up, in some cases where the thoughts might lend themselves to a misperception of reality, it might be wiser to further the cause of "reality" by simply telling the youngster the reason for the visit. The reason ought to be predicated upon the same reasons the parents sought treatment for the child in the first place. That is, when the parents let their child know they are concerned that he gets into "trouble" (I would spell out exactly what is meant in simple language in a concerned, kind, and compassionate tone of voice), the stage is set for the beginning of his learning cause and effect. At the same time, structure is subtly introduced in terms of setting up an appointment time, with the same person, in the same place.

When I see the child for the first time, I will follow up with the child and ask if he knows the reason for coming to see me and knows what it is that I do. Even a child as young as Randall was when he first came to see me (six-and-a-half years old) can understand a global description given by his parents, such as, "we're taking you to Dr. Seitler who likes to help children who sometimes have problems in school." So long as the child is aware of the difficulties he is having in school (or elsewhere) it is much easier for the child to apprehend the rationale behind the parents' concern and his visit to the doctor. It gives him a cognitive "handle" onto which to hold.

Mr. and Mrs. E. were very conscientious about their "assignment." They sat down with Randall and talked to him about how worried they were about him because they could tell from his behavior that something was bothering him. They then told him that they had found someone to talk with who would try to help him with whatever was bothering him. Almost immediately after their conversation with Randall, they called me to let me know that they had spoken with him and that everything was in place for me to begin therapy with him.

EARLY ENCOUNTERS WITH RAMBLIN' RANDALL

Randall came into my office, accompanied by his father, who then introduced his son to me. He then gently excused himself and assured Randall that he would be in the waiting room until Randall's first meeting with me was complete. Randall entered my office, looked up and down and back and forth, apparently sizing up the place. He then said he wanted to make sure that his father had remained. He opened the door, stuck his head out, and checked to see if his father was still there. Even though he saw that his father was in the waiting room as promised, Randall still seemed to be a bit restless. Randall then began to repeatedly say that he does not like having to sit down, as if he were responding to someone who was somehow barking orders at him to sit still. In the midst of this, he exclaimed, "I don't like to sit down and I don't like to be still." All of this was met with my response, "You're free to stand, and if you want to sit, that's OK too; whatever makes you feel most comfortable." I explained that *I was going to sit down*, but he did not have to sit until he felt comfortable enough to do so. Despite his initial protests, Randall eventually settled down. It should be pointed out that while Randall's protest against sitting down could easily be interpreted as negativistic or oppositional, or even as defiant by some, it did not seem to me to be any of the above. I did not insist that he sit down. Whatever coping function his standing up and being free to roam about the room might have served, could now remain intact, and there would be no need on his part to enter into a "power struggle" with me in order to maintain that presumed defense.

Right from the start, Randall was given the traditional three options that I offer to children. I told him (1) that we could talk, (2) we could play games, or (3) we could talk and play games. Like many children with whom I have worked, he elected to talk and play games. He was uncertain what to play with and wound up going from item to item, quickly scanning each one before moving on to the next. Finally, he decided to play the "Candy Land™" game. Unsure if his father was still in the waiting room, he continuously went to the door. I reassured him that his father would still be there when we were done. This seemed to hold him, but only for a few moments, until the next time when he felt the strong pull to check on his father's whereabouts. At the conclusion of the session, he rushed out of the office. I was momentarily uncertain how our first meeting went, as he speeded away. Then, as quickly as he left my office, he just as rapidly pivoted around halfway down the hallway and said, "That was fun, can I come back?" "Of course you can," I replied, adding, "I can't wait."

Randall's reaction was both unexpected and equally reassuring. Because youngsters who have been called hyperactive seem to be constantly in motion, it is not always easy to gauge, in those early sessions, if rapport, or even the most minimal, elementary of connections has been established. This alerted me to the fact that Randall was able to pick up subtle cues that he was welcome and that the environment is friendly. However, it appears that he does this "on the fly," so to speak. In other words, he comes to conclusions swiftly. Thus, even though he may be racing around, as if driven by his inner impulses, his behavioral "hyperactivity" may not be as aimless as it may appear at first blush.

I had already had experience working, or performing psychodiagnostic evaluations with children regarded to be hyperkinetic or having minimal cerebral impairments—terms that were in use many years ago and which are now subsumed under the ADHD nomethetic umbrella. Primarily, as a result of a considerable amount of testing that I had done in my life, I had begun to develop some notions about whether what we currently call ADHD existed, and if it did, whether it was a syndrome and what might give rise to it, and/or whether it was an overly used "grab-bag" term to cover any behavior that might "inconvenience" some adults.

FINDINGS FROM MY PSYCHODIAGNOSTIC EVALUATIONS

It seemed more than an intellectual oddity to me that most of the children that had been identified by neurologists as having "minimal brain damage" rarely showed much more than "soft signs" on a Bender Visual-Motor Gestalt test. Rather, they almost uniformly showed signs of depression and unrest on Rorschach inkblots that I had administered to them. I wondered about this. Moreover, since hyperkinetic children were not supposed to be able to maintain their attention for very long periods of time, one would think that they would be unable to do tasks that required them to sit still, such as being able to play on a computer. But the simple fact that I had always been able to administer a battery of tests with them, (even if I had to spread the test sequence over a few sessions) indicated that they *could* pay attention long enough to complete sections of the test, and then the entire examination. Accordingly, I was relatively confident that if something captured their interest they *would* be able to sit still and remain focused on it.

RANDALL'S TREMORS AND MY THEORETICAL TREPIDATIONS

My early theoretical formulations held that so-called hyperactive children, particularly boys, were hyperactive as a means by which they could deal with underlying feelings of sadness or depression (specifically speaking—*agitated depression*), and that it was not their neurological "wiring," so to speak, that was producing their excessive motoric activity. Yet Randall puzzled me. I observed that he had a noticeable tremor in his hands. It seemed to be much more than the "herky-jerky" impulsive movements that children often display who are anxious or not very coordinated. On the contrary, his tremors seemed to be similar to what are seen in people who are experiencing Parkinson's disease. Randall's tremors gave me pause. I wondered if I had been wrong about the psychological factors that gave rise to hyperactivity that I hypothesized. Could it be that the tremors that Randall exhibited were a sign that he did, indeed have a minimal neurological disorder? I remained open to the prospect of a neurological explanation for Randall's tremors, and kept alive the possibility my ideas about agitated depression being behind ADHD were wrong. If there were a neurological component inherent in Randall's condition that produced his hyperactivity, would he be able to focus on any task for very long?

I did not have to wait very long to find out. At our next session, Randall spotted my newly purchased Apple II C computer in the secretarial desk area. He asked if it worked, followed by a barrage of questions announced in rapid-fire succession, all of which centered around whether he could play on the computer; did I have games on the computer that he could play, and if so, what were they? I told Randall that I was sorry that I did not have any games on the computer (up until this point, I was using it for writing reports and sending out bills). Instantaneously, he seemed to become deflated by my response and quickly turned his attention away to something else.

RAPID RETREAT RELATED TO RANDALL'S RAMBLIN' REACTIVITY READINESS?

His reaction of quickly turning away was much like the way someone might act who had just been spurned by a good friend. I asked myself, had Randall been making a possible "petition for interaction" with me? If so, did he feel dismissed, or cast aside by my response? Did my response make him feel rejected? Was the reason he quickly diverted his attention away from our conversation his means of protecting himself both from his perception of being rejected, and the rapid transformation of that presumed perception into feelings of dejection?

So I then asked him if he would be interested in playing on the computer if I were somehow able to create a simple computer game for us to use? His reaction to my question was immediate. He exclaimed "yippee!" as though it was a *fait accompli.* Instead of continuing to divert his attention away from our previous interaction, as he had done just moments ago, Randall was now able to return to his original request and to our interaction.

Along with the above questions, I also wondered if my instructions to Randall might have been a source of confusion or provocation for him. That is, when I gave him the three options (i.e., talking, playing, talking, and playing), did he think that the computer was part of the playing? If so, did he then quickly interpret my saying the computer has no games on it as a contradiction or double message on my part? In other words, did I unsuspectingly introduce a "crazy-making situation" into the mix? If this were so, it might be a clue to the kinds of enactments that get set up and/or take place in his life—probably at blazing speed—to which he responds with equal celerity. Regrettably, because of the speed of his reactions, it may be difficult for adults in charge to spot, much less understand, these often-invisible processes that may give rise to his behavior in the first place. I decided to remain alert to these possibilities as well as remain open to any alternative explanations that may present themselves.

So long as the child remains in treatment, we are graced with the possibility that over time enough will happen for a pattern to emerge and that the child and I will figure it out together. As much as Randall's rapid reactions seemed to defy time, in the final analysis it would be our patience and collaborative work over the course of time that would ultimately prevail.

I kept my word. After learning Basic, an early and gratefully uncomplicated computer language, I was able to create a simple computer game, which I called "Space Debris." It was made up of a set of three dashes to form a crude-looking "spaceship." Essentially, it was little more than three lines that formed the shape of an "arrow." The rest of the game consisted of a series of dots that randomly descended from the top of the screen downward. As each dot came down, a programmed "counter" added up the number of dots that had "fallen." The "spaceship" could only move sideways. Its mission was to dodge the "space debris" dots as they descended. The score was based on the number of dots that were avoided. As the dots fell, the number of dots that were evaded was shown on the screen. The instant a dot touched the spaceship, the game ended and the total number of accumulated dots was displayed.

Randall was fascinated by the game and excitedly talked up a storm whenever we played it. We would take turns. Randall would go first, and then it was my turn. He had no trouble sharing. For the most part, he was slowly but indisputably developing the ability to wait until my turn was over. However, on the occasions when I was having success dodging the "debris," Randall became a little impatient. It seemed less a matter of competition regarding who got the highest score than what seemed like an "on edge" feeling on his part about possibly having to delay gratification by waiting. Of course, by definition, if my score was higher than usual, it meant that my turn was correspondingly longer. When this happened, I noticed that Randall would get up, roam the room, and find another game to play. The way I work with each child is for us to play one game at a time. It is perfectly fine to discontinue a game at any time, for any reason. However, before we move on to another game, the rule is that we put away whatever we are working on. So, at those moments when Randall started on another game, I would ask him if he was done with the one that was before us. If he said he was done, I would ask him to help put away the game, toy, and so on. Almost without exception, practically every child with whom I have ever worked has followed this regimen. It is a condition of playing with the materials in the office. Even more than that, it is a subtle but nevertheless integral part of the treatment. It helps the child develop and internalize a sense of structure, one built on uniform, unambiguous instructions, expectations, sameness, consistency, and constancy. I am always openly grateful and consistently express my appreciation for their helpfulness in the clean-up process.

Initially, Randall would simply walk away from a game without explanation. However, after a while, and with considerable encouragement, he began to talk about whatever he was feeling that seemed to propel him away from what we were doing. He explained, "It takes so long for my turn to come up. I just can't wait!" "It sounds like waiting is sometimes painful for you," I responded. "What does it feel like when you wait?" He said, "I hate it!" Eventually, this segued into discussions of what it must feel like to have to wait in other places such as, in school, at home, and so on—or with other people.

MOVING FROM READINESS TO ACT TO CONVERSATION ORIENTATION

Over time, Randall and I had many conversations about feelings he might have had that were associated with waiting, having to postpone gratification, tolerate frustration, or endure suspense. The object was to create an atmosphere for Randall to feel safe and comfortable enough to be able to freely express his feelings or thoughts. And express himself he did—often loudly, passionately, and unreservedly. He was beginning to substitute speaking for acting, in particular, speaking about his feelings. Instead of suppressing his inner urges, the emphasis on my part was to help him sublimate his energy into activities that would be meaningful and enjoyable for Randall. I felt the more conversation we could have that could replace action, the better.

We played on the computer many times. Initially, playing on the computer was one of his favorite things to do in the office. Each time we played, there was a great deal of spontaneous, excited conversation. As it turns out, his fantasy life was very rich. Sometimes, Randall became ideationally "flooded" by his own imaginings. Because talking was becoming a strong source of connection between us, a means by which we could speak about practically anything, Randall was able to express previously frightening thoughts he had been containing for a long time. Interestingly, at first, he seemed to be preoccupied with thoughts of aggression, usually involving people who were purposely being hurt or mistreated. He talked about topics involving violence in which someone was forcibly taken advantage of. Each time he began to bring up such topics, he became extremely agitated. At such moments he would rapidly get up, pace the floor, and roam from one part of the office to another and back, again and again. Whenever that occurred, it seemed as if Randall was reverting back to his "old standby" manner of handling his inner turmoil.

Talking about his feelings helped Randall safely share his frightening thoughts with me, obviating feelings of having to be alone with his disturbing thoughts. Moreover, Randall somehow was able to correctly perceive me as accepting, as being empathically attuned and nonjudgmental, thus permitting me to serve as a "good" (enough) transitional object for him. This, in turn, helped him build a bridge between himself, his parents, and others. By internalizing my general mien (of calmness, light-hearted humor, interest, and focus), he began to learn how to self-regulate his affect. In short, he could now be a "good parent" to himself, and in so doing, care for himself.

Nonetheless, the question about the origin of his unbearably frightening fantasies still needed to be understood and, if possible, worked through. There was an indefinable quality about Randall's fantasies that felt different to me somehow, from how I imagined Randall to be like. It felt like it was a different person telling me these horrible things, much like a separate or "false self" or introject of some kind.

GENERATIONAL TRANSMISSION OF TRAUMA

Fortunately, something his parents had told me in my history taking made me wonder if the nature of Randall's frightening fantasies had originated in their own fantasies that somehow were unconsciously transmitted to him. The nature of his fantasies involved sadistic material. While it is not out of the ordinary for children to have thoughts that we would call sadistic, the structure of the violent images that Randall expressed so closely resembled descriptions of World War II and concentration camps that I could not help but speculate if some of his thoughts had emanated from his parents' anxiety-related internalizations. It is not unusual for traumatic material to be *overtly* transmitted to a succeeding generation; it is less obvious—although no less possible—for such material to be silently or *covertly* passed on, as will be seen in the following description.

Although neither of Randall's parents ever agreed to my often-extended offers for them to be in their own psychotherapy with someone, they willingly came in for monthly consultations, ostensibly for the purpose of providing me with ongoing information regarding what they were experiencing with him at home and to discuss various kinds of ways they might be able to work with him. During those visits, they recited the litany of things that Randall had done. Typically, they would ask me what they could do in response to the behaviors Randall displayed. I would then focus on what they "felt" when Randall acted a certain way. This was designed to provide them with empathy for the difficulties they were experiencing with Randall, to let them know that I could appreciate what it must have been like for them whenever Randall got into trouble, and provide a sense that I was with them.

In the process of empathizing with their feelings, they began to recognize what they were feeling was, in all likelihood, being transmitted to them by Randall. Interestingly, because they were so sensitive and hyperalert to him, they picked up what he may have been feeling, albeit without realizing it.

Unfortunately, either because Randall was not aware what he was feeling or because he could not verbalize his feelings, he simply acted on his inner emotions. For example, there was an occasion when Randall perceived himself as being ridiculed. He started to scream uncontrollably at his mockers. At one point, right in the midst of this, he began to race around the classroom. When his parents informed me of these incidents, they told me, "We simply don't know what to do. We are beside ourselves." For them, the feeling was helplessness. When they were able to get in touch with their own vulnerability, defenselessness, and helplessness, they were able to consider whether Randall felt that way, too.

Although Mrs. E's tension level seemed to rise dramatically whenever she discussed Randall's behavior and the pain that she imagined was underneath it, Mr. E's reaction seemed more related to each incident in and of itself. He was visibly upset but not out of control. Mrs. E. said that, for some reason, her son being ridiculed reminded her of the humiliation that she imagined her parents undoubtedly felt when interrogated (or treated even worse) by the Nazis. I asked what she did with her feelings when she learned that her son had been mocked? She said she would scream at the top of her lungs in agony. She explained that her son being mocked felt exactly like being tortured.

If Mrs. E. vicariously overidentified with her parents, it is not inconceivable that she would use this "aptitude" with her son. In other words, she symbiotically merged with her son so that, in effect, his pain became her agony. Metaphorically speaking, if he accidentally got cut, she would bleed for him. By the same token, it is entirely plausible that Randall, in turn, would identify with the manner in which his mother would react. Thus, her agitation and possibly other repressed feelings became his.

Randall was bright and highly verbal. Because our talking together had taken on a fun quality for him, our meetings and light-hearted banter (i.e., exchanging stories, telling jokes, creating silly puns) over the years was something to which he looked forward. At the outset, the computer game was the prop that would get the conversation going. Later on, Randall found another interest. He went from our "space debris" game to a love of all things related to Star Trek.

He knew the names of all of the characters, by whom they were played, and their particular roles. He came to the session with drawings that he had made of the star ship Enterprise or stories that he wrote as possible episodes for the show. He and I would play the roles of various characters. At times, he was Captain Kirk and I would obey his instructions. Sometimes, I would be Scotty, the master engineer. I found myself saying to him, "Captain, we need more power, sir" (making sure to emphasize the "r" sound at the end of the word "power," much to his delight). He then would eagerly direct me to modify the engines. I remember asking him, at one point (a crucial turning point, as it turned out), "What I should do, sir, if the engines simply can't be changed?" His reply was telling. He said, "With patience we can figure anything out. Together, we can do it."

There is very little doubt in my mind that the multiple meanings contained in his statement were not lost on him, despite his tender young years. (He was nine years old by now.) I remember responding by telling him that our cooperation meant a great deal to me. At that moment, much to my surprise, he began to cry. I sat with him and waited. When the moment seemed right, I asked him if he wanted to talk about what he was feeling? He slowly replied. He said, "Nobody ever just listened to me without going crazy or telling me I'm doing something wrong. I can tell you really like me, no matter what." I replied, "I guess that's something that you haven't been used to, huh?" "Not really," he said. I then wondered out loud what it must have been like for him to have all these feelings inside and not be able to tell anyone because he thought nobody would be interested in them. He said, "I couldn't tell anybody. I just couldn't. My mother couldn't handle it, and my father was always busy with work or something, or I just got real shy with him." "So where did your feelings go?" "Inside, I guess," he replied. "Until they came out." "Yeah," he said, "until they came out and I got in trouble." "Are you afraid that if you talk about your feelings you will get in trouble here?" "Not with you I'm not." I then inquired, "What makes it hard to do it with others?" He said that he was a bit embarrassed that others would make fun of him, as they had done in the past, and that whenever they did he would feel lost and alone. "And angry?" I asked. "Yes, but not just angry. I mostly kept my feelings in until I couldn't anymore. And that's when I would explode. I really didn't want to blow up, but I just couldn't take it anymore."

If we cut to the chase, therein lies what I believe to be the crux of what most ADHD children experience, as well as the solution for their so-called excessive activity levels. Randall and I spent the next two years working through his underlying previously pent-up feelings of sadness, working on helping him recognize more consistently what he felt about something before he reacted. In so doing, he was able to develop an observing ego and was able to establish cause and effect connections between events, his feelings, and potential actions. Moreover, he was able to verbalize those hard-fought, newly obtained "insights." He was beginning to make—and keep—friends. His grades improved, and the tone of his teacher reports was more and more positive. As we know, the course of therapy is never smooth, and it had its share of starts and stops here as well. There were moments when Randall got angry with me when he thought that I had misunderstood something he was trying hard to tell me. But even those momentary "ruptures" were dealt with in the context of our relationship. If anything, he learned that (1) he was allowed to get angry with me and (2) he was capable of getting angry without hurting others or hurting himself (by getting into trouble). He also learned (3) how to get angry in a socially permissible manner, without it turning into uncontrollable rage.

FORTUITOUS FINDING

A serendipitous result occurred that I could not have anticipated in my wildest dreams. The tremor that Randall exhibited that I had observed early on in our sessions completely disappeared by the time therapy concluded. It seemed to happen so gradually (much the way a physical wound heals) that I barely took notice of the change until it was completely gone. Does this therefore mean that ADHD is not neurological? As much as I believe that to be the case, and as much as this occurrence could be interpreted to support that contention, there is no way to be certain.

THE IRRELEVANCY OF A NEUROLOGICAL ORIGIN

How can we account for the disappearance of the tremor so prominently displayed by Randall? One could argue that the neurological pathways that some say are associated with ADHD may have been "re-routed." Certainly, the new information that is being developed about the plasticity of the brain could render reasonable support for that position. Even if that were so, it indicates that a neurological explanation for the appearance of the ADHD symptom picture need not insure that only a neurological treatment would be effective. If anything, it strongly suggests that psychotherapy, particularly psychoanalytic psychotherapy, can be helpful.

What it essentially comes down to, as the case of Randall demonstrates, is that it is less relevant than we have been lead to believe if ADHD does or does not have a neurobiochemical substrate. What is important is that medication was not necessary in this case or any of the other cases I have treated, that psychoanalytically informed psychotherapy can be successful in effecting change with youngsters labeled with the ADHD appellation, and that it is the relationship that seems to be fundamental in fostering that change.

I wish to offer a final note. Practically all of the ADHD kids with whom I have worked have harbored a hidden inner sadness, which came out as hyperactivity. It is my view that the hyperactivity stemmed from sad feelings that were "bottled up" inside and which inexorably was expressed by the "court of last resort," the body—in the form of agitation and excessive motoric activity.

Being permitted to gain access to a child's inner feelings of depression and treating those feelings must, by necessity, be accomplished in the context and complexities of the child's family of origin, his extended family, his ancestral/generation family, his present and preceding cultural influences, and his own unique individual nature and internal phenomenology. All approaches must be tailored to the unique specifications of the child. One size cannot fit all. Manualized or formulaic treatments or medications cannot effectively or safely do more than suppress symptoms over time—if that. What made our work together work was our relationship, Randall's faith in me, and his resulting belief in himself.

REFERENCES

Arnold, L. E. (1996), Sex differences in ADHD: Conference summary. *J. Abnorm. Psychol.*, *24*: 555–69.

Barkley, R., Fischer, M., Edelbrock, C. & Smallish, L. (1990), The adolescent outcomes of hyperactive children diagnosed by research criteria. I: An 8-year old prospective follow-up study. *J. Am. Acad. Child Adol. Psychiat.*, *29*: 546–57.

Baughman, F. (1993), Treatment of attention deficit disorder. *JAMA*, *269*: 2368.

——— (2006), *The ADHD Fraud: How Psychiatry Makes Patients of Normal Children*. Bloomington, IN: Trafford Publishers.

Breggin, P. & Breggin, G. (1995), The hazards of treating "Attention-deficit/hyperactivity disorder" with methylphenidate (Ritalin). *J. Coll. Student Psychother.*, *10*(2): 55–72.

Connors, K. (1998), Overview of attention deficit hyperactivity Disorder. Presented at NIH Consensus Development Conference: Diagnosis and Treatment of Attention Deficit Hyperactivity Disorder, November 16–18, Bethesda, MD, pp. 21–4.

Flaherty, L. T., Arroyo, W., Chatoor, I., Edwards, R. D., Ferguson, Y. B., Ferguson, S., et al. (2005), Brain imagining and child and adolescent psychiatry with special emphasis on SPECT, viewed 9 July 2005, http://www.psych.org/psych_pract/clin_issues/populations/children/SPECT.pdf

Furman, L. (2002), Attention deficit/hyperactivity disorder: An alternative viewpoint. *J. Int. Child Adol. Psychiat.*, *2*: 125–44.
——— (2005), What is attention-deficit hyperactivity disorder (ADHD)? *J. Child Neurol.*, *20*(12): 994–1003.
Gaub, M. & Carlson, C. L. (1997), Gender differences in ADHD: A meta-analysis and critical review. *J. Amer. Acad. of Child and Adolescent Psychiat.*, *36*: 1036–45.
Goldman, L. S., Generl, M., Bezman, R. & Slanetz, P. (1998), Diagnosis and treatment of attention deficit/hyperactivity disorder in children and adolescents. *JAMA*, *279*: 1100–7.
Jachimowicz, G. & Geiselman, R. E. (2004), Comparison of ease of falsification of attention deficit hyperactivity disorder diagnosis using standard behavioral rating scales. *Cognitive Science Online*, *2*: 6–20.
Jackson, G. (2005), *Rethinking Psychiatric Drugs: A Guide for Informed Consent*. Bloomington, IN: AuthorHouse Press.
——— (2006), A curious consensus: "Brain scans prove disease?" *Ethical Human Psychology and Psychiatry*, *8*(1): 55–60.
——— (2009), *Drug Induced Dementia: The Perfect Crime*. Bloomington, IN: AuthorHouse.
Kaye, S. (1994), The place of depression in dysfunctional learning. *Psychoanal. Psychol.*, *11*(2): 265–74.
Lambert, N. M. (1998), Stimulant treatment as a risk factor for nicotine use and substance abuse. Overview of attention deficit hyperactivity disorder. Presented at NIH Consensus Development Conference: Diagnosis and Treatment of Attention Deficit Hyperactivity Disorder, Bethesda, MD, pp. 191–200.
——— (2005), The contribution of childhood ADHD, conduct problems, and stimulant treatment to adolescent and adult tobacco and psychoactive substance abuse. *Ethical Human Psychology and Psychiatry*, *7*(3): 197–221.
——— & Hartsough, C. (1998), Prospective study of tobacco smoking and substance dependence among samples of ADHD and non-ADHD subjects. *J. Learn Disabil.*, *6*: 533–44.
Raine, W. (2009, September), Western Australia Ministerial Implementation Committee for Attention Deficit Hyperactivity Disorder, Raine Attention Deficit Hyperactivity Disorder Study, Perth, Australia: Telethon Institute for Child Health Research.
——— (2010, January), *Attention Deficit Hyperactivity Disorder Study: Draft—Long-term Outcomes Associated with Stimulant Medication in the Treatment of ADHD in Children*. Perth, Australia: Telethon Institute for Child Health Research.
Rosemond, J. K. & Ravenel, D. (2008), *The Diseasing of America's Children: Exposing the ADHD Fiasco and Empowering Parents to Take Back Control*. Nashville, TN: Thomas Nelson Publishers.
Schore, D. (1991), Early superego development: The emergence of shame and narcissistic affect regulation in the practicing period. *Psychoanalysis and Contemporary Thought*, *14*(3): 188–250.
Seitler, B. N. (2006a), On the implications and consequences of a neurobiochemical etiology of ADHD. *Ethical Human Psychology and Psychiatry*, *8*(3): 229–40.
——— (2006b), Attention deficit hyperactive disorder: Its neurobiological aetiology put to question. Presented to the Philadelphia Society of Psychoanalytic Psychologists, January 29.
——— (2007), An alternative explanation of ADD/ADHD involving agitated depression and an illustration of successful psychotherapy without using medication. Presented to the Society for the Exploration of Psychotherapy Integration (SEPI) Conference, July 7, Lisbon, Portugal.
Seitler, B. N. (2008a), Successful treatment of an adolescent without medication, ECT, or psychosurgery. Presented at the International Center for the Study of Psychiatry and Psychology Conference, October 10, Tampa, FL.
——— (2008b), Successful child psychotherapy of ADHD: An agitated depression explanation. *Amer. J. of Psychoanal.*, *68*: 276–94.
Weinberg, W. A. & Brumback, W. (1992), The myth of attention deficit-hyperactivity disorder: Symptoms resulting from multiple causes. *J. Child Neurol.*, *7*: 431–5.

Psychodynamic Play Therapy With a Six-Year-Old African American Boy Diagnosed With ADHD

Gabrielle F. Cione, M.A.
Lila A. Coleburn, J.D., Ph.D.
Eric A. Fertuck, Ph.D.
Peter Fraenkel, Ph.D.

This article describes the effective, two-year psychodynamic treatment of Jaden, an African American boy diagnosed with Attention Deficit Hyperactivity Disorder (ADHD), Combined Type. Treatment began when Jaden was six years old and is currently in its second year. Play provided an understanding of his internal world and a holding environment (Winnicott, 1960) to contain and reflect Jaden's impulses and behavioral dyscontrol. Clinical material, which centers on character play, is presented to illustrate the evolution of Jaden's understanding of his diagnosis and his struggle to manage feelings of intense sibling rivalry, anger, envy, and frustration. Further, the transference-countertransference relationship was utilized in the clinical work and informed by a relational, integrative psychodynamic-systems perspective (Altman et al., 2002). This approach included ongoing collaboration with Jaden's family and his school, and the use of standardized psychological assessment. This integrative psychodynamic-systemic approach decreased Jaden's behavioral dyscontrol, aggression, and distractibility. These techniques fostered a realistic and more positive self-representation, enhanced his emotion and impulse regulation, and helped him improve his school performance. The implications for expanding treatment options and theoretical perspectives for ADHD are discussed.

Attention Deficit Hyperactivity Disorder (ADHD) is one of the most commonly diagnosed psychiatric disorders of childhood (American Psychiatric Association, 2000). The dominant etiological theory is that ADHD is a biologically based, genetic, and neurological disorder. Stimulant medications have been the most empirically supported intervention to date for the treatment of ADHD (Everett and Toff, 2008; MTA Cooperative Group, 1999; Rains and Scahill, 2004). Although acknowledging the efficacy of medication in many cases, other clinicians have argued forcefully that the psychosocial environment must be considered both when evaluating children for ADHD and when planning the appropriate treatment (Vaughan, Roberts and Needelman, 2009). When psychological interventions have been employed, either as the primary approach or in conjunction with stimulant medication, these have mostly been behavioral (Cousins and Weiss, 1993; Klein and Abikoff, 1997; Pelham et al., 2000; Friemoth, 2005). This article proposes that integrative psychodynamic play therapy can be effective in the treatment of children diagnosed with ADHD and that the symptoms can be understood in terms of intrapsychic conflicts and interpersonal issues. A detailed case example is presented in this article to illustrate psychodynamic play therapy coupled with parent consultation for ADHD.

DIAGNOSIS AND EPIDEMIOLOGY OF ATTENTION DEFICIT HYPERACTIVITY DISORDER

ADHD is defined clinically by the presence of developmentally or age-inappropriate levels of inattention, hyperactivity and/or impulsivity for at least six months.[1] Conservative estimates indicate that three to seven percent of school-aged children exhibit symptoms of ADHD (American Psychiatric Association, 2000) and that as many as 50 percent of children referred for psychological treatment are given this diagnosis (Gilmore, 2000). Not surprisingly, children who challenge parents and educators by exhibiting impulsive, inattentive, or hyperactive behavior at home or in the school setting, particularly in the classroom, form a steady stream of referrals to clinicians for evaluation and treatment (Hardy et al., 2007). In addition, children diagnosed with ADHD typically also present with social deficits, low self-esteem, and academic failures (Barkley, 2006).

Current clinical thinking about the functional issues presented by children diagnosed with ADHD focuses on their difficulties in the domain of executive function, that is, the skills through which the brain processes and organizes experience and plans adaptive behavior. Barkley (2011) identifies six dimensions of executive functioning which present problems for children with ADHD: self-awareness and monitoring of actions, emotional regulation, inhibition of behavior, nonverbal working memory, verbal working memory, and motivation. Impairment in these areas is marked by misperceptions about the self and others, decreased ability to monitor one's own actions, lack of adequate hindsight (the ability to activate and review memories of past maladaptive behavior), lack of adequate foresight (ability to use memories and a sense of time to predict and anticipate consequences), and impaired ability to regulate the expression of emotions. Children with ADHD typically lack the tools to inhibit or self-soothe in social situations.

[1] The Diagnostic and Statistical Manual of Mental Disorders, Fourth Edition-Text Revision (DSM IV-TR) defines ADHD as characterized by the presence of six or more of nine specific symptoms of inattention or hyperactivity coupled with functional impairment in two settings such as home and school. Three diagnostic subtypes are deliniated: primarily inattentive, primarily hyperactive/impulsive and combined type (American Psychiatric Association, 2000).

They come across as overly emotional individuals who are quick to become angry or upset or who are quick to get happy, silly, or clownish. Such attributes can be costly in the interpersonal realm, particularly when it comes to expressing anger. Others may forgive "class clowns" and silliness but be less forgiving of hostile and aggressive behavior. Hostile behavior contributes to the statistic that 50–70 percent of ADHD-diagnosed children have no friends at the third grade mark (Normand, Schneider and Robaey, 2007; Pelham and Bender, 1982).

Other studies documenting the strain in peer relationships associated with ADHD include one by Walcott and Landau (2004), who found that during peer competition, ADHD-diagnosed boys (in comparison to boys without the diagnosis) displayed greater disinhibition of emotions and were less successful at masking their feelings when instructed to do so. Similarly, Maedgen and Carlson (2000) found that children with ADHD (particularly Combined Type) had great difficulty adjusting their behavior in accordance with shifts in situational demands, whether due to others' overly negative or overly positive reactions.

Hallowell and Thompson observed that the presence of two or three ADHD children in a classroom can disrupt the learning experience for all and exhaust even the most dedicated teacher (1993). Given the high prevalence and the serious impact of these symptoms on children, families, and schools, the social costs of untreated or inadequately treated ADHD are high. As with other disorders involving school-aged children, effective treatment plans may necessitate cooperation from the patient, parents, and school and should be developed to suit the particular symptoms and situation of the individual child (Rube and Reddy, 2005).

A complicating factor in the reliance solely upon medication for treatment is that some parents and caregivers of children diagnosed with ADHD are concerned with both the short and the long-term effects of medication and either overtly or covertly reject the recommendation for such treatment (Berger et al., 2008; Friemoth, 2005). In addition, especially as they approach adolescence, some children become uncooperative and resistant to taking medication, which they view as evidence of their defectiveness and inadequacy (Chubinsky and Rappaport, 2006). Moreover, persistent concern exists, especially among African American parents of children with ADHD, about the overpathologizing of African American and other minority children, especially boys. There is also considerable parental wariness in minority communities about the use of medications as a form of social control (Carpenter-Song, 2009).

One study highlighting this concern among African American families surveyed parents of children treated for ADHD in an urban primary care setting. On average, all children in this study had taken stimulants for more than two years. Twenty-one percent felt that medications had bad side effects, and 23 percent believed that too many children were medicated for ADHD. Moreover, 71 percent were initially hesitant to use stimulants, 17 percent believed that stimulants led to drug abuse, and 21 percent preferred counseling over medication (dos Reis et al., 2006). Similarly, Schnittker (2003) found that compared to white families, African American families are more concerned about the use of psychotropic medications to treat their children, less likely to believe that psychotropic medications are efficacious, more likely to be concerned with side effects, and less likely to give these medications to their children.

In view of the estimate that at least 20 percent of ADHD children do not respond to stimulant medications (an optimistic estimate of its efficacy), it has become increasingly clear that there might be a stronger role for psychosocial interventions. Nathan (1992) states that although medication can assist in managing children's day-to-day functioning, it is less effective in producing long-lasting improvement. He notes that although little has been written about the use of psychodynamic therapy in the treatment of ADHD, such an empathic approach provides a more nuanced understanding of the emotions, resistances, fears, and estrangements that are prevalent in the lives of ADHD-diagnosed children. This approach also addresses interactional problems such as the child's difficulty reflecting upon and monitoring his or her affective states, which typically manifest as instability, short temper, aggression, and anxiety.

Similarly, Gilmore (2000) notes that behavioral interventions such as small classrooms, "shadow teachers," behavioral modification techniques, and medication can yield significant improvement in behavioral disturbances. However, the symptoms of inattention, impulsivity, and hyperactivity may be better understood from a psychodynamic perspective. She argues that ADHD disrupts children's basic ego functions, and that a psychoanalytic perspective provides a more useful understanding of the child's experience. Through empathy, limit setting, and attention to the expression of impulsive behavior in the treatment room, the psychodynamic therapist can verbalize and interpret the disorganized internal life of the child. Through providing insight, the attuned therapist can help the child develop the ability to modulate impulsive behavior and integrate discontinuities in affect and sense of self. ADHD children often suffer from pronounced narcissistic vulnerabilities, envy, and friction in sibling relationships, typically managed by identification with the aggressor and other problematic defenses, which create disturbances in the realm of object relations. The psychodynamic therapist can detect and work to modify these processes as they are enacted and understood in the transference.

From a psychoanalytic theoretical frame, Pine (1985) also proposes that disturbances in object relations have a causal connection to the common ADHD-type disruptions in learning and behavior. He identifies certain developmental achievements (and potential delays or failures) underlying the basic tools needed for learning, such as the capacity for sustained attention. These achievements must be forged in the developmental mix of object relatedness, drive-defense arrangements, and inborn capacities. Attentional problems necessarily arise in a developmental and psychological context. Moreover, sustained attention and learning in school develop only when children can modulate their affect and exert motoric control. When unharnessed, impulses and affects rapidly spill over into gross motor activity, and the state of receptivity for learning is negatively affected. This harnessing and modulation of affect, modulation of motoric expression, and reasonably accurate social perceptiveness are all crucial to the favorable development of the school-age child. Conversely, it is clear from his discussion that significant impairment of these capacities creates frustration and confusion for the child, parents, and teachers alike, which greatly amplifies the inevitable strains and crises of childhood and family life.

Concordant with these clinical theorists, Ladnier and Massanari (2000) consider ADHD to be in essence an attachment deficit disorder, arguing that since a child's neurological and emotional development is to a significant degree determined by the quality of interactions with primary caregivers, these relationships must be examined in depth. They point out that the main areas of dysfunction in ADHD-diagnosed children, their self-regulatory and social difficulties, can closely resemble the symptoms of an attachment-disordered child.

Jones (2002) also employs a psychodynamic understanding when working with ADHD-diagnosed children. Through this approach, the therapist can elaborate the conscious and unconscious family dynamics at work and interpret unacknowledged feelings and conflicting internal states utilizing knowledge of the child's idiosyncratic and subjective experience. Work with the parents is also critical to the process of exploring fantasies and feelings in the transference relationship with the child. Jones (2002) expresses concern that current treatment models, which focus primarily on external behaviors, may perpetuate a child's sense of not being understood. Instead of the common short-term, symptom-focused treatment frame, he suggests that a longer-term dynamic approach will often lead the child to more permanent symptom relief based in the child's development of a more stable and coherent sense of self.

CASE ILLUSTRATION

Jaden King[2] is an eight-year-old African American boy who lives with his mother, Mrs. King (age 39), his father, Mr. King (38), and his younger brother, Jordan (5). Jaden is currently in the third grade at a parochial school to which he transferred from a public charter school at the completion of the second grade. In his first grade year, at age six, the school referred Jaden for psychological treatment. Jaden had been removed from his initial first grade classroom and placed in another classroom due to behavioral and attentional problems which included difficulty focusing on academic material (specifically reading and writing), engaging in fights (both physical and verbal) with another boy (Peter), and having "meltdowns" in the classroom, where Jaden would cry hysterically and appear inconsolable.

PRESENTING PROBLEM

When Jaden presented for psychological treatment, his teachers described him as being easily distracted in the classroom, as having trouble staying in his seat, and as wanting to engage in negative behavior with other children during assignments. Jaden's parents agreed that he displayed similar distractibility at home, had difficulty completing homework and sustaining attention on tasks, and was always "on the go." I[3] also observed Jaden's distractibility during a school observation conducted during the intake process. Jaden struggled throughout the day to follow the teacher's instructions, was often scolded by her to listen, and told that he was not focused. Jaden appeared to have an extraordinary amount of physical energy compared to the other children: he was continuously fidgeting, putting his head down on the table, falling off his chair, and throwing karate chops.

Jaden also struggled with controlling his emotions and behaviors at school. Jaden's initial first grade teacher reported his "meltdowns" in the classroom, during which he would cry and become extremely upset. She described these "outbursts," which occurred often in relation to Peter or in response to being disciplined, as difficult to calm and contain. Mr. and Mrs. King also reported that Jaden was "quick to anger" and "argumentative" when he did not get his way or when he got in trouble. They stated that Jaden "always wants to have the last word" and felt "slighted if he doesn't get his way." He would "scream and cry" and "slam or throw things." When he became "bent up" in this way, he found it difficult to transition out of his "negative" and "sour display."

Jaden also struggled in his relationship with his younger brother, Jordan. His parents reported Jaden's jealousy of his brother and his repeated complaint that his parents "love Jordan more."

[2] All names and other identifying information have been changed or deleted to preserve confidentiality.

[3] Gabrielle Cione was the therapist on the case and Dr. Lila Coleburn served as her supervisor. Intake and treatment took place at an urban clinic staffed by doctoral students in clinical psychology.

Moreover, they felt that Jaden would frequently instigate physical and verbal fights with Jordan as he did at school with Peter. Jaden would often take food from Jordan's plate to eat himself and would sometimes hit Jordan when his brother was not looking.

Intake Sessions

During the intake sessions, Jaden was active, engaged, and energetic. He attended the first session with his mother and exhibited an abundance of excitement and eagerness to explore the room. His smile was full and he made eye contact with both his mother and me. He was also competitive and directive. For instance, he wanted to play with the bowling pins and directed me to set up all of the pins in a specific formation so that he could see who would be the "best bowler" among us.

At times, Jaden appeared distracted and unruly, becoming either overly aggressive or overly silly. He threw the toy bowling ball aggressively around the room rather than rolling it on the floor. Periodically, he became overly excited, dancing around the treatment room or falling to the ground and rolling on his back with exaggerated laughter.

Jaden could be creative and imaginative in his play, which convinced me that we could utilize the play as a way to communicate, playing out themes that were relevant to Jaden's experiences in school and with his family. For instance, in the second intake session, Jaden wanted to "play school," where he was the teacher and I was the student. He was authoritative as a teacher, ordering me to "raise my hand" and reminding me that I was a good student because I was "not like [him]." Jaden told me that he would give me a prize for getting the correct answer to the math problem "8+8=?" When I correctly answered the question, he told me to close my eyes and then gave me a baby doll as my prize, which provided some insight into his conviction that "the baby" (his younger brother) was the prize child in his family. During this session, Jaden also claimed that he actually did not have a brother, which suggested a wish to eliminate his envied brother. During his third and final intake session, Jaden held up an African American baby doll and declared, "I hate this one!" He then asked permission to put the doll outside of the room and into the hallway, which I granted. He wondered if his mom was outside the room—perhaps wanting to communicate his feelings about babies to her—and as he placed it in the hallway outside of the treatment room, announced, "I want to kill it."

Jaden was open in his communication with me. I explained to him that the reason for his coming to see me was the difficulty he had been having in school and that our time together would involve playing and talking about things with which he was having a hard time. I confirmed that I had met with his parents before our session together and that I had visited his school. He responded well to this conversation and soon after, simply wanted to continue playing. He was comfortable sharing his feelings about school—his struggles and his experience of being bullied. He revealed that in his view, he had "no friends at school . . . .only one . . . and he's stupid–skinny and stupid." Jaden went on to say, "School is hard for me."

Overall, Jaden presented as a curious and animated child who clearly expressed a desire to connect to me and to engage in the therapeutic process. In our first ever session together, Jaden had a hard time ending and asked, "Could I have more time with you?" and "Are you open on weekends, what about Sunday?" In our last intake session, Jaden again had difficulty ending, confiding, as he reluctantly helped clean up the toys, "I want to come here everyday."

Diagnosis and Treatment Plan

At the conclusion of the intake process, Jaden was diagnosed with Adjustment Disorder with Mixed Disturbance of Emotions and Conduct and referred for weekly psychodynamic play therapy (continuing with me as therapist). Subsequently, Jaden was given a battery of psychological tests as part of a neuropsychological assessment while treatment was underway. Based on the intake reports and test results, Jaden was diagnosed with ADHD, Combined Type, in addition to his initial diagnosis. The possibility of a trial of medication was discussed with Jaden's parents; they firmly rejected that option in favor of continuing psychotherapy without medication. They also agreed to meet periodically with me to collaborate in understanding Jaden's issues and to discuss his progress.

Course of Treatment: Themes, Transference and Countertransference

For the first several months of treatment, Jaden's behavior was characterized by significant levels of impulsivity and aggression as well as by narcissistic vulnerability and frustration as reported by his teacher, observed by his parents, and enacted during sessions. "Meltdowns" and "tantrums" continued with disturbing regularity. The difficulty with connecting with other children in a positive way also persisted, and Jaden seemed to have no friends or prospects for any, only tormentors. His reports of being bullied by a boy from his initial first grade classroom contrasted with his teacher's rendition of the exchange which she described as more of a "co-creation" in which Jaden often instigated the negative interactions. Jaden also engaged in fights with other children, teasing and provoking them, which ended in tears or rage, with him feeling like the victimized one. He was frustrated that adults (parents and teachers) did not see these incidents in the same way. His capacity for self-awareness and empathy seemed blunted and underdeveloped.

At this early stage of treatment, it was apparent that Jaden was trying to determine who I was in his life and what kind of role I would play. Could he trust me? Should he fear me? Would I tell on him? Was I like his teacher? Was I like his mother? Or was I more like a playmate? As the treatment progressed, I could see that I represented elements of both his mother and his teacher, but that I also represented a playmate whom he could trust with his feelings.

Jaden initially investigated my seeming role as a teacher figure by testing the limits of allowable behavior. I had established certain safety rules for the treatment space that were similar to a teacher's classroom rules—not hurting each other or ourselves, keeping the light turned on, not throwing toys at each other, and not destroying clinic property. Jaden continuously acted out against these rules as though attempting to elicit in me a representation of a punitive teacher.

For instance, when Jaden turned the lights off during a session and I instructed him to flip the switch back on for safety reasons, he called me a "loser" said that he hated me and then asked, "Are you a teacher?" which he followed by a verbal taunt: "Nah, ne-nah, nah-naaaah." The punitive teacher role became alive in the transference, as through the magic of projective identification, Jaden made me the "loser" in an attempt to rid himself of "loser" feelings provoked by teacher figures. I was a different figure who could contain Jaden's hatred and verbal taunts without becoming punitive. Jaden learned that he would not get in trouble with me for expressing these feelings. Thus in the transference, he acted out his aggression—and my therapeutic role was to contain and help him observe, describe, regulate, and metabolize those feelings by setting limits, tolerating his aggression, and verbalizing his affective experience. I interpreted his facial expressions, wondering aloud if my rules reminded him of the rules at school and stated that it seemed that he really did not want to follow them. I reflected his oppositional feelings and conveyed to him that it was safe to express anger about the rules, which he was nonetheless required to follow. I also said that maybe calling me a "loser" made him feel better. Jaden asserted that name-calling *did* make him feel better and then he announced that he did not want to talk anymore. He just wanted to play, and so we played. This sequence, repeated numerous times over the course of the therapy, captured Jaden's increasing ability to move between experiencing and expressing feelings that had the power to push me away and create attachment rifts, to experiencing and expressing feelings that could repair the relationship and reconnect us in shared positive affect. Together we learned that we could tolerate his expressions of negative emotions.

Jaden continued to explore my likeness to a teacher figure as the treatment unfolded by acting out various classroom scenarios in which he was the person in charge. This helped to modulate his rage against his teacher, whom he perceived as punitive, and seemed to assuage his feelings of being in a position of little power.

In one session Jaden introduced a character named Jake, who was "fooling around" in the classroom while the teacher was conducting a lesson "because he had poop in his pants." After several sessions featuring Jake's misbehavior, Jaden flung toys all around the therapy room and explained that Jake had exploded the classroom with secret bombs hidden in a suitcase.

It became clear through his play early in the treatment that Jaden was in part contending with powerful feelings of anxiety, dysphoria, and envy arising from his displacement within the family by his much-adored younger brother, who seemed to possess all the sweetness and winning ways that Jaden lacked (M. Klein, 1975). Jaden explicitly reiterated his wish not to have a brother as he had during the initial intake sessions when he exiled a baby doll from the treatment room. He acted out his wish to be the baby himself during sessions by being overtly silly and "baby-like," falling to the ground and crawling on the floor. He also described how at home he "tricked" his brother by swiping food from his plate, stealing his toys, and even hitting him when the opportunity arose.

The empathic acknowledgment and acceptance of these feelings in the treatment room seemed to help Jaden gain more tolerance and control over them. It became clear that his provocation of fights and adult censure at school provided a forum for his aggression and an opportunity to elicit punishment for his "badness" at home. At the same time, the anxiety stirred by his envious and hostile wishes toward his brother made it difficult for him to attend to more neutral subjects such as schoolwork or neutralized relationships such as friendships.

Meetings with Jaden's parents revealed that it was difficult for them to appreciate the extent of the personal sense of loss and hurt that Jaden was experiencing as attention and family pride shifted to the newer and seemingly more gifted favorite brother. Mr. King was skeptical of the idea that Jaden's upset feelings and behavior at school or home could have anything to do with a sense of displacement and loss, stating, "I didn't feel that way when it happened to me." Mrs. King also initially referenced her own childhood as a way to reject this idea, recalling that she had to "come out as an adult, no questions asked." Mrs. King had been separated from her own mother at age one when her mother had left their island country to work in the United States, leaving her in her grandmother's care until she was three and a half. Mrs. King described her parenting style as similar to that of her own mother: "strict and impatient." When I gently explored this further, Mrs. King remembered feeling confused by the second transition, which had in effect required her to adapt to losing a mother twice. She then began to cry when she spoke of the separation from her mother and her loneliness as a six-year-old "latch key kid" in New York City, coming home to an empty apartment to cook and do laundry herself.

I knew from my sessions with Jaden that he also felt loneliness at home where it was seldom possible to have a meal together and family time was brief. In one session he set up a family of dolls and directed me to "cook for the whole family." In other sessions Jaden cooked for *me* while instructing me to draw as though he were the mother and I the child. He placed a white baby doll at the table next to me during one of our play meals together and said, "He's white like you and your son," thus creating an image of me as a mother sharing a meal with her child. I had learned during the intake process that although Jaden's brother had been breastfed as Jaden watched at age three, Jaden himself had not due to his mother's physical discomfort. I wondered whether Jaden's mother's inability to breastfeed him had affected their early relationship and if her own experience as a child affected her attachment relationship with Jaden. Meanwhile in his sessions, Jaden spoke longingly of his desire for "more squishy hugs from Mom." When told of this longing, Mrs. King became amenable to making more time for Jaden and to arranging more family time.

As Jaden's anger and anxiety became less acute and as he felt more nurtured, he had more interest in his peers as playmates and more of a desire to engage in collaborative games with me. This was a step up developmentally from the days when he yelled out that he hated me for winning or that he hated himself for losing. Jaden reserved the right to call others names to make himself feel better—"you should try it!" he advised, only half in jest. Calling others "loser" (most often, me) barely masked his own sense of fragility. In one such memorable session, Jaden knocked our Connect Four game off the table and fell on the floor laughing maniacally and farting audibly for nearly ten minutes to show his rage at losing. In that session I was eventually able to persuade Jaden to try writing down words for the feelings he was having—"mad, mean and happy"—and to talk with me about what provoked those feelings. Over time we worked more on using words, spoken and written, to express (and modulate) intense feelings, in a way by creating our own school-like assignments.

I wanted to assist Jaden in differentiating and articulating feelings that seemed to be prompting his negative behavior but also to tolerate and negotiate having both positive and negative feelings for the same person. Through the transference, he had hated me (heard in his name-calling of me and seen in his aggressive behavior toward me), and he also loved me (seen in his more affectionate overtures such playing love songs in session that he had downloaded onto his cell phone). Our relationship helped Jaden achieve a new capacity to hold ambivalent feelings that had previously led to emotional outbursts. I also guided Jaden toward ways to soothe himself in moments when he felt overwhelmed by negative feelings. I proposed that maybe if he got mad he could think of a "squishy hug" from his mom, which he described as something that made him happy. He showed me what that the hug looked like by hugging himself tightly, then smiled and said, "Maybe." My goal in that moment was to foster Jaden's ability to conjure up a warm and benign image of his mother, that is, to build a more soothing capacity into the internalized representation of her that he could draw on consciously. I believe that Jaden also felt calmed and relieved by my acceptance and equanimity (which I often had to struggle to maintain) throughout the affect storms he brought to his sessions. While I actively participated in the play in each session, acting the part of characters, narrating aloud what they might be feeling and joining in the physical games Jaden favored (not always easy in our tiny, ill-equipped treatment room), I tried to speak in a calm but engaged tone even during aggressive play. I also tried to display a sense of humor and a willingness to appreciate humorous asides by him. It helped that I understood Jaden's more aggressive behavior as a way to defend against succumbing to the more vulnerable feelings he held inside. He may have wished to be the baby at home, but he did not want to be seen as baby-ish and weak, especially at school.

The previously unconscious feelings of shame and humiliation that plagued Jaden at school emerged most vividly one year into the treatment during a game of basketball when Jaden fell to his knees and began to throw the ball back and forth against the wall. He started at a slow pace then began to throw the ball harder and harder as he screamed, "I hate school! I hate school! I hate school!" While repeating these words, he broke into tears and started to cry hysterically. I kneeled down next to him and put my hand on his back while he continued to weep. I said, "I know. I know school's hard for you. I know you hate it." He began to cry harder. Tears were streaming down his face and mucus from his nose, as he moaned through his hyperventilating breaths, "I hate school . . . I hate school . . . They're mean to me . . . They're not nice to me . . . I hate school . . . I hate school . . . I hate school." Jaden then kicked off his shoes, crawled up on a chair, and curled into a fetal position. He continued to cry uncontrollably while drool dripped out of his mouth and onto the sleeve of his shirt. He then revealed more. "I hate my teacher. She rushes me and I can't focus . . . She rushes me . . . They yell at me for talking and not focusing but I can't focus . . . I can't . . . She rushes me. I hate her . . . I hate her . . . I hate school." As I sat on the floor next to him, I told him that I really cared about his feelings. As he began to calm down, I asked him if he would want me to tell his parents about how he was feeling at school. He replied, "They won't care." I told him that I was sure they would care and the conviction that he and I could talk about that in next session. He was then able to calm down. At the end of the session he asked if I would take him to the bathroom to "clean up." Notably, he walked into the women's restroom, where a mother might take a male child, and I followed him in. I helped him wash his face and blow his nose with a paper towel and tissue paper. I told him to take "deep breaths" and he did. I then walked him to the waiting room where a sullen teenage relative wearing headphones was waiting to pick him up. Jaden had turned to me to comfort him and to accept and hold his most intense emotions. He had come to rely on therapy to provide a safe "holding environment" (Winnicott, 1960), which in this instance included "live, human holding" (Winnicott, 1955) when I placed my hand on his back.

I disclosed the content of this pivotal session to Jaden's parents and reported his severe negative feelings about his school, his feeling of being "rushed" by the teachers, and his not being able to "focus." As a result, Mr. and Mrs. King began to actively look into more accommodating academic options and ultimately withdrew Jaden from his public school and enrolled him in a parochial school that was informed of his ADHD diagnosis and could better accommodate his needs. I realized the profundity of Jaden's feelings of being "rushed" and was able to better understand his experience through a psychodynamic and attachment-focused lens. In a way reminiscent of his mother's history of being rushed into adulthood and responsibility, Jaden seems to have felt rushed away from his mother's breast and out of her arms, rushed into relinquishing much of his parents' attention to a younger sibling, and rushed into being a first grade student—all without enough time or attunement from others for him to adapt to these changes and take on these roles.

Current Functioning and State of Therapy

In his new school, which has provided him with more individualized attention and closer physical proximity to the teacher, Jaden is doing much better academically and socially. He has made friends and is blossoming in his social world (e.g., talking to friends on the phone and having "play-dates" outside of school). In ongoing therapy, Jaden has asked to come twice a week, which his parents endorse theoretically but have found difficult to arrange. During a few weeks of absence from therapy he "got into trouble" at school for talking. When I asked whether he thought this lapse might have something to do with missing therapy, he said, "Exactly!"

Jaden's feelings of maternal deprivation appear to be lessening as he and his mother now spend more one-on-one time together, share family meals together, and exchange "squishy hugs" more often (something I have witnessed in the waiting room). Jaden has also begun to express a stronger identification with his father and a desire for his father's help in gaining certain skills. For instance, Jaden recently attended basketball camp, a response to the suggestion that better skills at a team sport might help him make friends on the playground as well as increase his sense of mastery and confidence as a growing boy at his urban school. He now enjoys playing basketball, which is his father's "favorite sport." Mrs. King has observed with pleasure that Jaden now "wants to be just like his father." Mr. King has responded positively to our discussion in parent sessions about Jaden's need for more "father time." After describing his own father as "not present for the smaller moments" during his childhood, he has made more time in his schedule to spend with Jaden, recognizing the importance he feels in sharing "all moments with a dad—big and small." Jaden and his father now enjoy playing basketball together which Jaden and I also play for some portion of our sessions.

Jaden's internal world is still marked by narcissistic injury, feelings of envy and jealousy toward his brother, and the conviction that he is at times unfairly singled out by both his parents and his new teacher, but less frequently. Jaden continues to express frustration and annoyance at having a brother but also has expressed moments of care and affection for him. They now attend the same parochial school.

Jaden also continues to express the fact that he "doesn't like to lose"—yet he is beginning to gain awareness of how to negotiate these feelings more successfully. As he has begun to make friends, he has developed interests in music, pop culture, and gadgets, which provide a basis for shared enjoyment less fraught with rivalrous feelings.

Jaden shows an increased capacity to identify his emotions and to communicate them verbally. He is also developing more positive ways to manage his impulses and his readiness to resort to physical fighting has diminished.

In a recent session, Jaden shared the "good news" about his report card, telling me that he "got all As and Bs," to which I replied, "Wow! That is great news!" He then put up his open palm for me to "slap him five." When I walked him back to the waiting room, his mother asked him if he told me about his report card and Jaden said that he had. Mrs. King exclaimed, "He did great!" Spontaneously, Jaden, his mother, and I all cheered and slapped each other five in the clinic's waiting room.

CONCLUSION

The treatment described in this article illustrates the way in which a psychodynamic approach to the difficulties associated with ADHD can be effective in improving the patient's capacity for affect and impulse regulation and realistically based self-esteem. Jaden's parents decided not to follow the recommendation to use medication to treat his symptoms of inattention, hyperactivity, and impulsivity, which were disrupting his school and family life. However, they were amenable to Jaden's participation in psychotherapy and to meeting with his therapist themselves in an effort to understand their son better and to consider changes they could implement in the family and in their own individual relationships with him.

This treatment, in contrast to medication or behavior-focused treatments, utilized play therapy and the transference relationship to illuminate and address Jaden's interpersonal and object relations. Jaden's aggressive and inattentive behaviors were understood to reflect developmental disruptions related to attachment, as well as the result of unresolved intrapsychic and interpersonal conflicts. Behavioral and pharmacological interventions alone may improve symptoms, yet leave the fundamental intrapsychic issues that fuel those symptoms unaddressed. Moreover, pharmacologic treatment for ADHD symptoms is often refused by parents and caregivers, particularly in the African American community. This detailed case study presents psychodynamic play therapy as a potentially effective alternative.

Case histories such as this one can provide guidance and encouragement for therapists to develop clinical theory and refine therapeutic techniques. We hope this article inspires others to explore and refine the psychodynamic approach to working with children diagnosed with ADHD and their parents. However, along with the clinical validity provided by in-depth qualitative case analysis (Stake, 2005), it is important to test or examine the effectiveness of this approach using rigorous empirical methods. This would include establishing a reliable training protocol for therapists, and clinical trials moving from case studies to randomized controlled trials comparing psychodynamic play therapy to more established approaches. Further, the mechanisms of action of this approach requires careful investigation to identify which individuals with ADHD are most likely to benefit from which approach in the growing number of treatment options (Kazdin and Nock, 2003). Further, the feasibility of combining psychodynamic play therapy with established approaches, both pharmacologic and psychosocial, remains uninvestigated beyond this and other clinical case reports. Despite these issues, clinical observation and case reports such as ours, and the limitations of current treatment options, implore us to expand our repertoire of treatment for this common and serious disorder.

ACKNOWLEDGMENTS

We would like to thank Eugenia Cherkasskaya for her suggestions on an earlier version of this article, Roisin O'Mara for her timeless emotional support, and John Weidman for his skilled and tireless technical support.

REFERENCES

Altman, N., Briggs, R., Frankel, J., Gensler, D. & Pantone, P. (2002), *Relational Child Psychotherapy*. New York: Other Press.

American Psychiatric Association. (2000), *Diagnostic and Statistical Manual of Mental Disorders*, 4th edition, text revision. Washington, DC: American Psychiatric Association.

Barkley, R. A. (2006). *Attention-deficit Hyperactivity Disorder: A Handbook for Diagnosis and Treatment*, 3rd edition. New York: Guilford Press.

——— (2011, January). Expert interview: ADHD as an executive function disorder. *The Carlat Child Psychiatry Report*, viewed 9 February 2011, www.thecarlatchildreport.com

Berger, I., Dor, T., Nevo, Y. & Goldzweig, G. (2008), Attitudes toward attention-deficit hyperactivity disorder (ADHD) treatment: Parents' and children's perspectives. *Journal of Child Neurology*, *23*(9): 1036–42.

Carpenter-Song, E. (2009), Caught in the psychiatric net: Meaning and experiences with ADHD, pediatric bipolar disorder and mental health treatment among a diverse group of families in the United States. *Cultural Medical Psychiatry, 33*: 61–85.
Chethik, M. (2000), *Techniques of Child Therapy: Psychodynamic Strategies*. New York: The Guilford Press.
Chubinsky, P. & Rappaport, N. (2006), Medication and the fragile alliance: The complex meanings of psychotropic medication to children, adolescents and families. *The Journal of Infant, Child and Adolescent Psychotherapy, 5*(11): 111–23.
Cousins, L. S. & Weiss, G. (1993). Parent training and social skills training for children with attention deficit hyperactivity disorder: How can they be combined for greater effectiveness? *Canadian Journal of Psychiatry, 38*: 449–57.
dosReis, S., Butz, A., Lipkin, P. H., Anixt, J. S., Weiner, C. L. & Chernoff, R. (2006), Attitudes about stimulant medication for attention-deficit/hyperactivity disorder among African American families in an inner city community. *Journal of Behavioral Health Services and Research, 33*(4): 423–30.
Everett, C. A. & Toff, H. D. (2008), Response to Sparks and Duncan's "do no harm" critique of the use of stimulant medications to treat ADHD in children and adolescents. *Journal of Family Psychotherapy, 19*(10): 27–35.
Friemoth, J. (2005). What is the most effective treatment for ADHD in children? *The Journal of Family Practice, 54*(2): 166–8.
Gilmore, K. (2000), A psychoanalytic perspective on attention-deficit/hyperactivity disorder. *Journal of the American Psychoanalytic Association, 48*: 1259–93.
Hallowell, E. M. & Thompson, M. G. (1993), *Finding the Heart of the Child: Essays on Children, Families and Schools*. Braintree, MA: Association of Independent Schools.
Hardy, K. K., Kollins, S. H., Murray, D. W., Riddle, M. A., Greenhill, L., Cunningham, C., et al. (2007), Factor structure of parent- and teacher-rated ADHD symptoms in preschoolers in the preschoolers with ADHD treatment study (PATS). *Journal of Child and Adolescent Psychopharmacology, 17*(5): 621–34.
Jones, J. D. (2002), Plea for a measure of understanding: The importance of intensive psychotherapy in the treatment of children with ADHD. *Psychotherapy: Theory, Research, Practice, Training, 39*(1): 12–20.
Kazdin, A. E. & Nock, M. K. (2003), Delineating mechanisms of change in child and adolescent therapy: Methodological issues and research recommendations. *Journal of Child Psychology and Psychiatry, 44*(8): 1116–29.
Klein, M. (1975). *Envy and Gratitude and Other Works 1946–1963*, M. Masud & R. Khan (eds.). The International Psycho-Analytical Library, 104: 1–346, London: The Hogarth Press and the Institute of Psycho-Analysis.
Klein, R. G. & Abikoff, H. (1997), Behavior therapy and methylphenidate in treatment of children with ADHD. *Journal of Attention Disorders, 2*(2): 89–114.
Ladnier, R. D. & Massanari, A. E. (2000). Treating ADHD as attachment deficit hyperactivity disorder. In: *Handbook of Attachment Interventions*, T. M. Levy (ed.). San Diego, CA: Academic Press, pp. 27–65.
Maedgen, J. W. & Carlson, C. L. (2000), Social functioning and emotional regulation n the attention deficit hyperactivity disorder subtypes. *Journal of Clinical Child Psychology, 29*(1): 30–42.
MTA Cooperative Group. (1999), A 14-month randomized clinical trial of treatment strategies for attention/hyperactivity disorder. The MTA Cooperative Group. Multimodal treatment study of children with ADHD. *Archives of General Psychiatry, 56*(12): 1073–86.
Nathan, W. A. (1992), Integrated multimodal therapy of children with attention-deficit hyperactivity disorder. *Bulletin of the Menninger Clinic, 56*(3): 283–312.
Normand, S., Schneider, B. H. & Robaey, P. (2007), Attention deficit/hyperactivity disorder and the challenges of close friendship. *Journal of the Canadian Academy of Child and Adolescent Psychiatry, 16*(2): 67–73.
Pelham, Jr., W. E. & Bender, M. E. (1982). Peer relationships in hyperactive children: Description and treatment. In K. Gadow & I. Bialer (Eds.) *Advances in Learning and Behavioral Disabilities*, K. Gadow & I. Bialer (eds.). Greenwich, CT: JAI Press, p. 366–436.
——— Gnagy, E. M., Greiner, A. R., Hoza, B., Hinshaw, S. P., Swanson, J. M., et al. (2000), Behavioral versus behavioral and pharmacological treatment in ADHD children attending a summer treatment program. *Journal of Abnormal Child Psychology, 28*(6): 507–25.
Pine, F. (1985), *Developmental Theory and Clinical Process*. New Haven, CT: Yale University Press.
Rains, A. & Scahill, L. (2004). New long-acting stimulants in children with ADHD. *Journal of Child and Adolescent Nursing, 17*(4): 177–9.
Rube, D. & Reddy, D. P. (2005). Attention deficit hyperactivity disorder. In: *Clinical Child Psychiatry*, 2nd edition, W. M. Klyklo & J. L. Kay (eds.). Chichester, UK: John Wiley & Sons Ltd., 153–89.

Schnittker, J. (2003), Misgivings of medicine?: African Americans' skepticism of psychiatric medicine. *Journal of Health and Social Behavior*, *44*: 506–24.

Stake, R. E. (2005). Qualitative case studies. In: *Handbook of Qualitative Research*, 3rd edition, N. K. Denzin & Y. S. Lincoln (eds.). Thousand Oaks, CA: Sage Publications, pp. 443–66.

Vaughan, B. S., Roberts, H. J. & Needelman, H. (2009), Current medications for the treatment of attention-deficit/hyperactivity disorder. *Psychology in the Schools*, *46*(9); 846–56.

Walcott, C. M. & Landau, S. (2004), The relation between disinhibition and emotion regulation in boys with attention deficit hyperactivity disorder. *Journal of Clinical Child and Adolescent Psychology*, *33* p(4): 772–82.

Winnicott, D. W. (1960). The theory of the parent-infant relationship. In: *The Maturational Processes and the Facilitating Environment*. Madison, CT: International Universities Press, pp. 37–55.

(1955). Group influences and the maladjusted child. In: *The Family and Individual Development*. London: Routledge, pp. 146–54.

Index

abandonment 63, 69
abuse 3, 52, 55, 61–9, 81, 108 *see also* trauma
Adderall 118
ADHD Rating Scale 117
Adjustment Disorder with Mixed Disturbance of Emotions and Conduct 136
adoption 53, 64–5, 104, 111, 113–14
Adverse Childhood Experiences (ACE study) 61–2
African American children 3, 63, 65, 130–2, 134–41
aggression: complex trauma 62; EVA Study 44, 46; Frankfurt Prevention Study 38, 39–42; integrated affective and cognitive model 23; Other 90; play therapy 130, 134–9, 141; psychosocial symptomatic behaviour, ADHD as 125; social and emotional functioning 19; trauma 52, 53–5
agitated depression 116, 122–3
amygdala 23, 107, 110
anger: parents 111; play therapy 130, 132, 134, 135–6, 138; trauma 53, 55, 62
antisocial behaviour 20
anxiety: attention 103, 108–9, 113; Frankfurt Prevention Study 38; internal object, psychoanalytic conceptualizations of 91–3; learning theory 10; play therapy 137–8; psychosocial symptomatic behaviour, ADHD as 122–3, 125; reality-sampling deficit 75; social and emotional functioning 20; stress, effect of early 10; trauma 52, 54, 62–3, 69
Anzieu, D 98
arithmetic 19
attachment theory 44–7: attachment deficit disorder 133; complex trauma 3, 60, 63, 65–9; disorganized attachment style 45–6, 68; EVA Study 44, 45–6; internal object in ADHD child 89; MCAST (Manchester Child Attachment Story Task) 44, 45–6; mirroring function 68–9; play 139; self-regulation 133; social difficulties 133; trauma 3
attention and concentration 103–15: anxiety 103, 108, 113; biological function 105–6; case study 3, 104–5, 111–14; complex trauma 3, 61, 63; diagnosis and epidemiology of ADHD 131; emotion dysfunction 20, 103, 108, 114; EVA Study 44; executive function 16, 103, 104–6, 112; functional MRI findings 15; illness 107–8; impulsivity 104–6; intelligence 103, 107–8; internal object in ADHD child 3, 87, 89; language disorder 103, 107–8; learning problems 103, 105, 107, 133; medication 103, 105, 112, 114; motivation 106–7; motor control 133; neuropsychology 3, 103, 105–6, 110, 114; oppositional defiant disorder 105, 112; play t130, 134, 140–1; Predominantly Hyperactive-Impulsive Type 107; Predominantly Inattentive Type 107, 108; psychoanalytical concepts 3, 103, 105; psychosocial symptomatic behaviour, ADHD as 116, 122–3; psychotherapists' attention 109–11, 114; reality-sampling deficit 73–4, 80; selective attention 16, 18, 103, 107, 109–10; self-soothing 103, 108; social functioning 20; sustained attention 2, 16, 17, 133; training programs 24; trauma 3, 52, 53–4, 103, 108, 114; visuospatial abilities 18–19
Aulagnier, P 96
Australia 118
autobiographical self 78
automaticity 107

Barkley, RA 2, 9, 29–30, 88, 90, 106–7
Beatty, WW 18
Beeghly, M 68
behavioural treatment 34, 61, 88
Bender Visual-Motor Gestalt test 122
Bick, E 75
bipolar disorder 2, 63
Blondis, T 17
borderline personality disorders 69
brain training programs 24

Brown ADD Rating Scale 117
Bürgin, Dieter 47

Callaghan, BL 10
caregivers *see* parents and caregivers
Carlson, CL 132
Carney, J 6, 8, 90
Carte, E 18
case studies: attention 3, 104–5, 111–14; internal object in ADHD child 3, 87, 91–100; play therapy 3, 130–1, 134–41; psychoanalysis as viable treatment option 8, 32–48; psychosocial symptomatic behaviour, ADHD as 3, 116, 119–28; psychotherapy 3, 116, 119–28; reality-sampling deficit 76–8, 82–4
Casey, BJ 22–3
cerebellum 9, 14–15, 22
Child Behaviour Checklist 37
Cicchetti, D 68
Cierpka, M 37
cognitive behavioural psychotherapies 1, 34
cognitive-energetic model 22
cognitive psychology, team approach to 5–12
communication *see* language, communication and speech
community violence, exposure to 3, 52, 61, 63, 64, 65–6
complex trauma 60–70: Abuse Complex Trauma 65; Adverse Childhood Experiences (ACE study) 61–2; attachment trauma 3, 60, 63, 65–9; attention 3, 61, 63; culture 60–1; definition 3, 61–2; domestic or community violence, exposure to 63, 64, 65–6; environmental trauma(chronic stress) 60–1, 65–7; hospitalized children in urban psychiatric hospital 60–70; mentalization 60–1, 67–70; method of research 63–7; National Child Traumatic Network 3; neglect or maltreatment 63, 64–9; reflective ability 67–70; results of research 65–6
computerized programs 24
concentration *see* attention and concentration
concentration camp survivors 119, 125–6
conduct disorder 23, 63, 88–9
Conners Rating Scale 37, 39, 117
Connors, K 117
containment 75, 91, 98–9
conversation orientation 124–5
Cooper, A 110
coping mechanisms 52, 54, 105, 121
core coupling 78, 82
cortex 9, 14, 17, 22–3, 80, 106–7, 110
countertransference 8, 78, 87, 94, 103, 110, 130, 136–40
Crawford, SG 2
culture 40–3, 48, 60–1, 117

Damasio, Antonio 48, 107
Daud, A 53
de Boo, GM 20
'dead' mother, ADHD as compensation for having 40
decentration 68
deductive reasoning 105
Demaree, HA 19
demographics 60, 64, 65 *see also* gender
depression 20, 40, 52, 54, 62, 63, 116, 122–3, 128
developmental milestones 120
development trauma disorder (DTD) 62
developmental models 23, 67
Dewey, D 2
Diagnostic and Statistical Manual of Mental Disorders (DSM-IV) 39, 52, 56, 60–1, 93, 105, 107, 116–17
diffusion tensor imaging (DTI) findings 15
disruptive behaviour disorders 2, 20, 28, 52–4
dissociation 19, 45, 52, 62, 68, 109–10
distraction *see* attention
divorce and separation 62, 104, 108, 114
domestic violence, exposure to 46, 52, 63, 64, 65–6, 104, 114
Döpfner Scale 37
drive, psychology of 107
drugs *see* medication
DSM-IV 39, 52, 56, 60–1, 93, 105, 107, 116–17
dual- or multiple-pathway models 22–3

EARLY STEPS project 35, 44
eating disorders 20
Edelman, Gerald D 48
ego: development 1, 2, 87, 97, 127, 133; Ego Psychology and Object Relations 3; functions 47–8, 107, 133; psychological perspective 3, 90–1; reality-sampling deficit 78, 80–1, 84; strength 74, 93; super-ego formation 97
The Ego and the Id. Freud, Sigmund 2
Embodied Cognitive Science 48
emotion dysregulation 2–3, 19–23, 40, 48, 53, 55, 62, 69, 103, 108, 113
environment 10, 14, 20, 48, 52–6, 60–1, 65–9, 73–6, 83–4, 89, 131
envy 130, 133–5, 137, 140
EVA Study 3, 35, 36, 43–7, 48
executive function: attention 6, 9, 103, 104–6, 112; complex trauma 61; developmental model 23; diagnosis and epidemiology of ADHD 131; hyperactivity 17; learning problems 19; neurocognitive research 17, 19; reality-sampling deficit 80; self-regulation problems 2
experimental psychology 105

extraclinical studies 32–48
extraordinary talented children 40

family interactions 40–8, 53, 89–93, 108–14, 128: caregiver system, disruption in 52, 63–9; EVA Study 35; play therapy 130, 132–41; sibling relationships 40–3, 130, 133–5, 137, 139; trauma 55 *see also* parents and caregivers
Famularo, R 53
FAUSTLOS project 35, 36, 46
Felton, RH 19
Ferenczi, S 3, 76
FIRST STEPS integration project for infants with migrant background 35–6
Fischmann, Tamara 90–1
Flaherty, LT 117
flashlight metaphor 106–7, 110
flexible adaptation to reality 79–85
Fonagy, P 6, 8, 67–70
foresight and hindsight 21, 131
foster care 52, 55, 64–6, 81–3
Frankfurt Prevention Study 3, 33–43, 48, 88, 90
Frazier, TW 19
free association 76–7, 109
Freud, Anna 1, 109
Freud, Sigmund 74–5, 89, 98–9, 103, 109
frustration 120, 124–5: attention 104–5, 111; play therapy 130, 133, 136, 140; psychoanalytic conceptualizations of the internal object 91; reality-sampling deficit 73, 76–80
functional MRI findings (fMRI) 15
Furman, L 62
fusion 76–8, 82

Gammill, James 96–7
Garcia-Sanchez, C 19
gender 38, 41, 56, 116–17, 122
generational transmission of trauma 119–20, 125–7, 128
genetics 6, 13–14, 42, 47, 48, 105, 114, 117
Gilmore, K 6, 48, 90, 133
Goldberg, E 106–7, 110
gratification 75, 80–1, 85, 106–7, 124

Hallowell, E 105, 132
Halperin, JM 23
handwriting 18
Hinshaw, S 18
Hospitalized Child and Adolescent Trauma and Psychopathology Questionnaire 60, 64
hospitalized children 51, 55–6, 60–70
Huether, G 48
hyperactivity: complex trauma 62; diagnosis and epidemiology of ADHD 131; DSM-IV 52; emotional functioning 20; executive function 17; Frankfurt Prevention Study 37–8, 42; internal object, psychoanalytical conceptualizations of 87, 89–90, 93; motor functions 17–18; play 140; psychoanalysis as viable treatment option 47; psychodynamic therapy 131, 133; psychosocial symptomatic behaviour, ADHD as 116, 118–23, 128; reality-sampling deficit 73–5, 80, 82, 85; social functioning 20; trauma 52, 53–6, 62; visuospatial abilities 19
hyperarousal 54, 55–6, 62
hyperkinetic impulse disorder 17

idiosyncratic life history of child 39–40, 47, 48
illness 2, 7, 41, 47, 52, 60, 107–8
impatience 105, 120, 124, 137
impulsivity 17–20, 23, 131: attention 104–6; complex trauma 62, 69; internal object in ADHD child 87, 91–4; play therapy 130, 136, 140; psychodynamic treatment 116, 122–3, 133; reality-sampling deficit 73, 75, 80; trauma 52, 56
inhibition 15–17, 20, 53, 68, 94, 105, 107, 131–2
inpatients 51, 55–6, 60–70
Institute for Psychoanalytical Child and Adolescent Psychotherapy (IAKJP) 33–6
integrated affective and cognitive model 22–3
intelligence 41, 103, 107–8
internal and external reality, disturbances at interface of 75, 80, 85
internal object 3, 87–100
Israel 45

Jones, JD 133–4

Kandel, Eric 48
Kaplan, BJ 2
Kernberg, OF 67–8
Klein, Melanie 90, 97, 100
Klingberg, T 24

Ladnier, RD 133
Landau, S 132
language, communication and speech 1, 8, 80: attention 103, 107–8; conversation orientation 124–5; impulsivity 94; internal object in ADHD child 87, 89, 91, 94, 97, 99; internalization of speech 20–1; listening 54, 77–8, 79, 82, 84, 109, 127; organization difficulties 18; play 135, 140; trauma 53–4; unconscious 1, 40
learning problems 8–10, 19, 63, 103, 105, 107, 133

Leuzinger-Bohleber, Marianne 90–1
Levenson, E 110
Levin, Fred 9
Levine, M 106
Li, Q 15
listening 54, 77–8, 79, 82, 84, 109, 127
Loge, DV 18
lying 111–12, 113–14

Maedgen, JW 132
magnetic resonance imaging (MRI) findings 14, 15
Massanari, AE 133
MCAST (Manchester Child Attachment Story Task) 44, 45–6
McVay, JC 9–10
manual dexterity 18
medicalization of social problems 33, 43
medication 18, 23–4, 61. 132–3: Adderall 118; African American and other minority children 132; after-affects 118; attention 103, 105, 112, 114; gender 116–17; internal object in ADHD child 88–9, 93, 95; methylphenidate 33, 74, 81–3, 88; neural and neurocognitive determinants 23–4; play 136, 140–1; psychoanalysis as viable treatment option 33, 41–3; psychosocial symptomatic behaviour, ADHD as 116–18, 120, 128; Raine Study 118; randomized control trials 34, 88; reality-sampling deficit 73–4, 76, 81–3; Ritalin 33, 41–3, 118; side-effects 7, 118, 132; social control 132; Straterra 118
Mehta, M 10
memory 2, 75, 91, 109: definition 20; forgetfulness 54, 116; learning problems 19; procedural memory 69; working memory 9, 15–17, 20–1, 24, 105–6, 131
mental energy 106–7
mentalization 60–1, 67–70, 73, 79, 80, 84–5
metallization based therapy 3
methylphenidate 33, 74, 81–3, 88
Mevorach, C 16
migrant background, children with 35–6, 43
mirroring 54, 68–9, 76, 82–5
mood disorders 63, 117
motivation 9, 20–2, 33, 55, 106–7, 112, 131
motor functions 15, 17–21, 133
mourning and depression 40
Multimodal Treatment of ADHD (MTA) Study 88
Murphy, KR 16

narcissism 41, 90, 105, 129, 133, 136, 140
Nathan, WA 132
National Child Traumatic Network 3
neglect or maltreatment 3, 40, 48, 51, 54, 63, 64–9
neural and neurocognitive determinants of ADHD 2, 13–24: current conceptualizations of ADHD 14; dual- or multiple-pathway models 22–3; executive dysfunction models 20–1; impaired motivation/reinforcement system model 22; medication 23–4; models 2, 14, 20–3; neurocognitive research 2, 15–20; parent training 23–4; neuroimaging research, review of 14–15; proposed theoretical frameworks 2, 14, 20–3; neurobiology 1, 33, 36–43, 48, 78, 116–20, 128
neurocognitive determinants *see* neural and neurocognitive determinants of ADHD
neurological disorders 3, 17, 23–4, 42, 61–2, 89, 123, 127–8, 131, 133
neuroimaging 14–15, 117
neuropsychiatric disorders 5, 12, 88, 90
neuropsychology: attention 3, 103, 105–6, 110, 114; complex trauma 61; flashlight metaphor 106–7, 110; internal object in ADHD child 87–8; psychosocial symptomatic behaviour, ADHD as 117; reality-sampling deficit 74–5 *see also* neural and neurocognitive determinants of ADHD
neuroscience, team approach to 5–12
New York Montreal (NYM) study 88
NICE guidelines 73–4
Nigg, J 18, 22–3

object relations 3, 46–8, 90, 97, 133, 141
oppositional defiant disorder (ODD) 23, 52, 53, 63, 105, 112
Other 90

Palombo, J 6, 91
Panksepp, Jaak 48, 81
parents and caregivers: ADHD, parents with 105, 108–9; adoption 53, 64–5, 104, 111, 113–14; attention 103, 111–14, 117–22; complex trauma 62–3; 'dead' mother, ADHD as compensation for having; diagnosis and epidemiology of ADHD 131–4; disruption in caregiver system 40–3, 52, 62–9, 81–2, 90, 104–5, 108, 111–14, 137; divorce and separation 62, 104, 108, 114; dysfunctional interaction styles 62; EARLY STEPS 35; EVA Study 44–6; FIRST STEPS 35; foster care 52, 55, 64–6, 81–3; Frankfurt Prevention Study 37, 40–3; generational transmission of trauma 119–20, 125–7, 128; internal object 87–8, 90–3, 95–7; maternal deprivation 10, 137–40; medication 7, 136; play 134–41; primary

skin container function 75; reality-sampling deficit 73–4, 76–7, 81–3; STARTHILFE 34; training 23–4, 73–4, 76, 81–2; trauma 35, 44–6, 53, 62–4, 111–14
Parsons, M 77–9
peer relationships 41, 53, 62–3, 70, 76, 104–5, 132, 134, 138–40
personality disorders 67, 69, 103
Piaget, J 68
Pine, F 109, 133
planning 11, 14, 17, 20, 107
play 3, 46, 81–4, 92, 96, 99, 113, 121–6, 130–41
pleasure principle 75, 80–1
post-traumatic stress disorder (PTSD) 52, 53–4, 56
poverty 35, 43, 46
Predominantly Hyperactive-Impulsive Type 107
Predominantly Inattentive Type 107, 108
prefrontal cortex 9, 14–17, 22–3, 80, 106–7, 110
pretend mode 68
primary process activity 74–6, 77–8, 84
Prins, PJM 20
processing speed 16–17
provocativeness 79, 82, 111–12, 137
psychoanalysis 1–12: attention 3, 103, 105; case studies 8, 32–48; EVA Study 3, 35, 36, 43–7, 48; extraclinical studies 32–48; FIRST STEPS 35–6; Frankfurt Prevention Study 3, 33–4, 36–43, 48, 88, 90; gaps in literature 6; internal object in ADHD child, conceptualizations of 87–100; neurobiology 36–43; psychosocial symptomatic behaviour, ADHD as 3, 116; psychotherapy, aims of 1–2; reality-sampling deficit 73; semiotic capacity 87, 91, 94, 97–9; signification and the internal object 98–100; team approach 5–12; transference 8, 46, 87–8, 89, 91, 94; trauma 40–8; viable treatment option, as 8, 32–48
psychodynamic play therapy 3, 130–41: African-American boy, case study of 3, 130–1, 134–41: aggression 130, 134–9, 141; anger 130, 134, 135–6, 138; anxiety 137–8; attachment 139; attention 130, 134, 140–1; case study 3, 130–1, 134–41; counter-transference 130; course of treatment 136–40; current functioning and state of therapy 139–40; diagnosis and epidemiology of ADHD 131–4; diagnosis and treatment plan 136; envy 130, 134–5, 137, 140; frustration 130, 136, 140; hyperactivity 140; impulsivity 130, 136, 140; interpersonal issues 130; intrapsychic conflicts 130; maternal deprivation 137–40; medication 136, 140–1; narcissism 136, 140; peer relationships 134, 138, 139–40; psychosocial environment 140; randomized controlled trials 141; self-regulation 130; self-representation 130; sibling rivalry 130, 134–5, 137, 139; transference 3, 130, 136
psychodynamic treatment 3, 103: attention 133; complex trauma 63, 67, 70; hyperactivity 131, 133; internal object in ADHD child 88–9; psychoanalysis 6 7; relevance 3–4; subgroups 38–40; transference 133 *see also* psychodynamic play therapy
psychology, team approach to cognitive 5–12
psychosocial environment 52, 74, 140
psychosocial symptomatic behaviours, ADHD as collection of 3, 116–28: agitated depression 116, 122–3; aggression 125; anxiety 122–3, 125; attention 116, 122–3; case study 3, 116, 119–28; conversation orientation 124–5; depression 116, 122–3, 128; developmental milestones 120; DSM-IV 116–17; functional neuroimaging studies 117; gender 116–17, 122; generational transmission of trauma 119–20, 125–7, 128; genetic markets 117; hyperactivity 116, 118–23, 128; impatience 120, 124; impulsivity 116, 122–3; medication 116–18, 120, 128; neurobiochemical origins of ADHD 116–19, 128; neurological disorders 123, 127, 128; neuropsychological test results 117; physiological pathology 117; psychodiagnostic evaluations 122; psychodynamic treatment 3, 116; psychotherapy 118–28; readiness to act 124–5; social skills 120; structural neuroimaging studies 117
psychostimulant medication *see* medication
psychotherapy: case study 3, 116, 119–28; dynamic psychotherapy 7; preparing the child 120–1
psychosocial symptomatic behaviour, ADHD as 118–28
PTSD 52, 53–4, 56
punishment 22–3, 40, 44, 82, 91, 111, 137

Rafalovich, A 23, 61
Raine Study 118
Rainwater, JB 90–1
randomized control trials (RCTs) 34, 36, 88, 141
Ratey, J 105
reaction times 16–17, 20, 123
reading comprehension 18–19, 105
reality-sampling deficit 73–85: analytic technique 73–8, 83–4; anxiety 75; attention 73–4, 80; biological influences 73, 75; case

studies 76–8, 82–4; container, reality sampling of 75; education programmes 73–4; environmental influences 75; excessive internal stimulation 81; excessive stimulation from external objects 74; executive dysfunction hypothesis 80; flexible adaptation to reality 79–85; free association 76; frustration 73, 76–80; fusion 76–8, 82; hyperactivity 73–5, 80, 82, 85; immediate gratification 81; impulsivity 73, 75, 80; internal and external reality, disturbances at interface of 75, 80, 85; medication 73–4, 81–3; mentalization 73, 84–5; mirroring 84–5; neuropsychological testing 74–5; NICE guidelines 73–4; parent training 73–4, 81–2; primary process activity 74–6, 77–8, 84; psychiatry 73–4; psychoanalytic theory 73; psychodynamic theory; psychological theory 73; psychosocial adversity 74; repression 74–5; rewards, delay of 75; second skin formation 75–6; secondary process activity 74–6, 78, 84–5; separation from analysts 76, 78–9, 82–3; socialisation 73; time, disturbed sense of 74–5
reflective ability 21, 67–70, 84, 133
regression 3, 75
reinforcement 22, 82, 107
repression 74–5, 126
reward 20, 22–3, 75, 82, 107, 111
risk factors for ADHD 10, 13–14, 35, 51–6
Ritalin 33, 41–3, 118
Romanian orphans 53, 69
Rommelse, NNJ 21
Rorschach inkblots 122
Rydelius, P-A 53

Salomonsson, Björn 6, 8
Sander, L 55
schizoaffective disorder 63
schizophrenia 63
Schneider-Rosen, K 68
Schnittker, J 132
Schore, A 69
Schulz, KP 23
secondary process activity 74–6, 78, 84–5
self-esteem 20, 88, 91, 131, 140
self-regulation 2–4, 20–3, 41, 48, 52–6, 62, 69, 90, 107,125, 130, 133
self-representation 69, 130
self-soothing 53, 55, 91, 103, 108, 131, 138
semiotics 8, 87, 91, 94, 97–9
separation 76, 78–9, 82–3
sexual abuse 3, 52, 61, 63–8
Shalev, L 16
shame 73, 95, 105, 112–14, 139
Shaw, P 14
sibling relationships 40–3, 130, 133–5, 137, 139
Sigmund-Freud Institut 33–6
signification and the internal object 98–100
social difficulties: attachment 133; EVA Study 43; hyperactivity 20; integrated affective and cognitive model 23; neural and neurocognitive determinants 19–20; psychosocial symptomatic behaviour, ADHD as 120; reality-sampling deficit 73
social high-risk populations 35, 36, 44
speech *see* language, communication and speech
spelling 19
Spence, D 109
STARTHILFE 34
Staton, RD 18
Staufenberg, AM 33
Steger, J 18
Stern, D 110
Stevens, SE 53
Straterra 118
stress 2–3, 10, 47, 52–4, 60, 62–7
structural magnetic resonance imaging (MRI) findings 14
structural neuroimaging 14, 117
subgroups of children 3, 38–40, 48
substance use disorder 6, 20, 52, 64–6, 108
Sugarman, A 90–1
Sullivan, HS 109–10
super-ego formation 97
supervision therapies 44–6

talented children 40
Tamm, L 24
Target, M 68, 69–70
team approach to psychoanalysis, neuroscience, and cognitive psychology 2, 5–12: achievements in each area 5–8; clinical intuition to conceptualize data, use of 11; cognitive psychology 7–8, 9–10; design of research 10–11; dominant risk model in developmental psychopathology 6; explanations for lack of approach 5, 6–8; neuroscience 7, 8, 9, 10; psychoanalysis 6–7, 8, 10; statistical tools as iterative 11; use of data 10–11; what disciplines have to offer 8–10
time, estimating 21, 74–5
transference 82, 85, 98, 141: countertransference 8, 78, 87, 94, 103, 110, 130, 136–40; emotional and cognitive deficits 3; internal object in ADHD child 87–8, 89, 91, 94; play 3, 130, 136; psychoanalysis 8, 46, 87–8, 89, 91, 94; psychodynamic treatment 133;

psychosocial symptomatic behaviour, ADHD as 3
Thompson, MG 132
trauma 51–6: aggression 52, 53–5, 62; anger 53, 55, 62; anxiety 52, 54, 62–3, 69; attachment problems 3, 60, 63, 65–9; attention 3, 52, 53–4, 61, 63, 103, 108, 114; clinical implications 56; complex trauma 60–70; concentration 3, 53; coping mechanisms 52, 54; depression 52, 54; DSM-IV 52, 56; emotion dysfunction 3, 55, 69; EVA Study 44–6; examples of trauma 51; gender 56, 65; hyperactivity 52, 53–6, 62; hyperarousal 54, 55–6, 62; impulsivity 52, 56, 62, 69; inpatient settings 51, 55–6; language difficulties 53–4; literature review 51, 53–4, 62; maltreatment 3, 51, 54; memory 9, 69; oppositional defiance disorder 52, 53, 63; parents 35, 44–6, 53, 62–4, 111–14; psychoanalysis as viable treatment option 40–8; PTSD 52, 53–4, 56; risk factor, trauma as 51, 53–4, 55; self-regulation 52, 53–6, 62, 69; subgroups 40–3, 47, 48; symptoms, ADHF masking trauma 51, 54, 56 *see also* abuse
Tsal, Y 16
twins 105

unconscious 1, 3, 40–2, 74, 125, 139: attention 106, 109–10; internal object, psychoanalytic conceptualizations of 88, 90–1, 94, 97; psychodynamics 133; semiotics 94; trauma 63, 67, 125

Van der Kolk, BA 62
Vane, MJ 9–10
verbal symbolizations, failure to learn to use 47–8
visual-motor skills 2, 18–19

Walcott, CM 132
Waldung, Christina 40–1
Wender Utah Rating Scale 117
Winnicott, DW 69, 83, 90
Witenberg, E 110
work situations 108
working memory 9, 15–17, 20–1, 24, 105–6, 131

Youngstrom, EA 19

Zinkann Foundation 33

FSC
www.fsc.org
MIX
Papier | Fördert
gute Waldnutzung
FSC® C083411

Kolibri 360 GmbH
Ferdinand-Jühlke-Straße 7
99095 Erfurt, Deutschland
produktsicherheit@kolibri360.de